The Divided Self

CHOICE   NOV. '69

Language & Literature

English & American

MIYOSHI, Masao. The Divided Self; a Perspective on the Literature of the Victorians. New York University, 1969. 348p 69-19261. 8.00

Miyoshi's book follows studies like E. D. H. Johnson's *The Alien Vision* (1952) and others in exploring the divided consciousness of Victorian writers. Where Smith concentrates on Tennyson in *The Two Voices* (CHOICE, June 1965), and Johnson examines Tennyson, Browning, and Arnold in illuminating detail, Miyoshi ranges far more broadly: from the gothic novel and the Romantic poets in the first third of his book, through varied works of the entire Victorian period. He thereby gains in scope, but loses a great deal in trying to do too much. As a result of his efforts to trace his theme through so many writers and genres, one often finds absurdly brief discussions (e.g. two paragraphs on Coleridge) or appallingly dull repetitions of what is well known. So too, instead of a coherent narrative with adequate development, we too often get only a snatch or a glance here, a quick survey or a hurried generalization there. This is a decidedly imperfect book that offers some interesting moments amid its often flatulent, plodding qualities, but it is not a book that smaller libraries need feel compelled to get. Helpful notes. Index.

in process

MASAO MIYOSHI, born and raised in Tokyo, came to the United States after graduation from the University of Tokyo. He pursued graduate studies at Yale and Bennington and received his Ph.D. from New York University. Since 1963 he has been a member of the English Department the University of California, Berkeley.

The Divided Self

A Perspective on
The Literature of the Victorians

Masao Miyoshi

New York · New York University Press
London · University of London Press Limited
1969

ACKNOWLEDGMENTS

Thanks are due the following for their kind permission to use passages from the works indicated:

From Eugene Ionesco's *The Killer and Other Plays*, translated by Donald Watson. Copyright © 1960 by John Calder (Publishers) Ltd. and Calder & Boyars (London). Reprinted by permission of John Calder (Publishers) Ltd., Grove Press, and Calder & Boyars (London).

From Douglas Bush's *Mythology and the Romantic Tradition in English Poetry*. Copyright © by Harvard University Press. Reprinted by permission of Harvard University Press.

From Thomas Hardy's *Tess of the D'Ubervilles* and *Jude the Obscure*. Copyright © by The Trustees of the Hardy Estate, The Macmillan Company of Canada Ltd., and Macmillan & Co. Ltd. (London). Reprinted by permission of The Trustees of the Hardy Estate, The Macmillan Company of Canada Ltd., and Macmillan & Co. Ltd.

From James R. Foster's *History of the Pre-Romantic Novel in England*. Copyright © 1949 by the Modern Language Association of America. Reprinted by permission of the Modern Language Association of America.

From James Hogg's *The Justified Sinner*. Copyright © by Cresset Press. Reprinted by permission of Cresset Press.

To Gay, Kathy, Owen,
and
Their Friend C.C.

Contents

Preface

The confusion, the perplexity, the deep unease of the English nineteenth century are impressed on all who study the period. Whether the text be poetry or technology, Higher Criticism or social revolution, twentieth-century readers of that time so recently past find it difficult to see its life steady and see it whole. As A. N. Whitehead points out, there were always "opposing camps" in modern intellectual life, which often developed bitter antagonisms on questions they felt were fundamental. But in the nineteenth century, each individual was "divided against himself." Whitehead sees the "deep thinkers" as "muddled thinkers," their assent "claimed by incompatible doctrines; and their efforts at reconciliation [producing] inevitable confusion." [1] "Dover Beach" is the emblem to him of the divided mind of the time.

In this book we are concerned with the ways in which Victorian men of letters experienced the self-division endemic to their times and gave expression to it in their writing. The discussion avoids any narrow definition of "divided self," attempting instead to keep the notion elastic enough to fit and relate in a broad scheme certain of its outstanding phenomena. In what is perhaps the most widespread manifestation of the war of the selves, a writer may not appear at all concerned with the problem—and this, whether it is his own or his character's—but the crisis of self-division is all too apparent in the breakdown of formal unity in his work, the so-called "dissociation of sensibility." In another type, less pervasive perhaps but much more conspicuous, the writer is very self-aware and indeed self-knowledgeable about his inner state. He may tailor specific themes (the self-duplication of the doppelgänger, the double, and the Romantic ideal, or the self-division of the Gothic villain, the Byronic hero, and the Jekyll-Hyde split personality) and whole new genres such as the Gothic romance to suit the experience, or he may simply become very verbal about self-alienation, creating a philosophical construct or system of the self and arguing the problem long and hard through the personae of his poem, novel, or essay. Although this experience of self-division is often very intense, it is in still a third type that the identity crisis is at its most severe. It is here that the boundary between life and art in the artist, always difficult to trace, becomes in the personality of a Byron or a Wilde indeterminate to the vanishing point.

It is my intention that none of these three broad categories, the formal, the thematic or ideological, and the biographical, will be slighted. Yet the plan of the book does not allow equal emphasis on all. In regard to the first type, I venture that its phenomena are too widespread and diffuse to be handled successfully in a study of this sort, although this does not necessarily mean that I subscribe to Eliot's understanding of modern English writing. The more purely formal aspects of a work—the only significant ones for criticism, given the dominant critical viewpoint today—are therefore discussed only where the text is a vital element in the writer's strategy for handling his sense of internal division. Thus, the poetics of Matthew Arnold or the structure of *Wuthering Heights* are treated at some length, even though literary structure and style as such are not the central subject of the book. As for the third broad category, the dual personality as a fact of the author's life, biographical references are made wherever interesting or illuminating for the theme of the book. Especially toward the end of the century, where the frontier between art and life becomes increasingly indistinct, the author's own double life is nearly as important as his work for any treatment of the theme of the divided self. Although the book as a whole is not of course meant as a composite biography of a literary era, it happens that in Chapter 6, which deals with the eighteen-nineties, a sort of pastiche of literary lives will be found useful to us in understanding this essential aspect of the writer's divided self.

It is with the second type, then, that the book is mainly concerned—the explicitly self-aware or self-conscious writer whose works are clearly defined in their embodiment of the self-consciousness. Although the focus adjusts most naturally to those works in which a dramatic persona is presented as double in the theme, certain of the great ideological tracts of the time, where there is no "double" and often no obvious persona, are not easily set aside. As regards *Culture and Anarchy,* for example, it must in my view be understood in the context of Arnold's earlier preoccupation in poetry with the problems and expression of self-division, and it is in this context that it is treated here.

Distinctions among the several themes of self-duplication and self-division arise from the source of the second self or partial self. In the case of duplication, the second self or double appears, as it were, from outside the first self; whereas in the case of division, as in the Jekyll-Hyde personality, it splits off from within. For our practical purposes here this difference is of only minor importance next to what is essential to both, the disintegration of the person. Common, too, to both duplication and division are the conflicting and often simultaneous impulses in the victim— the craving for and the fear of the encounter with the second self—each of which has its archetype in a traditional version of the double: the Platonic, or epipsychean, longing for unification of the severed halves of man, and the folkloristic fear of the double as an omen of death.

Certain distinctions between the novel and the romance in the nineteenth century are referred to throughout, yet, as has been suggested, the book should in no sense be construed as an attempt to treat a narrowly defined story genre on the theme of the supernatural double, a project which would be of limited scope though not inconsiderable interest.[2] One of the problems intrinsic to that approach would be the simple historical fact that by the time of the Victorians sharp genre distinctions had been fairly well blurred. The poet writing his sonnets found it impossible to put out of his mind the novels, idyls, and dramatic monologues he had been reading; and the novelist certainly learned a great deal from poetry. Indeed, border crossing among genres is one of the important features of Victorian writing: *The Ring and the Book* and the *Idylls of the King* in many respects remarkably resemble novels, whereas *Wuthering Heights, Bleak House,* and stories like Rossetti's "Hand and Soul" approach the domain of poetry very closely. This book then, while it may seem to take genre distinctions lightly, moving as it does from novel to poem, from Gothic romance to essay, and back again, nonetheless finds this method to its purpose in lifting some of the masks that our time has pasted on the times just past.

For any such broadly defined discussion, selection of materials and decision as to which should be emphasized are paramount. It could be argued that because no one is possibly independent of his place, moment, and milieu a book treating the Victorian writers should be no less inclusive than a full survey of the period. I will not pretend to cover the whole range of Victorian literature exhaustively, because for my purposes the general survey would of necessity blur the outline of the thesis. What I have found is that some writers and some works are decidedly more relevant to the theme than others and these are of course the ones selected for discussion.

The self has not always been the problem it was to the nineteenth-century men of letters, yet questions about its makeup and meaning have been among the most insistent concerns of Western thought. Socrates preferred that the whole world be "at odds with" him rather than that he be at odds with himself. In another context, yet in the same language of war, St. Paul described that other "law in my members, warring against the law of my mind." Augustine, too, confessed the two wills struggling within him that "by their discord, undid my soul." As against this, Tennyson's young man in *Maud* sees himself not only "at war with [him]self" but with the whole "wretched race." [3] The struggle within may be seen as part of man's struggle with the other. In the modern philosophical tradition, the opening cannon was fired by the New Astronomers, waging their war of the worlds against man. Pascal, for one, tells of his anguish at the loss of a definite and unquestioned place in being: "engulfed in the infinite immensity of space of which I am ignorant, and which know me not, I am frightened, and am astonished at being here rather than there." [4]

In the rich literature of England, the breaking of the great chain by the Copernican cosmology did not immediately entail the thoroughgoing angst of existence that is striking in so many writers of the nineteenth century. For all the identity crisis of a Thomas Browne or even a Hamlet for that matter, the humane vision with its supreme confidence in man would usually at a critical point intercept the darker muses. Pope, for one, as late as the eighteenth century could still sum up unperturbedly in those neat couplets of his man's unhappy "middle position": "With too much knowledge for the Sceptic side, / With too much weakness for the Stoic's pride, / He hangs between; in doubt to act, or rest; / In doubt to deem himself a God, or Beast." [5] But before long, this same "God" and "Beast" are joint tenants of the dark cave of the Gothic villain-hero.

Part I of this study, "The Man Within," treats Gothicism and Romanticism, traditions which together created the prototypes of man divided that are to reappear throughout Victorian literature: the Gothic villain, the Byronic hero, and the Shelleyan solipsist. Earliest on the scene, the Gothic villain is a character-type well instrumented to explore the evil and irrationality of man and his sharply personal sense of the war within, and with his advent in the late eighteenth century, feeling, long in eclipse, showed its face unashamedly for the making of a whole new literature, becoming part of that same structure of emotion that constitutes Romantic poetry.[6] Thus in a few short years the Byronic hero, that plagiarized Gothic villain, had replaced him in the imagination of a whole generation of Europeans. But the Byronic type is only one product of the Gothic influence on Romanticism. There

were many other things about the tales—their sensational-
ism, their introspectiveness—which were powerfully attractive to the creators of the myth of the infinite self. For the
Romantic poets, that "other self" once the villain was now
the "ideal," a fugitive beauty eternally attractive, forever
unreachable—until the gravity of the real world brought it
down to earth again. By the time of Dickens and the
Brontë sisters, it was the "unrealistic" romance that suggested new ways of exploring the unconscious and the irrational, the other self, within the framework of the novel.
And the revival of Gothicism in the last decade—in Wilde,
Stevenson, Hardy, and many other writers—is so prominent
that it scarcely needs mention here. The romance tradition
will be seen, therefore, as running parallel to the tradition
of the "realistic" novel throughout the nineteenth century,
until toward the turn of the twentieth the two traditions
blend and become almost undistinguishable.

It was a legacy of heartbreak that the Romantics left
the Victorians; on its flight to the Absolute the alone had
met only the alone, the self only the self. However the men
and women of Empire had to face up to a bewildering
array of alternatives quite specific to their own time: faith
or agnosticism, the old ways or progress, authority or freedom, privacy or community, mundane good sense or poetic
insight. There is a value in possibilities—the more the
better—but the Victorians too often saw them in rigid
pairs—all or nothing, white or black. For a Tennyson or
a Carlyle, to keep a grip on himself in the face of what he
took to be clear and pressing alternatives was difficult, and
achieved if at all only at the price of pleasure, spontaneity,
the sense of life itself. Part II, "Life Against Art," deals
with the method—moral commitment—the High Victorians
used to "solve" the problem of self-division and the effects
of such a life strategy on their work.

The chapters of Part II focus on the years 1830, 1850, and 1870—roughly the beginning ("Will as Form"), the midpoint ("The Colloquy of the Self"), and the end ("Broken Music") of the Victorian era as a definable literary period.[7] Such symmetry is not a scholar's caprice, but history's, for the books and poems that best express the writers' response to personal crisis happen to have appeared in clusters at or very near the opening years of these three decades.[8] Again, history must be called on for an explanation of the rapid change in the *Zeitgeist* during these forty years in the middle of the century: from 1830, when Tennyson, Browning, and Carlyle all felt very right about their "conversion," to 1850, with the endless equivocations of skeptics like Arnold and Clough, to 1870, when Thomson and Rossetti and the aging exhausted Dickens wrote as though mired inescapably in a dismal existence where any further struggle toward self-definition or effect in the world seemed useless. Thus the investment of the Victorians in moral commitment was gradually withdrawn, and with that their hope for a strong definable self-identity dwindled.

The men of the nineties could see in High Victorian commitment little else than self-delusion and hypocrisy. For every bourgeois Jekyll they promised to uncover a troglodyte Hyde. And perhaps because of this vaunted contempt for mid-Victorian values, the writers and artists of the nineties worked hard to make the self as different from the world as possible, namely, as much like an artifact as possible. Often, as it happened, it was a delicate balance indeed between life and art in their lives, the art of life and the life of art becoming practically interchangeable. Sooner or later, the lie of this artifice, too, would have to be exposed. Yet the nineteenth century ends, as the twentieth begins, with all the illusions and subterfuges of the divided self intact, taken as ordinary conditions of existence. Part III, "The Art of the Self," treats decadence and the phenomenon of art for art's sake as part of the larger movement to rejuvenate the tired broken life of the self in the play of art.

A note is in order here on my occasional appropriation of the Freudian vocabulary while disavowing a psycho-analytic explanation of literary works and literary men. As to the vocabulary, much of it is in such general use that it is quite innocuous theoretically. As to the psychoanalytic interpretation, it tends to become, like its terminology, more and more broadly applied and so less and less power-ful as an explanatory instrument. That the artist has much in common with the neurotic is axiomatic. There is plausi-bility in the notion that the use of the double theme may indicate the author's fear of sex, or perhaps his irrational desire for immortality.[9] In themselves, such interpretations of the phenomenon of the double allow little room for quarrel. However it does seem to me that psychoanalytic criticism in its purer form tends to fix on the writer as neurotic at the expense of his writing. Finally, it might be said in defense of the more traditional practice of literary criticism that Freud himself, that eminent Viennese Vic-torian, was practicing a style of literary art in his clinical studies. The hysterical girl sent for the cure to the well-known physician is lost forever to the "Dora" of his bril-liant case report. Literary studies may thus explain Freud almost as well as Freud explains the work of art.

Many good friends and teachers have read the manu-script of this book at various stages: William E. Buckler, Leslie A. Marchand, and Gordon N. Ray; more recently, Frederick C. Crews, Stanley Fish, Thomas Flanagan, Josephine Miles, John H. Raleigh, and Mark Schorer.

They spent many hours on the manuscript and provided me with detailed notes and commentary, and all were generous in their encouragement of the project. I am deeply indebted to them. Ulrich C. Knoepflmacher alternated raving and scolding through repeated readings of the manuscript; his arguments and counterarguments have been so freely appropriated that it is hard to indicate the extent of my debt. Several students assisted in research and proofreading, but I want to single out for special thanks Carole Berntsen, and Dennis Jarrett, both incorruptible critics but always sweet morale builders. I am grateful to the editors of *Victorian Studies, Studies in English Literature, College English,* and *Victorian Newsletter* for permission to use portions of my articles published in those journals. Thanks are also due to the University of California for two grants-in-aid. Finally, I owe a great debt to Elizabeth Ann Lester who edited the manuscript but perhaps more importantly helped me translate the world of my thought from Japanese to English over the past sixteen years.

M.M.
Berkeley, California

*N*otes

1. *Science and the Modern World* (New York, 1925), p. 119.
2. There is no satisfactory or comprehensive treatment of this subject. For a random listing of these two themes, see Ralph Tymms, *Doubles in Literary Psychology* (Cambridge, 1949).
3. The three quotations are, respectively, from: *Gorgias, The Dialogues,* 3rd ed., trans. Benjamin Jowett (London, 1892), II, 369; Romans vii.23; and *Confessions,* trans. Edward B. Pusey (New York, 1949), p. 153. For the text of *Maud,* see footnote 52, Chapter 4.

4. *Pascal's Pensées,* trans. W. F. Trotter (New York, 1958), p. 61.

5. *An Essay on Man,* Ep. II, 5–8. The Twickenham Edition, ed. Maynard Mack (London and New Haven, 1951), III, i. See also John Locke, who raises the question of self-identity only to dismiss it at once. *Human Understanding,* Book II, Chapter 27, p. 9.

6. The view that the collapse of Neoclassicism brought about the first expression of the divided self has been advanced by two critics with quite different approaches: Walter Jackson Bate, *From Classic to Romantic* (New York, 1961), p. 12, and Leslie A. Fiedler, *Love and Death in the American Novel* (New York, 1960), p. xxviii.

7. G. K. Chesterton argues in *The Victorian Age in Literature* (Notre Dame, 1962), pp. 108–109, that the year 1870 marks "the turn of the century." Walter E. Houghton, similarly, regards the four decades from 1830 to 1870 as the typically "Victorian" period. See *The Victorian Frame of Mind: 1830–1870* (New Haven, 1957), p. xv.

8. This is only a general scheme. The discussion of Tennyson's early poems, for instance, begins with his juvenile works written in the late 1820's, and moves on to *Poems, Chiefly Lyrical* (1830), *Poems* (1832), and *Poems* (1842), all in Chapter 3. Despite this telescoping, the scheme is maintained throughout—with the single notable exception of George Eliot's "The Lifted Veil" published in 1859, which is included for its treatment of the divided self.

9. See, for instance, Otto Rank, *Beyond Psychology* (New York, 1958).

Part I
The Man Within

Thou double-headed and four-legged monster!
Vathek

I.

The Castle of Catatonia:
The Gothic Tradition

English fiction of the eighteenth century shows a gradually deepening understanding of the often turbulent emotional life of the characters. In *Pamela* (1740), Richardson, to begin with, remains relatively uninvolved in developing Pamela's calculating nature or Mr. B's straightforwardness, and Fielding thought such characters almost ludicrously naive. Thus, when the literary world laughed at him, Richardson began to move cautiously to build characters of greater complexity. In *Clarissa* (1748), there are the conventional contrasts between Clarissa and Lovelace, and Lovelace and Belford, but added to this there is some degree of tension within the characters. To be sure, this tension is in no sense the fully scaled passion-remorse dichotomy of the Gothic villain, but at the same time it goes much beyond that of *Pamela*. Clarissa shows determination to preserve her chastity in the face of temptation that is more than a mere tactic toward securing a future reward. No prude, Clarissa has a will to set

3

off her femininity against Lovelace's manliness, to transform his carnality into love, all the while maintaining some sort of equilibrium within between her warring impulse and reason. Similarly, Lovelace is not a one-dimensional villain. He is without doubt capable of rage, not to say of rape, but he nonetheless really loves Clarissa and repents his numerous outrages quite sincerely.

By shrewd use of epistolary form Richardson could enhance the introspective and confessional qualities of his later work. Although the alternating moods of passion and remorse also appeared in the more clearly social novel, such as that of Fielding, it was Richardson's men and women of passion and sensibility, especially Lovelace and Clarissa, that gave the later romance writers and the Romantic poets their tortured lovers—men and women estranged from each other and society and distracted within themselves as well.

The form of the novel was, however, a child of the enlightenment, born of reaction against the fantastic romances that had dominated prose fiction since the previous century. Defoe, Richardson, and Fielding, having developed the Aristotelian notion of the probable, insisted on what for them constituted the main distinction between the novel and the romance: verisimilitude.[1] Defoe presented *Robinson Crusoe* as a "just history of the fact";[2] and Richardson, in his Preface to the continuation of *Pamela* (1741), hoped that the work would "be found equally written to Nature, avoiding all romantic flights, improbable surprises, and irrational machinery."[3] Their position is best stated by Fielding. The proper concern of the novel, he believed, is "nature from the just imitation of which will flow all . . . pleasure,"[4] and in the introductory chapters of *Tom Jones*, especially Book VIII, he opposed the romance genre for its indul-

gence in the marvelous, the extravagant, and the supernatural. It was powerful literary opinions such as these
that worked to keep the new narrative form free of
impurities. Unfortunately, its dedication to the portrayal
of character and action familiar in ordinary daily life was
typically at the expense of psychological depth. Even
Richardson, having made his preliminary round of the
psyche in *Clarissa,* felt obliged to present his findings in
such a way as to yield a recognizable and reasonable yarn.

But other impulses were astir.[5] The improbable situations of the Gothic romances established a genre running
parallel to the realistic novel of the nineteenth century.
Whereas the novel adhered to the ordinary and the everyday, the romance ventured into the dark night of the irrational. The novel's contemporary backdrop of village
squares and city streets is replaced in these tales by the
"barbarous" and "irregular" caves and dungeons of by-
gone days. Rejected, too, by the new Gothic is the virtuous
hero of the earlier romances in favor of a villain whose
remorse for his evildoing is often as thoroughgoing as his
villainy. It is this violent oscillation of evil deed and penitent mood that makes the Gothic villain a modern archetype for alienated man divided against himself.

I

Horace Walpole woke suddenly from a dream one
morning, possessed of a compelling image: "a gigantic
hand in armour"[6] on a banister at the top of a long
staircase. He began writing at once and in less than two
months finished the first version of *The Castle of Otranto*
(1765). Because of its dream genesis this work has been
declared "surrealistic," a product of its author's "uncon-

scious," [7] although a more complete critical picture should take into account its mechanical plot, pasteboard characters, and the unashamed improbability of its supernatural events. Walpole's amateur status carried a considerable advantage: With no particular audience to please, he could exploit all the more the experimental possibilities inherent in writing to please himself. Thus, if *The Castle of Otranto* is not a very good work, it is a very vigorous one, having established in those dungeons and vaults an attractive and in time legitimate line in eighteenth-century English fiction.

All the features we have come to call "Gothic" [8] are there in *Otranto*. The most conspicuous is of course the character of the villain. Manfred plans to divorce his faithful wife and marry a young princess who would have become his daughter-in-law had not his son been killed mysteriously. This ruthless fellow is determined to have an heir, although, as a grandson of an unrightful claimant to the title, he has no right to it himself. Retaining the usurped title in the family is, however, only the ostensible reason for his projected act, the plain truth being his lust for the innocent girl. The war of guilt and remorse is very prominent throughout this story of the ultimate downfall of a wicked and illegitimate prince. Manfred is alternately all goodness and reason, and passionate to the point of ferocity. At one moment he is admiring Friar Jerome's "saint-like virtue" [9] and wishing to emulate it, and at the next trembling with a "rage" strangely compounded with "shame" (p. 46).

To discuss Manfred as the prototype of the pre-Romantic villain may seem to commit an anachronism, for the new feature of the story at the time was its revival of medievalism. Walpole must have been quite conscious of this novelty because the first edition was

advanced as a sixteenth-century translation of an Italian
tale composed even earlier. Also, because villains of a
similar stamp had figured in English literature off and
on since the Renaissance, we might make a case for tracing Manfred's ancestry to such villains of the Elizabethan
drama as Barabas, Cassius, King John, Richard III, and
Webster's Cardinal,[10] and from there to the Satan of
Book IV of *Paradise Lost* who is tortured with self-
doubt and indecision.

Yet the Gothic villain is not to be explained satis-
factorily in terms of family history alone. For one thing,
the Elizabethan villain was usually portrayed as an unambiguously evil existence, the flaw in the scheme of
things. If he had occasional worries about his viciousness,
his misgivings were quickly resolved one way or the
other, either confirming him in evil or radically convert-
ing him, with the slate of past sins wiped clean. Manfred,
in contrast, is a very inconsistent villain. At times he
seems almost a villain in spite of himself; the real culprit
is his passion, which constitutes an identity practically
distinct from the Manfred who emerges at the end. The
agon of the Renaissance drama, acted out in the world
by identifiable villains and heroes, is played in a new
setting: Reason and passion here contend *within* the main
characters. Convention still required poetic justice for the
villain, but the author's main interest in a work like
Otranto lay less in the moral outcome of circumstance
and events than in exposing his villain's psychological con-
formation, his frightful appetites alternating with soul-
searching guilt and sorrow. Gradually, as the Gothic villain's oscillation between passion and remorse became accepted as a possible predicament for any man, he was in
a way universalized. The villain, beside whom the virtuous heroes and heroines of literature pale almost to non-

existence, begins to preempt the essence of man. This increasing representativeness of the Gothic personality is apparent in its transformation into the outcast (*Caleb Williams*, for example) and later the Byronic hero, with his glamor and on the whole sympathetic qualities.

The other conspicuous element of the new Gothic in *The Castle of Otranto* is its use of supernatural beings and marvelous events. Two years before the publication of *Otranto*, Richard Hurd in his *Letters on Chivalry and Romance* spoke favorably of Gothic poetry as well as medieval chivalry and architecture, all of which had long been held in contempt by the literati. Hurd's point was that the poet's world of the marvelous and the extraordinary, despite its absurdities, was an agreeable "imposture," and that if "reason" and "common sense" were allowed to drive the magic away, fancy would be forced to play along with "strict truth" as a fee of admission "into reasonable company." [11] Although his plan for a Gothic revival was concerned primarily with poetry, his ideas were naturally applicable to a program for the revival of the Gothic style of prose fiction. Walpole's romance may thus be read almost as a fulfillment of Hurd's prescription. In the Preface to the first edition of *Otranto* Walpole observes how the prose tradition has been thus far quite free of "miracles, visions, necromancy, dreams, and other preternatural events," [12] which will now be made use of. He remarks that such events were, after all, once believed in. Furthermore, he promises, "If this *air* of the *miraculous* is excused, the reader will find nothing else unworthy of perusal." "Allow the possibility of the facts," he continues, "and all the actors comport themselves as persons would do in their situation." [13] His Preface to the second edition is even more specific on the relative roles of imagination and probability in prose fiction, and distinguishes between the kind of fiction that indulges in imagination and fancy at the expense of verisimilitude and that whose "strict adherence to common life" (p. 7) results in imaginative deprivation. If the novel as defined by Fielding and others tends to be of the second type, *The Castle of Otranto* attempts a fusion of the two. It will do so, according to Walpole, by strict observation of the demands of probability in the creation of believable characters who are at the same time under the sway of incredible forces and events. A tale of the supernatural, but one in which the characters will be made to "think, speak, and act, as it might be supposed mere men and women would do in extraordinary positions" (p. 8). By this strategy Walpole attempts to accommodate the gradually reviving emotional life to the still dominant rationalism of his time. Although he was in advance of his time because of his acceptance of supernaturalism, he was bound to it because of his adherence to the strictures of verisimilitude.[14] This is not to say, of course, that a writer's respect for common sense and the laws of probability and credibility are characteristics solely or primarily of a rationalistic age. No writer can afford to ignore the general requirement that imaginary people not be allowed to "lose sight of their human character." And, from the earliest romancers —from Walpole to Beckford, Godwin, Scott, Shelley, Hawthorne—and on to the writers of the 1890's,[15] there was this insistence on the humanly credible character, however self-divided he might appear or however incredible the situation in which he might be found.

In connection with this, the nature of the belief in the supernatural, as it was presented by Walpole, is worth some attention. Apart from Thomas Gray, who, if we take his report entirely seriously, was so frightened by the apparitions that he was "afraid to go to bed o'nights," [16] the reviewers were, for the most part, quite expectedly disdainful of *Otranto's* "absurdities." [17] It would be a rare eighteenth-century gentleman who would find sufficient reason to give credence to a miracle. As for the author himself, there is no evidence that he lost any sleep for fear of ghostly visitations. Those who relished the tale, then—and there were many, even among eminent literary figures—were able to ignore the *"air* of the *miraculous"* and settle down to enjoy this new fare, which seemed to go a long way toward satisfying their craving for the sensational.[18] The gap thus begins to close between what Hurd called the "pleasant imposture" of the Gothics and the Romantics' suspension of disbelief. It is of some bearing on this point that Walpole, despite popular success, was convinced he was not writing for his own time—which wants, as he said, "only cold reason"— and that he was determined to compose what he liked despite "rules, critics, and philosophers." [19]

The incidental trappings of the Gothic are also quite complete in this book. There is the medieval setting with its castle and tyrant lord, the chivalrous hero whose identity is not revealed until the end of the story, the persecuted maiden, the subterranean vaults with secret passages and trapdoors, the loquacious servant, caves deep in the woods, the monastery, and many mementos from the supernatural world: a bleeding statue, a helmet falling out of the sky, a portrait that comes alive. Of note, too, is Walpole's interest in the incest motif. In *Otranto* it is only barely hinted at in the proposal of marriage between would-be in-laws. However, three years after the first book, Walpole worked the theme much more thoroughly in *The Mysterious Mother,* in which the title character has a daughter by her own son, who later unites with this daughter-sister.

The incest theme has a lineage as long as the Western literary tradition, but its appearance at this time, after a noticeable hiatus in the neoclassic period, and its frequent use since, takes on special significance. Violation of a taboo of this sort, even in fiction, tells as much about the temper of the time as about the author's own psychology. As perhaps the extreme expression of social defiance, incest was a serviceable symbol for the Romantics, who took seriously their obligation as rebels and social critics. What society finds distasteful or dangerous is often for that reason alone attractive to those who see that same society as corrupt and contemptible. Moreover, the sheer shock effect of violating in print such a strong taboo prepared the way for the attack on a whole range of other customs and complacencies. Incest was thus probably the most versatile weapon in the Romantics' antisocial arsenal. It was also, so they were discovering, a metaphor of the most astonishing correspondence to their own state of dual and undecided identity. The incestuous relation, in dissolving the usual familial as well as extrafamilial bonds between individuals, finally dissolves the identifying masks distinguishing one individual from another. Given the time-honored sense of the family as an extension of self, a larger self in a sense, the incestuous act becomes the moment for the self meeting with itself. At the same time, it provides a temporary escape from roles assigned by fate or society and now unwanted. In embracing his daughter as his mistress, the incestuous father denies his paternity. One can be, through incest, other than oneself, yet strangely, by virtue of this sense of the family as a "larger self," more completely oneself. The new role provides a freedom denied in everyday family experience.

In this double perspective, clear border lines of things shift and blur. Not only the familial identities of persons, which shift from daughter to mistress, or son to lover, in relation to the incestuous parent, but the moral categories derived from the family structure begin to transfuse— love into lust, kindness into cruelty.

Otranto's vaults must have seemed a well-stocked store indeed to later Gothic writers. Why is it then that a study of Walpole will not afford us a full perspective on the subsequent development of the Gothic romance? There is a sense in which the tale's Gothic panoply, however wild and wide it is, is strikingly underutilized. Improbable experiences are given no margin for development as genuine psychological possibilities. Nor is Manfred's war with himself developed in a way to indicate any significance beyond a mechanical alternation of mood. Where the fascination with the self and its states predisposed many later writers to the psychological possibilities of the Gothic medium, Walpole shows only elementary understanding of this potential. In the Postscript to *The Mysterious Mother* he says he intends to furnish not only a "contrast of characters, but a contrast of virtue and vice in the same character." [20] He clearly saw the fantastic mode as the best one, indeed the only one, for his purposes, there being little chance that the man with two selves, such as the Gothic villain-hero, would find himself at ease in the broad daylight of the novel of verisimilitude.

However, it is not at all clear that Walpole could see further possibilities in the villain-hero, such as the type who would appear later on, manifesting his self-division by projecting a shadow or duplication of an original self— as the doppelgänger of the folk tradition—or the one typically experiencing the self as incomplete, one half of the Platonic whole—which is the usual Romantic sense of self-division. Despite these relative weaknesses, Walpole's tales stake out a whole new territory for fiction, and it is certainly not to his discredit that other writers were able to mine it more thoroughly.

The Castle of Otranto continued enjoying popular success, and before 1800 twenty-one editions had been published. However, it was not until the publication of Clara Reeve's *The Champion of Virtue, A Gothic Tale* in 1777 (republished the following year as *The Old English Baron*) that the literary establishment paid much attention to Walpole. In her Preface, Reeve spoke of her debt to *Otranto,* referring to her story as the "literary offspring" of Walpole's. She also borrowed Walpole's theory, seeing her own work as an "attempt to unite the various merits and graces of the ancient Romance and modern Novel." Her recipe calls for "a sufficient degree of the marvelous to excite attention," along with "the manners of real life to give an air of probability," and enough of "the pathetic to engage the heart." [21] Her rules of probability are certainly, however, more demanding than Walpole's: For Reeve the marvelous must be, paradoxically, reasonable. Although she approves of an occasional ghost or enchanted sword or helmet, they must be "of reasonable size." [22] Indeed, the charm of her tale lies not so much in these "reasonable" terrors—the ghost's appearances are made for the most part only in dreams—but in the refreshing details of domestic life and the rather pleasant sentimentality of the whole project. This use of the supernatural is little more than a come-on for what is essentially a domestic tale and represents a continuing insistence on reason and common sense in fiction —an eighteenth-century orthodoxy that is apparent well into the nineties, most especially in Ann Radcliffe's tales.

Beckford's works, *Vathek* (begun in 1782) and *The*

Episodes of Vathek (written concurrently), in contrast, are part of the same counterclassicism that had shown itself in the poetry of melancholy and the school of sensibility as well as in the pervasive longing for times past and exotic places in the whole literature of the period.

II

Vathek proper, obviously inspired by the *Arabian Nights,* recounts the Caliph Vathek's on-again off-again adventures with evil and final punishment. The motive of this oriental Faust is the wish "to know everything; even sciences that [do] not exist." [23] At the outset, Eblis invites Vathek to share his domain and its treasures, but his invitation, which is pleasant enough at first, inexplicably changes into a warning: "Woe to the rash mortal who seeks to know that of which he should remain ignorant; and to undertake that which surpasseth his power!" (p. 21). Thus, the main paradox of the story is indicated: the Caliph's lust, insatiable as it is, will bring him nothing but agony.

Vathek learns the hard lesson that he cannot bargain something for nothing, or even for a fair price, where there's the devil to be paid. The Giaour, Eblis' messenger, having told Vathek that he must devote himself exclusively to Eblis in return for the "talismans that control the world" (p. 41), requires an additional sacrifice: the fifty most beautiful children in the world. The Caliph complies, swearing his eternal worship of the dark powers. Yet his devotion proves somewhat unsteady. When he finds himself starving and is fed and taken care of by the devout Emir, he switches loyalties and curses the

Giaour; he then falls in love with the Emir's daughter and vows to renounce the satanic power forever; and when, after having resumed his original course, he comes within sight of the gate of hell, he is struck with fear and repentance for that resumption of evil ways. Vathek's mother, in contrast, is undeviating in her enthusiasm for the dark powers. "Thou double-headed and four-legged monster!" she thunders at her opportunistic son, "What means this winding and writhing?" (pp. 176–177).

Vathek is sometimes whimsical, sometimes grotesque, and is written for the most part with a sure ironic touch. The plump and accommodating Giaour turns himself into a football, to the vast amusement of the harem; at one point, Vathek is so depressed that "of the three hundred dishes that were daily placed before him, he could taste of no more than thirty-two." There are many such episodes in *Vathek,* and a few of them are very good parodies of literary themes. In Beckford's parody of *Romeo and Juliet* the young lovers, waking from the effects of a narcotic, make love quite freely, believing they had been poisoned and had passed on to the next world. *Paradise Lost* is mildly satirized in the scene of the great prophet Mahomet sitting in heaven and occasionally intervening quite gratuitously in the affairs of mortals such as Vathek; there is even a forbidden fruit—not apples but melons. Nor does Beckford's sense of fun spare the main theme of Faustian egotism and intellectual pride. When the Caliph finds himself failing in his search for knowledge, his intellectual greed is transformed into such a terrible thirst that it cannot be slaked even by the practically endless supply of water furnished by his numerous wives.

Such horseplay continues to the point where Vathek reaches the Palace of Eblis when, quite abruptly, there is an unmistakable change in tone. The doomed pilgrims are overwhelmed with remorse, and there is no room for burlesque or tongue-in-cheek sophistication. Vathek and his companions in hell, utterly estranged from each other, wander about quite without purpose, each of them—like Roderick Ellison in Hawthorne's tale or one of the night walkers of "The City of Dreadful Night"—lost to hope and gnawed by the pangs of fear and the necessity of a perpetual penance:

> In the midst of this immense hall, a vast multitude was incessantly passing; who severally kept their right hands on their hearts; without once regarding anything around them. They had all, the livid paleness of death, their eyes, deep sunk in their sockets, resembled those of phosphoric meteors, that glimmer by night, in places of interment. Some talked slowly on; absorbed in profound reverie: some shrieking with agony, ran furiously about like tigers, wounded with poisoned arrow; whilst others, grinding their teeth in rage, foamed along more frantic than the wildest maniac. They all avoided each other; and though surrounded by a multitude that no one could number, each wandered at random, unheedful of the rest, as if alone on a desert which no foot had trodden (pp. 207–208).

Apart from this tonal discord so near the end of the story,[24] there is the problem of the nature of the creative mode that required it just at this juncture.

Several years before he wrote *Vathek* Beckford had written a long prose tale in which a young man tells of his solitary escape into nature and subsequent encounter with heavenly spirits. In this "Long Story," [25] as he called it, young William is first put through initiation ordeals, and then rewarded with a gift of the "Eternal Records of Truth," after which he is led to a grotto by the goddess-like Nouronihar, who initiates him into further mysteries. This journey, like Vathek's, begins with a thorough self-examination and uncovers the same sort of Faustian curiosity that was to send Vathek down to the Palace of Eblis: "Where am I? By what strange Impulse am I driven? For what end am I come here? . . . A sort of madness has hurried me here and I strive in vain to reason with myself." [26] Guilt, too, hounds this young man as it did Vathek: "It was to such a solitude, to such a dreary waste that Cain fled, reeking from the murder of his brother, and what murder have I committed, what crime have I perpetrated that I should conceal myself like him from everything human?" (p. 11). For a few moments he manages to escape such dark considerations of his crime. Moisasour brings him back to them by reminding him of the fate of the angels who challenged the gods (Beckford's youthful vision has the Fall recurring time after time). Vathek's union with Nouronihar is also prefigured in this early story. And yet, whereas *Vathek* is mainly a satire on this archetypal Romantic quest, "The Long Story" is a deadly earnest document of an adolescent trembling in expectation of such a pilgrimage. For one thing, Vathek's Nouronihar shows herself to be a coquette goading her man on to the promised loot. However, the girl in the prose tale is the sheer ideal beauty of a type that comes to predominate in poetry a few years later, most conspicuously in Keats's *Endymion* and Shelley's *Alastor*. Furthermore, "The Long Story" is charged with a rhapsodic sexuality that has the effect of drastically shrinking the conventional distance between the fictional narrator's passion and consequent guilt and the writer's own; between the writer Beckford and the young William of the tale there is no mediating grace of either irony or broad comedy.

Certain events in Beckford's life during the period from 1777 to 1782 may help account for this difference. In 1777 he was still, despite wide reading and other advantages typical of his class, pretty much the neophyte of life, dreaming about experience, while the Beckford of 1782, only five years older, was if not wiser, certainly a great deal more sophisticated. His debaucheries were, in fact, about to bring down upon him scandal and exile not altogether unlike Byron's thirty years later.[27] Whereas the adolescent author took the fate of his Faust and Fallen Angels seriously, his own anxiety being all too apparent in the tale, the Beckford of *Vathek* can only be amused at such worries. Still, the personal chronology does not provide an altogether satisfying explanation of the difference (in fact, it is undermined by the circumstance that the *Biographical Memoirs of Extraordinary Painters*, written about the same time as "The Long Story," was a book by turns introspective and ironic), nor does it explain the sudden shift in tone toward the end of *Vathek*.

Like the Romantics for whom there exists a choice of self-styles and attitudes on the world, Beckford found himself at once the enlightened and somewhat detached eye on the world and the hypersensitive and rather gloomy observer of his own interior states. Also, one could say, in Beckford there coexist the worldly-wise and immensely wealthy man about town, the eighteenth-century connoisseur and traveler for whom personal distress is typically grist for the mill of satire, and the Romantic recluse, brooding in his Fonthill estate carefully enclosed by a six-mile long fence. In his work he does not seem really secure in either role. When he finds himself unable to sustain full emotional intensity in a tale like "The Long Story" he simply stops writing, leaving an unpruned, over-long fragment. In *Vathek* the author's ironic attitude collapses at the point where punishment becomes an actu-ality for the hero. A relentless despair takes over which involves hero and author alike. The story-teller can no longer hide behind his mask of fiction; he must speak for himself about himself. Thus, between *Otranto* and *Vathek* the Gothic genre adds this new element of the confessional. There is in *Vathek* the same alternation of passion and remorse, but here the perspective itself al-ternates—between the cool and ironic and the confessional and introspective. In this sense Beckford points to Byron as well, in whom the divided sensibility, ironic and senti-mental in turn, appears more dualistic than in any other poet of his time.

Beckford's plan to finish *The Episodes of Vathek* and then work them into *Vathek* proper so as to fashion a kind of *Arabian Nights* was not achieved, and in any case only two of the three episodes were ever finished. As they stand, they are quite preponderantly gloomy in outlook,[28] being first-person confessions narrated by con-demned pilgrims now at journey's end.

"The Story of Prince Alasi and the Princess Firouzkah" is much like *Vathek*. The prince is torn be-tween fidelity to his virtuous wife and the embrace of an evil princess. Firouzkah is disguised as a boy most of the time, moreover a boy who bears a striking resemblance to the prince. Aside from these suggestions of compounded homosexuality and incest, the character of the prince bears out the basic Beckford theme. He is steadily driven to unspeakable depravities yet never free of self-doubt and remorse. "Prince Alasi" is, on balance, an inferior tale, being too crammed with incident and too empty of psychological insight. Much bolder is "The Story of Prince Barkiarokh." Although Beckford seems to have made no great efforts to control the voices or otherwise achieve any unity in the work, the overwhelming sexual guilt is more forcefully brought out here than in his other stories. The protagonist of the tale is the son of a poor fisherman who weds a good and faithful peri and proceeds to put her extraordinary gifts to very bad use. He deceives the king's daughter, marries her, and murders the king, thereby ascending the throne. His first wife still has the power to afflict Barkiarokh with an acute pain in the chest each time she finds him doing something wrong. However, because her innocence bars her from knowledge of his motives, he is able to trick her by pretending sincerely to repent. In fact, his shame after raping his princess wife while she is in a fainting fit only works to fan his passion:

> The woman I sought to embrace was always inert and seemingly dead, and I always quitted her with horror. Often, after issuing from Gazahidé's apartment, I rushed away to the Mosque, and there beat my breast with such violence that the spectators were lost in admiration at seeing a king as zealous, as much a martyr in the cause of penitence, as the most enthusiastic of fakirs.[29]

Any genuine remorse he may have felt dissolves into an empty show the minute he is aware of being observed. The next moment his returning lust drives any pretense of repentance quite out of his thoughts. With such a wide-ranging emotional repertory Barkiarokh comes to be simultaneously fascinated and disgusted with both the passion and the remorse, which is at once sincere and insincere. More and more there is a randomness about even his incest. Things, people, vices, and virtues begin to lose discrete identity; repentance is more like hypocrisy, deceit resembles remorse, beauty is filth, and filth beauty, and even the foul trough, the great Miry Desert, is suddenly transformed into a softly flowing wine stream. It is this slippery doubleness that Beckford almost monomaniacally examines in all these tales. The *Vathek* cycle, as a whole, is not concerned so much with the war of sin and guilt, reason and passion, as it is with this ambiguous identity of things by which ultimately everything is plunged into a murky limbo, all distinctions annihilated.

Because Beckford stages his Gothic drama in the magical east, Reeve's conception of probability and its application to fiction is no longer relevant. That is, Beckford certainly was not interested in making the marvelous seem reasonable or the exotic familiar in *Vathek*, where children are transformed into swine and the evil eye shines death rays, with no apparent reason and not even an attempt at explanation. Nor is the terror of the story dependent on its fantastic elements. Oriental counterparts of the typical Gothic paraphernalia are all there, certainly, but Beckford's use of them is usually quite incidental and, at that, ironic. In those passages where he does not sustain this spirit of parody the fantastic element often assumes much deeper human significance. What was, in *The Castle of Otranto*, the usual Gothic underground vault is, in *Vathek*, a vast netherworld whose sojourners can know only an eternity of despair. It is Beckford's relentless preoccupation with the anguish of the human condition that achieves for his tales their undeniable impact.

The moral significance of the tales serves to differentiate Beckford's work from the *Arabian Nights* as well. Sensuality, for Beckford, is not considered an end in itself. Instead, by careful descriptive work on the sensual in man he is able to suggest the full moral range, one that shades all the stark goods and evils of the Gothic ethos. It is the same with his sensuous evocations: The subtle shadings of lights and darks, the decay and chill stone of the Palace of Eblis, the fragrance of incense, the stench of burning bodies, the icy sweat of necrophilia, the reverberating groans of men in their last agony, the pervasive slime—in such passages the prose is heightened at times to poetry, as if to conceal a certain confessional element.[30] In any case they bear as little resemblance to the usual Gothic crudities as they do to the bold stories told by Scheherazade.

Vathek throughout suggests the autobiographical reference.[31] Author and character share many traits: lively curiosity, egotism, self-indulgence, and homosexuality. (It turns out that Beckford's adventure with the tower he was at such pains to construct on his estate is an ironic support for the moral verdict he passed upon the Caliph. "The Grand Babel," as he called it, collapsed before it was finished, and the second Babel, sham Gothic in wood and stone, crumbled some years later.) However, more than mere parallels between an author's life and his work, we see in Beckford an extraordinary involvement of himself in his work. Story-telling, for Beckford, is not so much the detached craftsmanly activity aimed at turning out a first-rate yarn as it is a highly personal means of self-study, a process by which the *making* of something is quite secondary to the *discovery* of something, and this discovery more of oneself than of the world. When the writer laughs, as Beckford does in his Gothic parodies, it is at himself; however, when the joke is finished, an uncomfortable intensity builds up, and the tale is told as in a confessional. Thus do the *Vathek* tales reflect without deception the fundamental ambivalence of Beckford the man.[32]

The romance tradition developed very rapidly after *Vathek*. Other tales by Clara Reeve; Sophia Lee's *The Recess* (1785) and *Warbeck* (1786); Charlotte Smith's *Manon Lescaut* (1786), *Desmond* (1792), and *The Old Manor House* (1793); and Dr. John Moore's *Zeluco* (1786) are prominent. Ann Radcliffe began her career with *Castles of Athlin and Dunbayne,* published in 1789, and quickly followed it with *A Sicilian Romance* (1790), *The Romance of the Forest* (1791), and *The Mysteries of Udolpho* (1794).

Between 1794 and 1797, five of the best known tales of the period were published: William Godwin's *Things As They Are; or, The Adventures of Caleb Williams* (1794); Radcliffe's *The Mysteries of Udolpho* and *The Italian* (1797); Matthew G. Lewis' *The Monk* (1796); and the first volume of Sophia and Harriet Lee's *Canterbury Tales* (1797). Three of these (*Caleb Williams, The Monk,* and *The Italian*) are interesting transitional works connecting the Gothic tradition with the main currents of nineteenth-century literature.

III

"Man is like those twin-births, that have two heads indeed, and four hands; but, if you attempt to detach them from each other, they are inevitably subjected to miserable and lingering destruction." [33] So speculates Caleb Williams just as his story is about to close. He sees man as beset by the twin demands of personal integrity, or truth-to-self, and social esteem, both of which must be satisfied if he is to maintain his equilibrium of existence in the world. Godwin's novel *Caleb Williams* presents the two extremes of this destructive unbalance by the stratagem of two characters, Caleb and Falkland.

All his life Falkland has felt the compulsion, immoderate to the point of crowding out any other concern, to keep up his good reputation. His mentor Mr. Clare worries about this and on his deathbed admonishes him against his "impatience of imagined dishonor" (I,v). However, Falkland's moral sense continues to deal exclusively in appearances. When he saves the young girl from the fire and she embraces him passionately right there in the middle of the conflagration that would symbolically endorse her love for him, he reacts with a cool decorum that denies this possibility of a balanced richness in his life. After the murder of Tyrrel, Falkland is disgraced by the criminal charge against him, and even when the trial returns an "innocent" verdict his reputation has been weakened. What is more, the peace, the rather pleasant inner emptiness protected by his impeccable manners, is lost to him. Finding himself burdened by guilt and remorse for the first time in his life, he becomes a stranger to himself and to others. "Mr. Falkland was sometimes seen climbing among the rocks, reclining motionless for hours together upon the edge of a precipice, or lulled into a kind of nameless lethargy of despair by the dashing of the torrents" (II,iv). Gradually he recognizes in his developing friendship with Caleb an antidote to this Byronic loneliness. It occurs to him that the peasant youth's unspoiled outlook on life might somehow help him come to terms with himself. He resolves to be "more of a man," and promises to "forget the past, and do better for the time to come." "The future," he tells Caleb, "the future is always our own" (II,ii). The hollowness of this resolve becomes apparent as Falkland continues to hide like a guilt-ridden Dr. Jekyll behind the "phantom of departed honor" (Postscript), not allowing even his friend to glimpse the reality behind the ghost. Caleb, meanwhile, is possessed by the desire to know; he is the hunter, the "spring of [his] action . . . [is] curiosity" (I,i). As Godwin remarks elsewhere, in regard to the motivations of these two, the Bluebeard's job is, after all, to hide, his wife's to find.[34]

Caleb is usually seen as the innocent victim and Falkland as the relentless persecutor, but the evidence of the tale will not support this easy judgment. Caleb's guilt derives from his uncontrollable curiosity, and though he insists that in digging into his master's past he is only seeking "justice," he admits there is an "alluring pungency" to his spying, a "kind of tingling sensation, not altogether unallied to enjoyment" (II,i). At heart Caleb is less a wholesome country boy than a voyeur with a touch of the morbid about him. Until just before the end of the tale, this spiritual Peeping Tom remains quite blind to the depravity of his project, unable to see that such regard for the spiritual wounds of another amounts to an obscene invasion of that other, a crime that Hawthorne would describe so well as a violation of the "sanctity of a human heart."

In this role of self-appointed investigator Caleb is a kind of "second conscience"[35] to Falkland. Going about everywhere together, they become almost indistinguishable. Then, for a time, the tables are turned, and Caleb is shadowed by Falkland. The two locked together in their strange drama have little to do with the rest of society, and are isolated within it. In this respect they are much like Frankenstein and his monster in the tale by Godwin's daughter, Mary Shelley. Falkland is out to destroy Caleb to protect what is left of his reputation, and Caleb must run to keep alive his exclusive knowledge of Falkland. The contrapuntal plan of the work becomes apparent when Caleb, having been imprisoned for an alleged theft, finds himself disgraced by a conviction. After his escape from prison he in turn becomes "a solitary being, cut off from the expectation of sympathy, kindness, and the good will of mankind" (III,vii), and in this wretched state he curses the "whole system of human existence" (III,vii). Only his strong personality and rigid sense of justice keep him from despair. "The more I am destitute of the esteem of mankind, the more careful I will be to preserve my own. I will never from fear, or any other mistaken motive, do anything of which I ought to be ashamed" (III,xii). As long as he remains an outcast he can believe unequivocally in his own righteousness. It is only when he is at last able to vindicate himself and expose Falkland's crime that he can no longer fight what he calls the "prejudices of my species," and he caves in. He is forced to confront the dark place in his own heart, where he understands for the first time how he "wantonly inflicted on him an anguish a thousand times worse than death." More important, he comes to question his habitual self-consciousness: "Why should my reflection perpetually center upon myself?—self, an overweening regard to which has been the source of my errors!" (Postscript).

At the end, after the long struggle against injustice and his own loneliness, Caleb realizes the futility of "self-esteem"; conversely, Falkland, who had held tight to that "phantom of departed honor," wastes away, becoming himself a "skeleton," a ghost of his former self. "Death and infamy" have claimed him together, but not before the two men embrace, recognizing the essential equilibrium that exists in the union of their characters.

There is little question but that *Caleb Williams* was

begun as a propaganda piece for the type of rationalism
Godwin set forth in his *Political Justice,* published the
previous year. The prefaces to the novels [36] support this,
and *Caleb Williams* itself is evidence enough, for if Caleb
is Falkland's victim, Falkland is brought to his knees by
a feudalistic code of honor. He is by necessity "fitted to
be an assassin; . . . a dagger . . . fitted to be his instrument." The murder is not *his* crime in the sense that he
could freely will it, and so the punishment Caleb wants
for him is just so much "useless torture." [37] At the root of
every crime is the social structure the corruption of which
eats into the individual and prevents him from going on
to realize his innate perfection. To help make his point
Godwin has refurbished the Gothic castle dungeon as a
prison for the incarceration and torture of minor criminals, many of whom are innocent victims of bad laws.
And yet, if the author began the book for the purpose of
railing against social evils while proclaiming his strident
reformative doctrines, the novel outgrew that intent.
Caleb Williams is a quite different reading of life than
that expressed in *Political Justice.*[38]

What will help to explain the difference in outlook expressed by *Caleb Williams* and *Political Justice*
is the fact that some of Godwin's views had begun to
change about the time that *Political Justice* was published.
Revisions in the second edition (1795) were carefully
pointed out in the Preface, and in *St. Leon* (1799) he
makes a self-conscious apology for this "inconsistency" [39]
in his ideas. In the second edition, he is no longer an
out-and-out rationalist and makes some allowance for the
"culture of the heart." Thus, *Caleb Williams* was started
at an early stage of this broadening of Godwin's intellectual sympathies. The discrepancy between intention

and outcome is best explained by reference to this change in Godwin's thought and its mode.

For Godwin, as for most artists, the imaginative process is very different from the discursive. It is one thing to formulate the concept of a despotic aristocrat, and quite another to create a convincing fictional embodiment of that concept, such as Falkland. To work his theories into the texture of an imaginative work—into, one might say, the real lives of imaginary people—Godwin had to put to work an insight into the vagaries and defects of personality which in his philosophical writings could be dismissed as transitional imperfections of man in an imperfect society. Thus were the premises of his systematic work subtly undermined and shifted. Godwin himself describes exactly, if somewhat heavily, his discovery of this process: ". . . the thing in which my imagination revelled the most freely, was the analysis of the private and internal operations of the mind, employing my metaphysical dissecting knife in tracing and laying bare the involutions of motive, and recording the gradually accumulating impulses, which led the personages I had to describe primarily to adopt the particular way of proceeding in which they afterwards embarked." [40] *Caleb Williams* is prominent in that tradition of modern literature which regards the imaginative work—whether novel or poem—as a testing ground of the self, and the whole imaginative process as a kind of *Denkenexperiment* bent on discovery of nothing less than the writer's own mode of existing in the world. Godwin's change from necessitarian theory toward a deeper and less dogmatic understanding of the human affections may thus be read into the *Zeitgeist* of early nineteenth-century Romanticism. (It is interesting that not only Godwin but the young Wordsworth and Coleridge, once under his influence, were at that time carefully examining and challenging their Godwinian intellectual legacy.) *Caleb Williams* in fact develops one of the fundamental themes of the Romantic poets, the simultaneous attractiveness and anguish of isolation.[41]

However, Godwin's greater significance for this study lies in his interesting new use of various Gothic conventions. In *The Castle of Otranto* remorse belonged to the individual alone, whereas remorse and shame in *Caleb Williams* go a great way toward placing the characters in a definite social milieu. Then there is Godwin's new use of the maiden-in-distress motif: Emily's rescue from the fire is included less for its episodic excitement than for its value in revealing Falkland as a man unable to respond to a lovely young woman and come to some self-recognition through her. Similarly, the stock situation of a villain tormenting an innocent hero—a motif that will be used time and again in Dickens and Dostoevsky—is here used as a means of getting at the workings of the aberrant mind. (Related to this is his adaptation of the Gothic dungeon in his prison motif, which anticipates later use—Dickens' in *Little Dorrit,* for instance—as a symbol for man's inescapable self-identity.) Still another feature, the manhunt in which pursuer and pursued change roles, is put to good use to suggest two aspects of a single personality at war with each other.[42]

IV

In September 1794 Matthew Lewis was reminding his mother to be sure to read *Caleb Williams,* a book "in a new style, and well written." [43] At that time he had just finished his own romance, *The Monk,* which was to become sensationally successful following his election to Parliament (succeeding Beckford, incidentally) from the pocket borough of Hindon in Wiltshire. Soon everybody was reading the book by the young M.P., and nearly everybody found something in it to complain loudly about. Coleridge, although granting it a few merits, was generally unsympathetic in his review; [44] Mathias compared it to Cleland's *Memoirs of a Woman of Pleasure;* [45] Carlyle some years later stayed up till four in the morning to finish it and then concluded it was the "most stupid and villainous" [46] thing he had read in a long time; Hazlitt, slightly better disposed toward it, still charged *The Monk* for its "unpardonable grossness." [47]

These writers were disturbed by what they felt was the book's corruption. There is no doubt that *The Monk* is offensive, even revolting in places. There is a dwelling on unsavory scenes, certainly, but is it a deliberate defiance of prevailing moral standards? In fact, the work as a whole is informed with a rather sedate morality: Pride, especially spiritual pride, leads to damnation. Early in the book Ambrosio's arrogance and cruelty provide the devil's agent, Matilda, with an opportunity to seduce him; once seduced, he inevitably continues in his sinful ways until he is so wicked as apparently to have missed out on God's reasonable punishment and to have warranted something else from Satan—he is hurled from the sky to instant death. Considering Lewis' conventional treatment of crime and punishment, there is no reason to doubt the authenticity of his defense of the book to his father: "But though I did not expect much benefit to arise from the perusal of a trifling romance, written by a youth of twenty, I was in my own mind quite certain that no harm could be produced by a work whose subject was furnished by one of our best moralists, and in the composition of which I did not introduce a single incident, or a single character, without meaning to inculcate some maxim universally allowed." [48] Before writing this, he had gone so far as to expunge the most offensive passages to make the next edition more acceptable.[49] Thus, there is no basis for reading the monk of the tale as a moral spokesman for the "Monk" Lewis known to family and friends, although, through his nightly adventures, he does seem at times a sexual alter ego for the young man from Hindon. Ambrosio is an extravagant villain, and the verdict Lewis and his readers pass on his kind assures finally a comfortable distinction between author and character.

For the same reason—Lewis' conventional morality—there is no point in looking for a Marquis de Sade in Matthew Lewis, or, for that matter, a *Justine* in *The Monk,* however much Lewis may indulge himself vicariously in Ambrosio's perversions. Sade made an all-out attack on what he felt was the utter hypocrisy of the bourgeoisie; Lewis disguised his dream world behind the cloak of respectability. Still, he was not entirely lacking insight into this split between the ordinary negative judgment on his character's behavior and the simultaneous overwhelming compulsion of his pathological sexuality: "I perceive that I have put too much confidence in the accuracy of my own judgment; that, convinced of my object being unexceptionable, I did not sufficiently examine whether the means by which I attained that object were generally so. . . ." [50] It is not only that Lewis' treatment of aberrant sexuality is so insistently dwelt upon—he includes rape, incest, sodomy, necrophilia, voyeurism, and of course sadomasochism—but that the detailing of it goes so unrelieved by any touch of irony or humor. In *Vathek* there is often some very good comedy made of the Caliph's insatiable sensuality, but in *The Monk* it is the unfailing energy of the sexual alone that sustains the pace of the story. Lewis documents Ambrosio's relentless libido with all the determination of a Krafft-Ebing spelling out the definitive *psychopathia sexualis. The Monk* is interesting, then, primarily as a document of an adolescent's sexual fantasy; certainly its particular slant on the netherworld cannot be confused with the bold exploration of the unconscious and the irrational achieved in much twentieth-century literature.

In regard to Ambrosio's double life, one begins to suspect that the device was pressed into service in the tale primarily to intensify the excitement of perversion by contrast with ordinary everyday life.[51] It is all according to prescription: the publicly respected "man of Holiness" tormented by remorse while being driven, paradoxically, to even greater atrocities by this same remorse. Ambrosio then presents very little that is new in the Gothic tradition; Matilda also is imperfectly conceived. As Coleridge was quick to perceive, she is by far the more attractive figure, but her relationship with the monk becomes unintelligible when later on in the story she is presented as in fact Satan's functionary,[52] a sort of female Mephistopheles out to tempt him and bring about his downfall. Lucifer's transfiguration, too—from splendid angel of light to the darkest of devils—contributes nothing to the work except as a reminder of Lewis' artistic cowardice.

Lewis was a voluminous reader, and, whether legitimate borrower or outright plagiarist,[53] he did introduce many new features into English Gothicism from the lurid and violent spirit of the *Schauerroman,* which he absorbed during his sojourns on the continent. In Lewis, the German descendants of Walpole thus rejoin the native lineage of Clara Reeve and Mrs. Radcliffe, to form what may be looked upon as a second stage of the English romance

development. The haunted castle is now a Catholic abbey, with a little Inquisition atmosphere thrown in; the
subterranean dungeon becomes a catacomb filled with
the stench of putrid corpses; Lucifer, who had not had
much to say since Milton's time, bargains in *The Monk*
for man's soul; the Wandering Jew and the Bleeding Nun
are recruited from folklore and legend; and all the old
paraphernalia are there, from magic portraits to prophetic
dreams, moving statues, trapdoors, and sleeping potions.
The work is practically an encyclopedia of the Gothic
romance, documenting, as it does, the Protestant dualism
of flesh and soul projected onto imagined Catholic orgies.
Despite the fact that many elements in *The Monk* may
have been borrowed from earlier sources, they were
copied in turn by countless writers, especially on the continent. In this way Lewis' tale becomes for us a convenient *terminus a quo* in English Gothic, especially in regard to such archetypal characters as the priest-villain
and the *Diable Amoureux*.[54]

At the time Ann Radcliffe published *The Italian,*
the best of her works, she had already completed four
others, at least one of which was tremendously successful;
one reviewer thought *The Mysteries of Udolpho* "the
most interesting novel in the English language." [55] The
reader today, dutifully attentive through over six hundred
pages of *The Mysteries,* finds it difficult to understand
just how the enchantress managed to work her charms
on practically the entire English-reading public of her
time. The stagy terror especially tends to put one off.
Terror, for Radcliffe, is quite simply a trick up the
sleeve, and to this entertainment she judiciously adds the
proper mix of edifying ingredients, so that her tales inevitably end with a victory for love, virtue, and common

sense. The terrifying events have all been explained away as really quite ordinary occurrences that were only misconstrued by the frightened maiden of the tale. Radcliffe's best writing is found in her natural descriptions. Characteristically lyrical and sometimes elegiac, these passages heighten the melancholy of her situations and at times achieve momentarily a real fusion of beauty and terror for the tale.

Unfortunately, the misty landscapes Radcliffe describes [56] bog down her dramatic development at crucial places, for the Radcliffe people are mostly tiresome puppets. In her earlier romances, heroes and villains alike are subordinated to set situations and plot machinations. Schedoni, of *The Italian,* begins to come alive and is certainly the best of her characters. He has all the earmarks of the Gothic villain—the mysterious origin; the pale, handsome face; the melancholy; and above all, the fierce passion and remorse. In form a priest, in substance a devil, Schedoni is Ambrosio again, but with another dimension to his anguish:

> Had it been possible to have shut out all consciousness of himself, also, how willingly would he have done so! He threw himself into a chair, and remained for a considerable time motionless and lost in thought, yet the emotions of his mind were violent and contradictory. At the very instant when his heart reproached him with the crime he had meditated, he regretted the ambitious views he must relinquish if he failed to perpetrate it, and regarded himself with some degree of contempt for having hitherto hesitated on the subject. He considered the character of his own mind with astonishment, for circumstances had drawn forth

traits, of which, till now, he had no suspicion. He knew not by what doctrine to explain the inconsistencies, the contradictions, he experienced, and perhaps, it was not one of the least, that in these moments of direful and conflicting passions, his reason could still look down upon their operations, and lead him to a cool, though brief examination of his own nature.[57]

The fascination here is not with the *fait accompli,* to judge it or brood on it, but rather with the decisive moments prior to any act. Schedoni's confusions and contradictions divert his attention from the matter at hand; the effect of such inopportune deliberation is to weaken, often paralyze his will to act at all, sometimes to cut the very nerve of passion. The interesting thing in Schedoni is his Hamlet-like habit of simultaneously examining himself and then determining to cut short such inconvenient self-examination. One might also say that the Gothic villain in this work is deprived of both the strong impulse and the will to act, first by an awareness, or self-consciousness, and then by *the awareness of the self-consciousness*—a totally immobilizing condition. In this way Schedoni's psychological impotence anticipates that of Victorian personae like Clough's Dipsychus who are bewildered and in vital ways paralyzed by the conflicting forces of their time.

In most other respects, Radcliffe's work is quite eighteenth century in outlook. There is her continual explanation of supernatural phenomena as mere ordinary, though misunderstood, happenings—a mannerism traceable to her strict observance of Reeve's rules for establishing probability in the genre. In a way, she is probably the last of those who can be called pre-Romantic Gothicists,[58] for her love of nature is more in the deistic-sentimental tradition of Thomson, Gray, and Collins than 'in the Wordsworthian transcendentalism that was to follow.

V

The love of Gothic terror continued to be strong in the first several decades of the nineteenth century. Although parodies and lampoons of the genre by Jane Austen, Maria Edgeworth, Peacock, and others appeared frequently, these were far outnumbered by the cheap digests of the Gothic classics and other outright plagiarisms being published at this time in the form of "bluebooks" or "shilling shockers." [59] Maturin's *Melmoth the Wanderer* (1820) is usually considered the last great Gothic romance proper,[60] but the tradition survived in the "penny dreadfuls" and popular periodicals [61] and flourished anew at one point in the Newgate novels and at another in the domestic melodramas. Sir Walter Scott, influenced by "Monk" Lewis and other romancers, modified the Gothic terror to his purposes in the historical romance, with fortunate consequences throughout the Victorian age.

Although it is true that only a handful of Gothic romances seem much worth reading now, Gothicism did manage to stimulate the imagination of many important nineteenth-century writers in Europe as well as in England and America. To cite only the plainest evidence, the imaginative constitution of a Byron would seem very definitely traceable to the romances. Byron explicitly acknowledged Walpole as the *"Ultimus Romanorum,"* the "father of the first romance and of the last tragedy in our language," [62] and recognized Beckford as his spiritual kin.[63] To "Monk" Lewis he is in debt for far more than the source for *Manfred*.[64] His debt to Ann Radcliffe is really more than a literary one: Byron's incest with his half-sister was, to borrow from Praz, a "plagiarism." [65] Poe is another beneficiary of the Gothic; his tales are inconceivable without the romances, probably introduced to him by Charles Brockden Brown, and his "Philosophy of Composition" begins with a letter he received from Dickens treating the supposed writing method employed in *Caleb Williams*. Poe in turn transmitted Gothicism to French literature through his influence on Baudelaire.[66] Then there are the French writers, Baudelaire among these too, who stand in debt directly to "Monk" Lewis and Mrs. Radcliffe—Chateaubriand, Balzac, Hugo, Merimée, Sue, Gautier, and Flaubert.[67] Similarly, Beckford found a strong advocate in Mallarmé,[68] as did Godwin in Chateaubriand and Sainte-Beuve.[69] The result of all such crossings was that French Gothicism was returned to England toward the end of the nineteenth century as symbolism, to join the indigenous Gothic that had persisted through such writers as Byron, Shelley, James Hogg, Bulwer-Lytton, the Brontës, Dickens, Rossetti, Swinburne, Hardy, Stevenson, and Wilde. In other literatures, the work of E. T. A. Hoffmann, Chamisso, Hawthorne, Melville, and Dostoevsky cannot be overlooked in any discussion of the Gothic and its migrations and transmogrifications.

There is a great deal more to such "influences" than can be dealt with here. The writers were wide readers and in no sense limited by a single prevailing influence on their work. Goethe read Byron; Byron knew his Goethe well. Poe learned from Byron and then "taught" Baudelaire, who was also acquainted with all that Goethe and

Byron had been formed on. The history of literature is an organic development which withholds its essence from the statement of mere isolated relationships. Nor does English Gothicism constitute the only source for the nineteenth-century literature of spiritual distress, for the continental writers found materials in their own traditions that functioned similarly for them in their poems and novels.[70] However, English Gothicism does stand at the beginning of a larger development that may be called the romance tradition in nineteenth-century English literature, a tradition marked unmistakably by its practitioners' overriding concern with the problems of the self in the modern world. Early Gothic is a necessary part of this broader tradition by virtue of its exploration of the irrational in man and consequent liberation of the novelist's imagination. More specifically, it was the first modern prose form disposed to fairly intensive concern with the various phenomena of the divided self. (What realistic novel, after all, could convincingly present a Jekyll and Hyde, or an Ambrosio torn between everyday piety and nocturnal atrocities?) The poets and novelists of the succeeding generations were to make new use of this extraordinary form in their attempt to set down their sense of the widening rift in the self—between imagination and reason, feeling and thought, belief and agnosticism, and increasingly between private experience and public responsibility.

Notes

1. One of the earliest examples of this distinction may be seen in the Preface to *Incognita* by Congreve. See Bonamy Dobrée's edition (London, 1928), p. 5. In these definitions, there is hardly a mention of Aristotle, but their final source is undoubtedly his *Poetics*, Chapters 9 and 24.

2. *Romances and Narratives by Daniel Defoe,* ed. G. A. Aitken (London, 1895), I, p. lxvii.
3. *Novels,* ed. Austin Dobson and W. L. Phelps (London, 1902), II, p. 284.
4. Preface to *Joseph Andrews, Complete Works,* Drury Lane Edition (New York, 1902), I, p. 19.
5. The vogue of the orthodox novel had declined by then. During this period there are few important novels, the chief titles being Smollett's *Humphry Clinker,* Goldsmith's *Vicar of Wakefield,* and Mackenzie's *Man of Feeling.*
6. Walpole's letter to Cole, March 9, 1765. *The Yale Edition of Horace Walpole's Correspondence,* ed. W. S. Lewis (New Haven, 1937), I, p. 88.
7. Devendra P. Varma, *The Gothic Flame* (London, 1956), p. 67. Romance writers are fond of claiming inspired writing. Walpole says elsewhere that he finished his first version in eight days, and Beckford says *Vathek* took but "three days and two nights." This implied unconscious writing persists among poets and romance writers up to the present time. Yeats's "automatic" writing is a good example.
8. The term "Gothic" has been much debated: many of these Gothic tales are not Gothic, or medieval, in the least, nor, more importantly, are supernatural elements unfailingly present in them. To break down the fantastic genre into subtypes, such as the oriental story, the novel of suspense, the Gothic tale, and the story of doctrine, does not solve the problem, for many tales belonging to other subtypes share not only the properly Gothic trappings established by Walpole and Miss Reeve, but the Gothic spirit as well—the melancholy, the wonder, the suspense, and the terror. Thus, because these elements overlap the categories, the best strategy seems to be simply to include all these books under the heading of "Gothic" or "romance," and treat them all as more or less the descendants of *Otranto.* For a discussion of this, see Edith Birkhead, *The Tale of Terror* (London, 1921); Eino Railo, *The Haunted Castle: A Study of the Elements of English Romanticism* (London and New York, 1927); Montague Summers, *The Gothic Quest: A History of the Gothic Novel* (London, [1928]); Ernest A. Baker, *The History of the English Novel* (London, 1929), V; J. M. S. Tompkins, *The Popular Novel in England: 1770–1800* (London, 1932); Walter F. Wright, *Sensibility in English Prose Fiction: 1760–1814* (Urbana, 1937); James R. Foster, *History of the Pre-Romantic Novel in England* (New York, 1949).
9. *The Castle of Otranto: A Gothic Story,* ed. W. S. Lewis (London, 1964), p. 45. This edition is referred to throughout.

10. Clara Frances McIntyre, in particular, eyed the Elizabethan dramas as the main source of Mrs. Radcliffe's romances in her *Ann Radcliffe in Relation to Her Time* (New Haven, 1920), and increasingly emphasized the Elizabethan origin of Radcliffe and others in subsequent articles, "Were the 'Gothic Novels' Gothic?" *PMLA*, XXXVI (1921), pp. 644–667, and "The Later Career of the Elizabethan Villain Hero," *PMLA*, XL (1925), pp. 874–880. According to the last article, the term "Gothic" is almost synonymous with "Elizabethan." For a view similar to mine, see Robert Langbaum's *The Poetry of Experience* (New York, 1957), pp. 58–59.

11. *Letters on Chivalry and Romance*, 2nd ed. (London, 1772), p. 119.

12. *Otranto*, p. 4.

13. *Otranto*, p. 4. Italics Walpole's.

14. This is Professor Wright's interpretation. See his *Sensibility in English Prose Fiction*, p. 98.

15. See Clara Reeve's Preface to *The Old English Baron* and *The Progress of Romance*, her digest of Warton and Beattie; Godwin, Preface to *The Travels of St. Leon;* Sir Walter Scott, "Romance," an article contributed to the *Supplement to the Fourth, Fifth, and Sixth Editions of the Encyclopaedia Britannica* (London, 1824), VI, pp. 435–456; Shelley's Preface to his wife's *Frankenstein;* and Nathaniel Hawthorne, Preface to *The House of the Seven Gables*. The genre battle between novel and romance was revived toward the end of the nineteenth century, corollary to the struggle between realism and naturalism among writers such as Hardy, James, Stevenson, and others. For a discussion of this, see Chapter 6. In the twentieth century, this distinction has lost much of its significance, but some vestiges of the old argument are in evidence in, for instance, E. M. Forster's *Aspects of the Novel*.

16. Gray's letter to Walpole, December 30, 1764. Quoted by Lewis in his Introduction, p. vii.

17. The *Critical Review*, XIX (1765), p. 51, and the *Monthly Review*, XXXII (1765), p. 97.

18. Earlier examples of the eighteenth-century use of the supernatural are Defoe's *A True Relation of the Apparition of Mrs. Veal* (1706), *The Political History of the Devil* (1726), and *History and Reality of Apparitions* (1727). Later on, we might read Collins' *Ode on Popular Superstitions of the Highlands* (written in 1749?), Macpherson's poems, and Percy's *Reliques* (1765) as expressions of the enlightened man's nostalgia for incredulity, what he cannot believe with his own eyes. As such it makes up still another tributary of an ever-widening Romanticism.

19. Walpole to Mme du Deffand, March 13, 1767, written originally in French; quoted by Lewis in his Introduction, p. x.

20. *The Castle of Otranto and the Mysterious Mother,* ed. Montague Summers (Boston and London, 1925), p. 253.

21. *The Old English Baron: A Gothic Story* (London, 1883), p. 13.

22. Walpole would not let this remark go without some comment. He wrote to Robert Jephson on January 27, 1830, "It [*The Old English Baron*] was totally void of imagination and interest, had scarce any incidents, and, though it condemned the marvelous, admitted ghost. I suppose the author thought a tame ghost might come within the laws of probability." *The Letters of Horace Walpole, Fourth Earl of Oxford,* ed. Peter Cunningham (Edinburgh, 1906), VII, p. 319. This complaint was later seconded by Scott. See his "Clara Reeve," *Lives of Eminent Novelists and Dramatists* (London and New York, 1887), p. 547.

23. Beckford wrote both *Vathek* and the *Episodes* in French. *Vathek* was translated by Samuel Henley under Beckford's supervision, and, in England at least, Henley's version has been the accepted text. The text referred to here is the third edition (London, 1816), p. 5.

24. Many scholars have noticed this shift. See, for example, Birkhead, p. 95; J. W. Oliver, *The Life of William Beckford* (London, 1932), pp. 101–102; Baker, *History,* V, p. 75.

25. See Oliver, p. 24. The tale was published for the first time in 1930 under the title "The Vision" given it by the editor Guy Chapman.

26. *The Vision* and *Liber Veritatis,* ed. Guy Chapman (London and New York, 1930), p. 11.

27. For a good account of the Powderham scandal, see Guy Chapman, *Beckford* (New York, 1937), and Boyd Alexander, *England's Wealthiest Son* (London, 1962). See also J. W. Oliver, *Life.*

28. Characteristically, however, Beckford is unable to maintain his intensity in the third episode; the tale, perhaps reflecting the author's awareness of tonal flaw, breaks off abruptly.

29. *The Episodes of Vathek,* trans. Sir Frank T. Marzials (London, 1912), pp. 128–129.

30. In fact *Vathek* was put into couplets with the title of "The Palace of Istaker" by "A.V." (who thought the subject "more adapted to poetry than to prose") in the *Gentleman's Magazine,* LX (1790), pp. 69–70, 163–165, 258–259.

31. See Baker, V, p. 75; Oliver, p. 101; Chapman, p. 108. A recent Beckford scholar, Boyd Alexander, draws close parallels between the man and the work; see *England's Wealthiest Son,* pp. 92–99.

32. Another man of ambivalence about this time is, of course,

Laurence Sterne, whose sense of the self comes across as two quite distinguishable tempers—the sentimental and the comical. They are so smoothly worked, however, that neither book nor man seems the least disrupted by the contest. For an incisive discussion of Sterne, see Gardner D. Stout, Jr., "Yorick's *Sentimental Journey:* A Comic 'Pilgrim's Progress' for the Man of Feeling," *ELH* (1963), pp. 395–412.

33. Book III, Chapter 14, *Caleb Williams* (London, 1831). This edition is used throughout.

34. "Falkland was my Bluebeard, who had perpetrated atrocious crimes, which if discovered, he might expect to have all the world roused to revenge against him. Caleb Williams was the wife, who in spite of warning, persisted in his attempts to discover the forbidden secret. . . ." Preface to *Fleetwood,* 2nd ed. (London, 1832), p. xii.

35. Hazlitt's words. "William Godwin," *The Spirit of the Age, The Complete Works,* ed. P. P. Howe (London and Toronto, 1930–34), VII, p. 24.

36. See the Preface written (though withdrawn in 1794) for the first edition and the Preface to the 1832 edition of *Fleetwood.* Elsewhere he said that *Caleb Williams* was the "offspring of that temper of mind in which the composition of *Political Justice* left me." Quoted from Godwin's diary by C. Kegan Paul, *William Godwin: His Friends and Contemporaries* (Boston, 1876), I, p. 78.

37. *Enquiry Concerning Political Justice,* 3rd ed. (London, 1798), II, pp. 323, 325. This argument appears in Book VII which is entitled "Of Crimes and Punishments."

38. Caleb's outbursts in the prison are often cited as the best evidence that the work is a "novel of doctrine." See, for example, Rosalie Glynn Grylls, *William Godwin and His World* (London, 1953), p. 46, and George Woodcock, *William Godwin: A Biographical Study* (London, 1946), p. 121.

39. Preface to *St. Leon: A Tale of the Sixteenth Century,* 3rd ed. (London, 1831), p. ix.

40. *Fleetwood,* p. xi.

41. Isolation is one of the most important themes in all of his novels. In *St. Leon,* written after his wife's death, the agony of loneliness is the central concern. D. H. Monro sees this obsession with solitude in the context of his personal life. *Godwin's Moral Philosophy: An Interpretation of William Godwin* (London, 1953), p. 67.

42. This use of romance conventions puts *Caleb Williams* more properly in the romance genre despite the fact that it has so much in common with the novel of the time, with its contemporary setting, general adherence to verisimilitude, and disdain of out-and-out

supernaturalism. Thus, owing to their romance origin and role as villain-heroes, Falkland and Caleb both remain generic rather than specific, mythical rather than individual; or, to borrow Northrop Frye's words, not " 'real people' so much as stylized figures which expand into psychological archetypes." See *Anatomy of Criticism: Four Essays* (Princeton, 1957), p. 304. Godwin was one of the first to see the possibilities these romance conventions held for the psychological novel, possibilities that later romancers such as Mary Shelley, Poe, Bulwer-Lytton, Dickens, and Hawthorne would further exploit in the darker psychological terror of their tales.

43. "Selected Letters" in Louis F. Peck, *A Life of Matthew G. Lewis* (Cambridge, Mass., 1961), p. 213.

44. The *Critical Review,* XIX (February 1797), pp. 194–200.

45. *The Pursuits of Literature: A Satirical Poem in Four Dialogues,* 7th ed. (London, 1798), pp. 239–243.

46. A letter to James Johnstone, *Early Letters of Thomas Carlyle,* ed. Charles Eliot Norton (London and New York, 1886), I, p. 121.

47. "On the English Novelists," *Lectures on the English Comic Writers, The Complete Works,* VI, p. 127.

48. A letter of February 23, 1798. *The Life and Correspondence of M. G. Lewis,* ed. Mrs. Cornwall Baron-Wilson (London, 1839), I, pp. 156–157.

49. The various readings are reproduced in the Grove Press edition (New York, 1952), by Louis F. Peck.

50. *Life and Correspondence,* I, p. 155.

51. Lewis' interest in the dual personality theme is evident in some of his other works as well. See *The Twins* and *Rugantino; or, The Bravo of Venice,* his translation of *Aballino der Grosse Bandit* by Heinrich Zschokke.

52. Byron was no doubt right in saying that she should have been "really in love with Ambrosio: this would have given it a human interest." Thomas Medwin, *Conversations of Lord Byron,* 2nd ed. (London, 1824), p. 229.

53. The sources of *The Monk* have been quite thoroughly reconstructed. A convenient list appears in Peck's *Life of Matthew G. Lewis,* pp. 292–293.

54. This is why, despite its slight literary value, the book, together with its author, occupies a dominant position in the most comprehensive studies of Gothicism by its two greatest enthusiasts, Montague Summers and Eino Railo. The longest chapter in *The Gothic Quest* (pp. 202–308) is devoted to Lewis, and Railo's *The Haunted Castle* treats Lewis as the high point of the earlier development and the matrix of the later.

55. The *Critical Review,* 2nd Ser., XII (November 1794), p. 359. The review was long assumed to be Coleridge's by many scholars (T. M. Raysor in his *Coleridge's Miscellaneous Criticism,* for instance), until Charles I. Patterson found evidence to the contrary. See his "The Authenticity of Coleridge's Review of Gothic Romances," *JEGP,* L (1951), pp. 517–521. Another reviewer in the *Monthly* was also full of praise. See *Monthly,* XV (November 1794), pp. 278–283.

56. The heroes and heroines of *The Mysteries of Udolpho* and *The Italian* often ignore imminent danger to dawdle in appreciation of the beauties of nature. As Ellena in *The Italian* says to herself, while being abducted, "If I am condemned to misery, surely I could endure it with more fortitude in scenes like these, than amidst the tamer landscapes of nature! . . . It is scarcely possible to yield to the pressure of misfortune while we walk, as with the Deity, amidst his most stupendous works!" *The Italian; or, The Confessional of the Black Penitents: A Romance* (London, 1797), I, vi, pp. 154–155.

57. *The Italian,* II, pp. ix, 267–268.

58. "There was, of course, no exact date when the Pre-Romantic Period came to an end and the Romantic began, yet it is convenient to designate the last decade of the eighteenth century as the time, for it was then that the Gothicists decided it was no longer necessary to pay homage to reason and give rational explanations of their supernatural phenomena; and it was then that those twin idols of the century, Reason and Sensibility, were toppled to the dust." James R. Foster, p. 1.

59. The best account of the "bluebooks" remains that found in William W. Watt's *Shilling Shockers of the Gothic School: A Study of Chapbook Gothic Romances* (Cambridge, Mass., 1932).

60. See note 8 above.

61. Concerning the popularity of the Gothic romance in the early nineteenth century, see Walter C. Phillips, *Dickens, Reade, and Collins: Sensation Novelists* (New York, 1919); Amy Cruse, *The Englishman and His Books in the Early Nineteenth Century* (New York, 1930); E. S. Turner, *Boys Will Be Boys* (London, 1948); Richard D. Altick, *The English Common Reader: A Social History of the Mass Reading Public 1800–1900* (Chicago and London, 1957).

62. "The Preface to *Marino Faliero: Doge of Venice." The Works of Lord Byron, Poetry,* ed. E. H. Coleridge (London, 1901), IV, p. 339.

63. Byron's affection for Beckford is evident in *Childe Harold,* Canto I, Stanzas 22 and 23. The kinship between the two has often

been pointed out. See, for example, Sacheverell Sitwell, *Beckford and Beckfordism* (London, 1930), p. 9.

64. It is Lewis who orally translated *Faust* for Byron, unwittingly initiating a scholarly question about the indebtedness of *Manfred* to Goethe. Actually the two were affectionate friends despite Byron's pillorying of Lewis as "Apollo's sexton" in *English Bards and Scotch Reviewers,* and Byron valued Lewis' literary advice. See Peck, p. 55.

65. Mario Praz, *The Romantic Agony,* trans. Angus Davidson (New York, 1956), p. 69.

66. The fullest study on this subject is in Patrick F. Quinn, *The French Face of Edgar Poe* (Carbondale, 1957).

67. See Praz, especially Chapters 2, 3, and 4; Summers, Chapter 6 and "Surrealism and the Gothic Novel"; Railo, pp. 183–189.

68. Mallarmé wrote an enthusiastic introduction to a French edition of *Vathek* (Paris, 1893).

69. Praz, pp. 194 and 272; also Baker, V, p. 244.

70. There is no full-length treatment of the romance development in the nineteenth century except for Summers' and Railo's books, both unsatisfactory. Four more books, though, should be mentioned in this connection: George Brandes, *Main Currents in Nineteenth Century Literature,* 6 vols. (New York, 1902), especially II; Dorothy Scarsborough, *The Supernatural in Modern English Fiction* (New York and London, 1917); M. G. Devonshire, *The English Novel in France: 1830–1870* (London 1929); and Ralph Tymms, *Doubles in Literary Psychology.*

Even as a broken Mirror, which the glass
In every fragment multiplies—and makes
A thousand images of one that was,
The same—and still the more, the more it
   breaks. . . .
                                Childe Harold's Pilgrimage

2.

The Logic of Passion:
Romanticism

The polarization of the insane and the wholesome in human character, which had fascinated the Gothic writers, is reformulated by the Romantics as a problem involving much more than the psychological. To the Romantic poets, the imagination is a mode of transcending raw reality, a means of overcoming the world as given. No longer a feature of the passive mind, the *tabula rasa* of Locke and Hartley, the imagination is here the active agent, shaping the world as it finds it, creating it anew with each vision. The world as given is continually being transformed into a Higher Reality of the poet's own making. Since, in the Kantian tradition, the world—the thing itself—is ultimately unknowable, there can be no final certification of this transcendental and creative function of the imagination (as there is none for its counterpart, reason); it must be taken on faith. The Romantic poets were generally not Kantians in this sense, for they were more than believers. For a Wordsworth or a Coleridge, there was certainty in the immediacy and joy of imaginative play, in the experience of Nature's beauty. With this certainty, the imagination can well sustain the poet's Higher Reality as creator of the world and as perfectly one with it. By a Plotinian equation, the "I" sees the Many enfolded in the One, the One comprising the Many, subject meeting object, and time resolving into eternity. By this process, too, the old God, whom the deists had tactfully retired, was restored to his full glory and activity in Nature.

Despite such brave Romantic theology, it is hardly the Higher Reality that daily confronts the poet. His joyful communion with Nature is seldom matched by communion with his fellow beings; unlike Nature, which in its dimensionless inertia he finds amenable to his shaping powers, other people talk back to him. Moreover, they are occasionally sordid and often stupid in their talk, and, having their own worlds to discover and address, they rarely enter the poet's world very fully, however sublime its attractions. As prophesied by Blake's Isaiah, persuasion can remove mountains in the Higher Reality, but it will seldom move men. Thus, between the poet's longing for otherness and his continuing drama of the self lies the sheer and final face of human obstinacy. Again, between his lofty ideas, analytic and public, and his feelings, diffuse and private, there rush treacherous rapids, negotiable only where the creative imagination is powerful enough to gird the poetic vision in the swirl of worldly confusion. The balance is a delicate one: The more baffled the poet, the more desperately he reaches for oneness, and the tighter he holds to his vision, the greater his awareness of discrepant reality. Gradually, because the moment of truth is so rare and transient at best, the poet seeks his Higher Reality at a more down-to-earth level. God, recognized in every cloud and meadow, is soon indistinguishable from a whole host of spirits and demigods, indeed from the poet-seer himself, who after all aspires to the angelic condition. In an unfortunate irony, it is this Romantic atmosphere of apparent fusion of all being that refracts the poet's vision and breaks his self-image into two.

This montage of the Romantics no doubt overgeneralizes many of the problems specific to one or another of the poets, but for all alike there is no question but that their experience of their own self-identity was profoundly related to this tension between imagination and reason, the Higher Reality and the external world. And, by the time the second-wave Romantics—Byron, Shelley, and Keats—were coming of age, the poles of the self had stretched into a clearly articulated dilemma. Joy in a transcendental union of mind and matter was suspect to them, an uneasy indulgence, even as they trusted in the imagination as the great unifier. Looking inward, they searched for Divinity; not finding it immediately, these poets turned their gaze outward to the world. The abbreviated lives of the three record their various attempts to bridge the dilemma of the self.

The prose fiction of this time infused new spirit into the by then worn conventions of Gothicism. As we can see from the work of Mary Shelley and James Hogg, these fabulists breathed the same air as the Romantic poets; thus the established Gothic modes of self-division were inevitably different in their hands. It is hardly surprising that both *Frankenstein* and *The Justified Sinner* should be in many ways more interesting books than their predecessors, preparing the ground for later novels which would put the Gothic conventions to still other uses.

I

Wordsworth was a Gothic child. Like his friend Coleridge, he drank deep of the magic and melodrama, the gloom and the sickness of soul of the romancers. But with Wordsworth especially, the transition away from this youthful Gothicism and self-preoccupation toward his remarkable discovery of Nature tells a good deal about the literary changes we are documenting. Godwinism was an important way station for this adventure.

The year 1794–1795 was preeminently a Godwin year for Wordsworth. *Political Justice* was his moral and political textbook, and the great rationalist's ideas on benevolism and social justice were incorporated in "Guilt and Sorrow" (first called "Salisbury Plain" and published in part as "The Female Vagrant" in 1798). The poem deals with "an atrocious crime" committed, as William Godwin would have explained it, by a man "previously of the most exemplary habits." [1] Again, utilizing some of the Gothic paraphernalia that had already appeared in earlier works such as "The Vale of Esthwaite" and "Fragment of a 'Gothic' Tale," this Godwinian poem introduces the shame and fear of the criminal against the shadowy scene of the ruined castle. The poem is, however, rent by ambiguities. Since the sailor's crime is presented as a necessary one and not really his anyway but that of society, his remorse is pointless and his ultimate penance and heroic death [2] something of a puzzle. Guilt is an attribute of society, a general guilt represented, in the first version, by the crowd who gather around the gallows for the "festive" [3] spectacle of a hanging. It is these two objectives of the poem—to investigate the guilt and sorrow of a particular accused and to disclose the true guilt of society—that are not sufficiently fused.

However, just as Godwin felt the need to modify his views after the publication of *Political Justice,* Wordsworth, too, wished to escape from such a strict necessitarianism. His next work makes clear he has at last put behind him the many stages of his youthful *Sturm und Drang,* not least among them his Godwinian philosophy. *The Borderers,* although once again an enquiry into the "morbid and tortured" [4] motives of the criminal, deviates sharply from the guilt and remorse pattern of the prototype romance. The villain is here an intellectual type who boasts complete mastery of the emotions. It happened that as a young seaman he had been deceived by the crew into a plot to lure the captain onto a barren uninhabited rock far out at sea. Later on, having discovered the treachery and its evil effects—the captain's daughter had gone mad—he was stricken with guilt and prescribed for himself a philosophy rejecting all human emotion as weakness and the opinions of his fellowman as the "abject counter part" of reality. The opening scene shows Oswald succeeding in restoring some of his energy through such sophistry, and it is fitting that at this point this "moral sceptic," this "daring and unfeeling empiric," [5] freed now of the customs of the tribe, should come upon a band of philanthropic outlaws and their Robin Hood leader Marmaduke. Recognizing immediately in Marmaduke "a mirror of [his] youthful self" (IV.1865; *Works,* I, 202), he schemes to duplicate in that noble young life the same changes he had undergone. The ingenious plot succeeds in building event by event an exact reproduction of Oswald's own past. But what is Marmaduke's understanding of these events? What especially is his feeling about his crimes? Will Oswald's program to make of his friend a "shadow of myself—made by myself" (V.2009; *Works*, I, 208) finally fail due to the special quality of Marmaduke's remorse?

Oswald's motive for self-duplication at one time appears quite simply as a villain's great love of evil and at another as the quite reasonable desire to share one's bounty, however ill-begotten, with a friend. That Wordsworth was aware of the need for an analysis of character and motivation is apparent from the Introduction he provided, yet the play itself offers very little in the way of hints or explanations.[6] Oswald's motivation is perhaps not so important in itself: but whatever his shortcomings as a character, this villain's failure as a moral experimentalist is significant for a view of the young author's growth as a poet. Marmaduke turns out to have quite a different way of responding to his criminal impulses. For instance, as he is about to murder the old baron, he glances up for an instant, and

> . . . through a crevice,
> Beheld a star twinkling above my head,
> And, by the living God, I could not do it.
> (II.988–990; *Works*, I, 168)

This is not the paralysis of will of a Schedoni tormented with unceasing self-examination; what stays Marmaduke's hand is the utterly unanalyzed (if not unanalyzable) surfuse of sympathy with Nature, an "ennobling interchange / Of action from within and from without."[7] Oswald advises his friend to drive out remorse with speculation: "Remorse— / It cannot live with thought; think on, think on, / And it will die" (III.1560–62; *Works*, I, 189). But such Mephistophelian counsel goes unheeded.

Marmaduke would restore his spiritual calm by recourse to Nature, and retreats to the wilderness.

For Wordsworth, *The Borderers* provided a stage for the performance of his own moral dilemma, the moral doubles Oswald and Marmaduke being the two possibilities that seemed available to him in his struggle to escape the general sense of apathy and guilt that had been dominating his life. True, when Marmaduke says at the end of the play, "a wanderer *must* I go," he does not yet go off alone, but between Marmaduke and those wanderers soon-to-be, such as the Leech-Gatherer, the Old Man Travelling, or the "sylvan Wye," there is little real difference. For, soon Wordsworth would be proclaiming "How exquisitely the individual Mind . . . to the external World / Is fitted:—and how exquisitely, too . . . / The external World is fitted to the Mind" (Preface to *Excursion,* 63–68; *The Works,* V, 5). Indeed, within a year he composed "Tintern Abbey" in celebration of man's unity with Nature.

The Borderers owes some debt to the prose romances, although not certainly an exclusive one. Wordsworth has said that the model for Oswald is to be found in the character of Iago, and there are also several unmistakable imprints of *King Lear* on the work. Still, an acknowledgment of Shakespearean sources is not a denial of the play's obvious kinship to the romances of Godwin, Mrs. Radcliffe, and others.[8] What makes the play relevant to this study is then not so much its use of the Gothic motif of the double as its transitional place between the romance dualism of passion and remorse and the Romantic dualism of imagination and reality.

Wordsworth's great achievement is in his celebration of the fusion of the self with harmonious Nature, yet to look at his career is to see that this remarkably unified sense of himself in communion with mute, insensate things soon ceased to be a rich reality to him. The "Ode to Duty," the "Elegiac Stanzas," and "Intimations of Immortality" are his farewell to the transcendental imagination, after which he withdrew in order to remember instead of experience, teach instead of search, almost as though fulfilling his own youthful prophesy: "Cataracts and mountains are good occasional society, but they will not do for constant companions. . . ." [9]

Coleridge, too, who had gone through this same conversion, held all his life to a craving for "something *great—something one & indivisible.*" [10] Out of this craving his imagination shaped that pleasure dome in Xanadu. But the dome stayed afloat in the air, and the poet found that he would have to abandon it, bid goodbye to that "shaping spirit of Imagination," no matter how much he would reaffirm it in his *Biographia Literaria*.

Coleridge suffered acute psychological distress from self-division and turmoil. All too aware of his many evasions and deceits and worried about them, he dosed himself with opium to escape his awareness again. [11] He admitted to having at least a "smack of Hamlet" [12] in him. The unhappy prince seemed, to Coleridge, "forever occupied with the world within him," [13] and his notebooks carry a number of entries analyzing and castigating himself for this same trait. In one he questions, "Who that thus lives with a continually divided Being can remain healthy!" [14] In fact, his writings, taken together, form irresistibly the impression of an enormous preoccupation with the notion of the divided self. [15] Perhaps with his predilection for the "supernatural" and the "romantic," he might have put together a poem on the theme. [16] He spoke occasionally of writing a new *Faust,* [17] although, as with his other projects, nothing came of it. In his case, the failure reminds us all the more pointedly of the possibility.

II

We have Byron's word for it that the craniologist who once examined his skull reported to him that his faculties and dispositions were "strongly marked—but very antithetical; for every thing developed in & on this same skull of mine has its *opposite* in great force. . . ." [18] The contradictions of this man's character have been well publicized. To celebrate the partial restoration of his ancestral Newstead, he sat down unceremoniously to bacon and eggs and a pint of ale. Hazlitt condemned Byron's liberal politics as affectation in 1824, only to admit, on news of his death, that the poet had "died a martyr to his zeal in the cause of freedom." [19] With the Byronic myth raging over the whole of Europe, Lockhart told him to his face that he considered his misanthropy "humbug." [20] Byron was continually defending the "great little Queen Anne's man," all the while turning out poems of a sort Pope could not possibly have approved. There is no end of such paradox in Byron's character—his naivete and yet his cynicism, a fierce antiorthodoxy, at the same time a hypersensitivity to criticism amounting almost to paranoia. Many of his contemporaries—Dallas, Moore, Scott, Stanhope—found such antitheses in his character bewildering, and readers today who grapple with his tempestuous life and work are all drawn to the puzzle. For some, the contradiction lies mainly between the intellectual Byron of the tradition of Voltaire and the emotional Byron who, like Werther, suffered agonies of *Weltschmerz*.[21] For

others, the Byronic quest is in the direction of his conflicting impulses toward Nature: the Romantic's indulgence in it and the Calvinist's distrust of it that, gradually gaining ascendancy, was manifest in the comic vision of *Don Juan*.[22] In still another view, Byron remained
unresolved to the end, almost flippant in first taking up
and then discarding a mood, an attitude or a creed, as
though it were a mere pose or gesture of the moment.
This might be interpreted as the buffoonery of the shallow man [23] or alternatively as the dead seriousness of the
farceur who finds his truth by laughing at everything and
everyone, not least of all himself.[24]

It will help to begin at the start of the pilgrimage
and examine the relationship between Byron and the
characters he created. Just who Childe Harold is constituted a very troublesome question not only for Byron's
readers but inevitably for the poet himself. In fact, he frequently complained about the facile identification of the
poet with his hero: In the Preface to the first and second
cantos, dated February 1812, he demanded that Childe
Harold be understood as a fictional character, and in the
Addition to the Preface, written the following year, repeated the request. Still later on, he wrote Dallas, "I by
no means intend to identify myself with *Harold,* but to
deny all connection with him. . . . I would not be such
a fellow as I have made my hero for all the world." [25]
From these assertions it should be clear that at least at
some early stage of composition, Byron intended to create
a character quite unlike himself. For one thing, Stanzas ii
to xiii in Canto I sketch in the hero's biography, which is
not Byron's. However, after "Childe Harold's Good Night"
(spoken in Harold's voice and twice answered by his
"little page" who never appears again), inserted between
Stanzas xiii and xiv, the hero seems to disappear for

awhile, leaving the stanzas entirely to the poet (or the narrator). In Stanza xxvii, the line "So deemed the Childe" abruptly reminds the reader of what he might well have forgotten by that time, that all the foregoing was not the poet's (or the narrator's) but the hero's reflection. Two stanzas later, with Harold again behind the scenes, the poet is urging Spain to "awake" and "arise" against "Tyrants and Tyrants' slaves"—an unlikely call from a world-weary "shameless wight." The third-person narrative continues awhile, but the first person suddenly appears at Stanza lix:

> Match me, ye climes! which poets love to laud;
> Match me, ye harems of the land! where now
> I strike my strain, far distant, to applaud
> Beauties that ev'n a cynic must avow. . . .[26]

Is this "I" the same narrator who briefly introduces the poem in Stanza i: "Yet there I've wandered by thy vaunted rill"? Or is the "I" here a fiction quite distinct from the person of the poet? In these early stanzas, it would seem very hard indeed to distinguish the "I" from Byron himself, whereas in Stanza lxiii the first-person narrator who declares "Now to my theme" is incontrovertibly no one but Byron. Nor is there any effort on the poet's part to disguise or otherwise characterize this "narrator." The Byronic first person continues fairly constant through Stanza lxxi, after which the third person takes over, until in lxxxii the line, "Oh! many a time and oft, had Harold loved," stops one short with the realization that after all it had been Harold's tale throughout. The muddle persists, except for the last stanza of Canto I where the "he" in the fourth line clearly refers to the author, thus for the first—and last—time distinguishing the narrator "I" from the "he" who is Byron. Immediately afterward, the "he" is ambiguous again.

The following cantos are scarcely more encouraging. Stanza xvi in Canto II begins, "But where is Harold?" And the reader, looking for a stable point of view in the poem, joins in the search, however hopelessly. In the prefatory letter to Canto IV, written in 1818, Byron finally admits being forced to abandon his "pilgrim" and speak in the final canto "in his own person":

> The fact is, that I had become weary of drawing a line which every one seemed determined not to perceive: like the Chinese in Goldsmith's *Citizen of the World,* whom nobody would believe to be a Chinese, it was in vain that I asserted, and imagined that I had drawn, a distinction between the author and the pilgrim; and the very anxiety to preserve this difference, and disappointment at finding it unavailing, so far crushed my efforts in the composition, that I determined to abandon it altogether—and have done so.
>
> (*Works,* II, 323)

However, from the beginning Harold had no real life of his own as a character. The author, in fact, had no clear notion of what a dramatic character should be. Harold never acts, he never does anything. The accomplishments attributed to him in the biographical stanzas of Canto I had been made at some point in the past, before the time of the poem proper during which he does nothing but muse and reflect and regret. Harold is more a mood associated with a certain type of character, rather than a character full-bodied and providing some hint of his less introspective moods and behavior. Aside from this dramatic defect, one forms the unmistakable impression that as long as Harold represents a mood not precisely corresponding to Byron's own at the moment, the poet could regard Harold as completely fictitious. Then, too, the very mood that stalks this wandering hero may be all too sufficient a reason for the whole muddle. Byron tells us in the 1813 Preface that Childe Harold was modeled after Timon and Zeluco, but even without this clue the hero's ancestry should be obvious: "Strange pangs" would furrow his brow or "Cain's unresting doom" settle upon it. Often tortured by a "secret woe," he was without question a man who had, like Dr. Jekyll, "known the worst" for years on end. These features are the familiar ones of the romantic villain-hero,[27] and in fact the only place for Harold finally is the weary world of the Gothic romance, whose mood, Byron insisted, did not necessarily correspond to his own. In fact, at this early period in his life, however wild his escapades, Byron did not appear to suffer those Haroldian "strange pangs"; surrounded by his many friends, he was by no means the sorrowing outcast under the curse of Cain. In this sense at least, Byron's own word is persuasive.

Still, if Harold is fictitious, the mood of the poem is perilously infectious. The world, for Harold, is a wearisome place where passion or indeed any involvement necessarily leads only to agonizing remorse. As he sees it, he has every right to postpone decision, disengage himself, pack up and wander for a time. If this is the answer for the young Harold, if a gloomy indecisiveness provides the adolescent hero with an easy, if temporary, answer to his problem, why not for Byron too? There are glimpses in the poem of the curious drama of the poet who first trailed his hero like a doppelgänger, then gradually overtook and assimilated the persona. It is there in both the poet's unsureness of his control of narrator and character alike and in the eventual transformation of the poem into a first-person diary-travelogue. Remembering especially how Byron emerged as a literary lion with the phenomenal success of the poem, we can see how he saw himself destined to be the symbol of melancholy and passion that the taste of his age had so long been craving. In a sense he was not yet fully Byron until he had become Childe Harold. A Romantic nature will imitate his art.[28]

In the Turkish Tales (*The Giaour* and *The Bride of Abydos* published in 1813, *The Corsair* and *Lara* in 1814) Byron was working toward several kinds of villain-heroes who, as characters, would be rather better realized than Harold. Familiar suppressed, tormented types, they are rent by guilt and melancholy, at the same time haughty and rebellious. Here is the hero's remorse, as described by the narrator in *The Giaour:*

> So do the dark in soul expire,
> Or live like Scorpion girt by fire;
> So writhes the mind Remorse hath riven,
> Unfit for earth, undoomed for heaven,
> Darkness above, despair beneath,
> Around it flame, within it death!
>
> (433–438)

In *The Bride of Abydos*, the hero's alternation between passion and remorse is given in terms of self-alienation:

> "Think not thou art what thou appearest!
> My Selim, thou art sadly changed:
> This morn I saw thee gentle—dearest—
> But now thou'rt from thyself estranged."
>
> (I.383–386)

And for Conrad in *The Corsair* the world of the feelings is a dangerously unstable one:

> Strange though it seem—yet with extremest grief
> Is link'd a mirth—it doth not bring relief—
> That playfulness of Sorrow ne'er beguiles,
> And smiles in bitterness—but still it smiles;
> And sometimes with the wisest and the best,
> Till even the scaffold echoes with their jest!
> Yet not the joy to which it seems akin—
> It may deceive all hearts, save that within.
>
> (II.446–453)

These romances are overtheatrical, and Byron was perhaps tossing them off casually to cash in on his sudden fame. But if he was aware of their falseness, he took little care to guard his imagination, whether for art or for life. The mood began to eat deep into the substance of his own character.

The tales were being distributed and read by the thousands of copies, and Byron's personal life was approaching a crisis. Whatever the actual content of his relationship with Augusta Leigh, it can hardly be denied that the hint of incest in *The Bride of Abydos* was as much autobiographical in source as it was suggested by countless Gothic romances with the same theme by Walpole, Lewis, Mrs. Radcliffe, and others. His fiction grew out of his personal experience, while the person was simultaneously living his fiction. What is more interesting than incest in this connection is the inability of the Gothic character to "paint gray" on the moral canvas of a fictional work, mediate good and evil, black and white. Falling victim to each of his conflicting impulses in turn, such a character can see no way out of the morass of suspended action, a state of mind which is more and more noticeable in the less fictional framework of *Childe Harold,* especially as it moves on to Cantos III (1816) and IV (1818).

> Even as a broken Mirror, which the glass
> In every fragment multiplies—and makes
> A thousand images of one that was,
> The same—and still the more, the more it breaks;
> And thus the heart will do which not forsakes,
> Living in shattered guise; and still, and cold,
> And bloodless, with its sleepless sorrow aches,
> Yet withers on till all without is old,
> Showing no visible sign, for such things are untold.
>   (III.xxxiii)

To be able to forget the "earthborn jars, / And human frailties" would be a great relief. Very much like Empedocles in Arnold's poem, however, he cannot forget, knows he cannot forget, and, most upsetting of all, cannot forget that he knows. Nature (Byron was re-reading Wordsworth with Shelley) brought momentary relief ("I live not in myself, but I become / Portion of that around me . . ." [III.lxxii]), only to be rejected as mere self-illusion, as he returns to the old ritual of defiance and regret.

In the guise of *Manfred* (1817), Childe Harold attains a premature yet almost sublime dignity. The man's past, shrouded in mystery, apparently involves consort with the dark powers and worse: the "deadliest sin" of incest. Like Harold, he is burdened with remorse and because of this stands apart from his fellow beings. Like Harold, too, and their Gothic ancestors, he has a mortal sense of division within. But in Manfred this self-division is more grandiose:

But we, who name ourselves its sovereigns, we,
Half dust, half deity, alike unfit
To sink or soar, with our mixed essence make
A conflict of its elements, and breathe
The breath of degradation and of pride,
Contending with low wants and lofty will,
Till our Mortality predominates,
And men are—what they name not to themselves,
And trust not to each other.

(I.ii.39–47)

Unlike Harold, Manfred is capable of action. While the external drama moves on such events as his suicide attempt and his meeting with the Demons, the expected internal action, which should help to resolve Manfred's deadening remorse, has come to a halt. Even his "defiance" of the Demons comes to naught. The Demons find they have no power over him, and fly away before Manfred expires, and the Abbott's last lines show that this soul's destination is not really certain: "He's gone—his soul hath ta'en its earthless flight; / Whither? I dread to think— but he is gone." If Manfred defies both heaven and hell (and presumably both heaven and hell reject him as well), where does his "earthless flight" lead him? To take Manfred's own words, "[I] will be / My own hereafter" (III.iv.139–40). His egotism, a ruthless assertion of a self emptied of its being, is inherently impossible of fulfillment. Manfred's relationship with Astarte symbolizes this contradiction of being at once oneself and out of oneself. An irrevocable regret is the only possible denouement, however fierce the desire or sublime the defiance. In what is very nearly the *reductio ad absurdum* of Romantic egotism, Manfred's rejection of heaven and hell ends in a rejection of his own divided self.

Carlyle may not have been fully aware of all the implications of his advice, "Close thy Byron and open thy Goethe," but there is one vital difference between the two. Here is Faust in an apparently similar situation:

My bosom, of its thirst for knowledge sated,
Shall not, henceforth, from any pang be wrested,
And all of life for all mankind created
Shall be within mine inmost being tested:
The highest, lowest forms my soul shall borrow,
Shall heap upon itself their bliss and sorrow,
And thus, my own sole self to all their selves expanded
I too, at last, shall with them all be stranded.[29]

Dr. Faust's egotism is not the sort to exclude consideration of otherness; indeed, his pact with the devil aside, the Faustian quest is motivated by the desire for the total good. Thus his crimes contain at least the possibility of redemption and hence some movement and drama, as we see in *Faust II*. With Manfred, the search is circular, leading him nowhere but incessantly back upon himself.[30]

In *Cain* (1821) the hero is a Manfred writ large, and one even more neatly cleft between a "nothing" and an "all":

I look
Around a world where I seem nothing, with
Thoughts which arise within me, as if they
Could master all things. . . .
(I.i.175–178)

Again the antitheses never come to terms. When Lucifer explains the Manichaean situation to him, Cain makes it clear that he would worship neither God nor Satan. Again he disdains the proffered choice between Love and Knowledge. This seems to be still another declaration of independence of man from both God and Satan. But Lucifer is at a loss:

> and *thou* wouldst go on aspiring
> To the great double Mysteries! the *two Principles!*
> And gaze upon them on their secret thrones!
> Dust! limit thy ambition; for to see
> Either of these would be for thee to perish!
> (II.ii.403–407)

So free is Cain of both great "Principles" that after the murder he is not granted God's forgiveness nor is he embraced by Satan. Instead he is shown laboriously making his way "eastward in Eden," but no destination is indicated, whether heaven, hell, or only deeper into the limbo of his own remorse.

In these Romantic works, Byron is, for all practical critical uses, indistinguishable from his characters. Childe Harold, Manfred, Cain, all embody the Byronic moral values that polarize the whole range of lovely possibles into stark either-or's. Caught in the austere pageantry of Puritan saints and Puritan devils, the protagonists naturally recoil from the choice.

Still, Byron is larger than the host of Byronic heroes. He tried on one after another scowling or sneering masks, but there were moments, too, when he went forth naked-faced laughing at the absurdity of those masks. The comic poetry is his attempt to reconcile all those hopelessly unstable personae. With brutal clarity he saw through the human condition of sham and complacency. His comic vision might have given him exit from bitterness, the cancellation of the self from life which he had sought so long. However, he seemed doomed to ambiguity to the end. It was as though he were unable to sustain the responsibility of being the utter irresponsible, the absolute fool, and he had always to lean back on that other mood, which more and more with a dangerously deceptive ease he would identify as himself. Up to the moment of Missolonghi, his poetry kept shifting between the perspectives of laughter and lament, and his ultimate and tragic involvement in the Greek cause was in a sense his only way of resolving the lifelong dilemma once and for all—a task he had not been able to accomplish through his work.

Byron's genius lay in his savagely clear comic vision, but nineteenth-century readers held to the Byronic myth and forgot the poems, except for an occasional bad one. *Childe Harold* was the one that most evoked Byron for them, and in the "pageant of his bleeding heart," they tended to read, as Arnold did, the frightening possibility that they, too, should their grip on faith and commitment ease, might lose their very selves. That Byron was a gigantic threat to them we know from Carlyle's thoughts on the scowling devil-man. Arthur Hugh Clough was probably the one who most closely approached Byron's comic vision, and he was, for his friends, perhaps the biggest disappointment of his time.

III

Shelley's juvenile preoccupation with the tales of terror culminated in two early stories—*Zastrozzi* (1810) and *St. Irvyne; Or, The Rosicrucian* (1811). In *Zastrozzi* the hero is torn between the vampire Matilda (a direct descendant of Lewis' Matilda) and the conventional pure maiden, while Zastrozzi himself is the defiant "atheist" supposedly speaking the author's convictions. In *St. Irvyne* the main plot and divergent subplot are abruptly connected at the very end of the story by a totally unprepared identity statement: "Ginotti is Nempere,"[31] meant to indicate that the Wandering Jew of the main plot and the mysterious degenerate are two personalities of the same man—an explanation that notoriously failed to persuade even the publisher. This early venture into terrorism left unmistakable imprints on the poet's later work: certain diction and imagery, a liking for the plainly gruesome (in "The Sensitive Plant," *The Revolt of Islam,* and *The Cenci,* for example), and, more especially, Satanism and the incest theme. However, his sense of the divided self is manifest in a much more essential aspect of his poetry.

Shelley's experience of the fragmented self is probably no more acute than Byron's, but the Shelleyan self reaches so intensely for the ideal that nothing can sway it, nothing distract it from its goal. Furthermore, because the ideal is distant and necessarily elusive, the yearning for it is bound to frustration. Where the Byronic hero pulverized his being in the face of choice, the Shelleyan hero overreaches himself and ends by being sacrificed at the stake of his ideal just at the moment of achievement, when it presents itself as sheer illusion. Without the ideal, the self is unthinkable; with it, unrealizable. Significantly then, the ideal appears in his poems as a vision or an epipsyche (a "soul within the soul"), and the climax of meeting one's double, death, is the always impending doom of the Shelleyan hero:

> This fiend, whose ghastly presence ever
> Beside thee like thy shadow hangs,
> Dream not to chase;—the mad endeavor
> Would scourge thee to severer pangs.
> Be as thou art. Thy settled fate,
> Dark as it is, all change would aggravate.[32]

The warning was too early, in 1816, for Coleridge, as it was for Shelley himself. Even Matthew Arnold, a generation later, found that the "Resolve to be thyself" took a lifetime to accomplish and cost him his poetry as well. The "fiend" haunts Shelley's work. Both *Alastor* (1816) and *Epipsychidion* (1821)—to one reader probably his "most egotistic"[33] poems—show the poet's "mad endeavor" in his company.

Aside from the problem of obscurity in *Alastor,* which is at least in part due to its complex and at times confused imagery, there is another difficulty in the poem, located in its peculiarly self-conscious approach. The story of the Poet's[34] quest (67–670) is preceded by a first-person invocation (1–49) by the narrator, and set between these two parts is a kind of epitaph recapitulating the Poet's life, which is then again repeated in the final passage (671–720). In addition, there is the Preface explaining, in prose, the poem's intention. These parts may be construed as supplementing one another, yet they do not really jibe.[35] The first paragraph of the Preface explains the poem as a follow-up to the Poet's tragic career after his "farewell to Nature," whereas the second paragraph shows no concern at all with the hero and only with those who after the "death of joy" live along to an abject and inglorious decay. Unlike the Poet, they are doomed, so says the Preface, because while "loving nothing on this earth, and cherishing no hopes beyond, yet [they] keep aloof from sympathies with their kind, rejoicing neither in human joy nor mourning with human grief. . . ." Of the two possible choices available to those who have written their "Dejection" ode, the second is not dealt with in the poem itself, nor is the main point of the Preface, the hopelessness of either choice, at issue in the poem itself where the hero's tragic death is eulogized. What is more, Wordsworth is the villain of the Preface; at the same time, confusingly, *The Excursion* is the source of the lines attached to the Preface, and in the invocation the "I" adopts the voice of his master primarily. Apparently, hoping to avoid misunderstanding, Shelley inserted his comments in the poem itself, and then, still not assured of complete clarity, added the Preface. If such self-conscious efforts are for clearness, the obscurity of the total effect is even harder to understand—unless, of course, Shelley himself was unclear about the meaning of the Poet's tragic death. With an eye to this issue and to the possibility of Shelley's mistaken diagnosis of the Romantic self, we might look more closely at the poem itself.

In the first passages, the Poet is shown wandering about in unknown lands and times. Like the Wordsworthian Romantic, he seeks the supernatural in Nature's unity. His imagination both perceives and creates, but the balance of the two is precarious, to say the least, and in *Alastor* it collapses almost immediately when the Poet encounters the Arab maiden. For the first time, he realizes that the response of a human existence differs from Nature's apparently passive being, and from this, the Poet begins to question the basis of the imagination. It requires, he finds, substantiation in another being, not in mere "objects" (Preface). Here the Romantic paradox shows itself. If he were to meet others on their terms or even on some compromised middle ground, he would have to relinquish his own "shapership," the creative imagination that is the foundation of his existence. Conversely, if he meets them on his own terms, and this is what he chooses to do, he would not be meeting *others,* only himself. The *Alastor* Poet's answer is to conjure the other from within himself. The vision the Poet sees (that is, half creates) is, therefore, not only an "ideal beauty" like Endymion's Diana, but a creature uniting all that is "wonderful, or wise, or beautiful" (Preface). She is thus provided with the three cognitive faculties that the Poet already possesses but that he also requires of others: intellect, imagination, and the senses (Preface). In his moment of union with her, he is convinced that he has truly met otherness. Yet however accomplished the vision may be, and however perfect his union with her, she turns out to be, after all, only a vision, a projection of himself. His experience is inevitably narcissistic, nympholeptic, a mere meeting of the "I" with the "I."

Immediately upon losing his ideal beauty, the hero begins his indefatigable search for her. He wanders, utterly consumed by his ideal, unconsoled by Nature or by ordinary give-and-take with other people. Even the sight of a swan homeward bound reminds him of his own total alienation, from himself as well as from Nature: "And what am I that I should linger here. . . ." Tucked in his boat, this estranged Hiawatha flies on, through storms at sea, under perilous cliffs and darkest caverns, as desperate on his deathward course as *"Le Bateau Ivre."* Coleridge's Mariner voyages to a kind of redemption, but Shelley's Poet, resting for a moment in a quiet wood, finds only his own image everywhere, a Nature reflecting only himself:

> His eyes beheld
> Their own wan light through the reflected lines
> Of his thin hair, distinct in the dark depth
> Of that still fountain; as the human heart,
> Gazing in dreams over the gloomy grave,
> Sees its own treacherous likeness there.
>
> (469–474)

He is doomed, not because of a character flaw such as his indifference to others would suggest, but for the inescapable tautology presented by his very existence: "Thou imagest my life" (505), he tells the mirroring stream, and dies without ever seeing his vision again.

If the earlier part of *Alastor* can represent for us an earlier Romanticism, the later part, describing his encounter with his vision and futile pursuit of her, carries all the implications of Romantic solipsism. The Poet is Shelley's answer to the Wordsworth and Coleridge odes, although by this analysis he is seen to anticipate his own ultimate defeat. In fact, the poem celebrates the defeat. He is aware of the self-destruction implicit in his poetic principle, yet he knows that his hero's way is the only way his poetry could go. Shelley's expressed uncertainties in the commentary parts of *Alastor* grow out of his ambivalent attitude about the Poet's tragic courage and the ultimate failure of the Romantic shapership.

Alastor also programs Shelley's personal experience. In each attempt at finding his ideal love, he began by projecting on the poor lady his vision of the ideal woman, and after judging her reality not so ideal after all, rejected her. In this case, the two ladies—Elizabeth Hitchner and Emilia Viviani—were presently discovered to be, respectively, a "Brown Demon" and "a cloud" rather than the Juno he had envisioned. To Shelley, the actual

relationship between himself and his ideal woman is identical with that between the Poet and his vision. The
lover images his ideal woman and then tests the real
one against her, just as the imagination creates its vision
and then tests Nature against it the better to savor its
reality. Because the epipsyche [36] dwells in an actual body-
and-soul woman, union with it, as with one's double, is
impossible this side of death. Anyway the aspiration for
death is more interesting by far than death itself: One
prolongs the prelude, postpones the rendezvous, perhaps
from impotence, perhaps from some other nameless fear.
As one reader has understood it, the Shelleyan nympholepsy "appears to signify the fulfillment or rounding out
of the unfinished self." [37] But the self, waking from a
dream, finds itself unfinished as before, unfulfilled and
fragmented.

Like his "scorner of the ground," Shelley had to soar
higher and still higher in his quest. In *Epipsychidion*
the search for the self-duplicate is once again the theme,
but with a few important differences: since the poem
is, above all, a plea for love, it makes no comment on
the outcome of any particular quest (except for the brief
ironic Advertisement). *Alastor* is a tragedy, yet in *Epipsychidion* knowledge of the outcome is withheld from
the reader. Different also from the earlier poem is the
hero's assumption of Shelley's own voice with its more
direct articulation of his love-imagination principle. There
is no need to refer to Shelley's life to understand the poem,
identifying "the Moon" with Mary, "the Comet" with
Claire Clairmont, and so forth, but these, together with
his "many mortal forms," are the ones in whom the
psyche (or the "I") has attempted at some point to discover his epipsyche, and has failed. Here they provide
the dramatic framework to carry the argument of the
poem. However, there is still a much more important

new feature. The earlier poem shows the hero excluding everything but his vision, but in this one the "I" is constantly mindful of all his discarded epipsyches: "the Moon," "the Comet," other "mortal forms," all that might have been yet are not. This is represented dramatically as the husband's plea to his mistress for an elopement—on which they will be joined by his wife and several others. Such an attitude toward monogamy is commonly thought to be the essence of the poem:

> I never was attached to that great sect,
> Whose doctrine is, that each one should select
> Out of the crowd a mistress or a friend,
> And all the rest, though fair and wise, commend
> To cold oblivion, though it is in the code
> Of modern morals, and the beaten road
> Which those poor slaves with weary footsteps tread,
> Who travel to their home among the dead
> By the broad highway of the world, and so
> With one chained friend, perhaps a jealous foe,
> The dreariest and the longest journey go.
>
> (149–159)

However, this is still not the whole of it. Immediately afterwards, the "I" is comparing love with the understanding and the imagination, and making the point that one must always be careful to "divide" them properly. He attacks the visionary life style just as he had monogamy:

> Narrow
> The heart that loves, the brain that contemplates,
> The life that wears, the spirit that creates
> One object, and one form, and builds thereby
> A sepulchre for its eternity.
>
> (169–173)

For a love song the notion of such a multiple love would
be preposterously ineffectual. However, in terms of his
principle of the imagination, he is simply urging that the
spirit should create not "one object, and one form," but
many. Such devotion to a single vision as the *Alastor*
poet showed spells death to the imagination. Shelley seems
mindful now of others outside his chosen epipsyches.
No longer the sole reality of the universe, the imagination of the "I" is here seen simply as one among many
possible. Like Keats, Shelley struggles to overtake his
own shadow—to learn, in short, that negative capability.

   Epipsychidion remains the "I's" love song to his "Emily"; and as long as his goal is union, man's being must
still—regardless of doctrine, antisolipsistic or polygamis-
tic—be defined as the union of psyche and epipsyche,
the self and the self-created other. For "Emily" is only
what the "I" imagines her to be: [38]

> We shall become the same, we shall be one
> Spirit within two frames, oh! wherefore two?
> One passion in twin-hearts, which grows and grew,
> 'Till like two meteors of expanding flame,
> Those spheres instinct with it become the same,
> Touch, mingle, are transfigured; ever still
> Burning, yet ever inconsumable:
> In one another's substance finding food,
> Like flames too pure and light and unimbued
> To nourish their bright lives with baser prey,
> Which point to Heaven and cannot pass away:
> One hope within two wills, one will beneath
> Two overshadowing minds, one life, one death,
> One Heaven, one Hell, one immortality,
> And one annihilation.
>
>   (573–587)

With rapidly rising pitch, the "I's" anticipation of the union brings on the frenzy of nympholepsy itself.[39] "I pant, I sink, I tremble, I expire!" (591). With the subsidence of this self-generated ecstasy, "Emily" again shows herself a false vision; as she rejoins the planets, the "I" again finds himself unfinished, partial, and helplessly divided. Such self-division is the heart of the Shelleyan tragedy, not unique to Shelley but a forlorn pattern shared by many of the Victorians.

IV

In *Endymion* (1818) Keats comes as close as he ever does to this same frenzy of the disembodied imagination. Although it is a poem about a youth's quest after his ideal beauty, it is Keats's denial, not his acceptance, of the Shelleyan principle as set forth in *Alastor*.[40] In the Shelley poem, the Poet's pursuit of his vision precludes any other concern, but the *Endymion* hero, after his first absorption, begins to vacillate between hope for reunion with his goddess and despair of it and learns finally to resign himself to what is available on earth. In Keats's hero, there is no rejection of love or friendship, pity or compassion for his fellow beings, although they are mere humans and so less attractive than the divine Diana. Thus his quest for a "fellowship with essence" [41] is not wrecked on the Shelleyan tautology; on the contrary, only through the acceptance of existence does the essence make itself known. When Endymion encounters his lonely Indian maid (the counterpart to the Arab Maid who was practically ignored in *Alastor*) in Book IV, he almost at once falls in love with her, only to recall his love for Diana.

> I have a triple soul! O fond pretence—
> For both, for both my love is so immense,
> I feel my heart is cut for them in twain.
>
> (IV.95–97)

He sees he is unable to reconcile his conflicting loyalties and begins to lose his sense of identity.

> What is this soul then? Whence
> Came it? It does not seem my own, and I
> Have no self-passion or identity.
> Some fearful end must be: where, where is it?
> By Nemesis! I see my spirit flit
> Alone about the dark—
>
> (IV.475–480)

Keats himself believes that Endymion's salvation lies in this very circumstance. He is capable of aspiring to the highest ideal without renouncing the world. As it turns out, on account of his humility and compassion, he deserves the love of both visionary goddess and earthly maid, who are at the end the same person anyway.

Endymion, ending on the fulfillment of the hero's quest, affirms that divine and human, imagination and reality can be reconciled. As an answer to Shelley, it is not entirely a fair one, however. The hero's dedication to the higher reality in *Alastor,* although quite narrow, is at least clearly definable. The vision consistently represents an ideal that has no possible earthly existence. Diana in *Endymion,* in contrast, is everything a young poet could desire—wanton but virginal, beautiful *and* virtuous, in some respects utterly and tragically evanescent, in others immortal. Unfortunately, her dazzlingly rapid metamorphoses are confusing to reader and Endymion

as well. It is as though he were presented with a host
of ideal beauties, all of whom he is allowed to possess
simply because he loves them and then told that they
are all the same girl after all. The Romantic paradox is
taken quite lightly, not so much resolved as glossed over.

Yet even Keats's way of posing the question is different
from Shelley's. He does not typically ask if what the imagination seizes as truth is indeed truth; he accepts experience
and, when second thoughts about its authenticity come to
him, he takes comfort in the thought of their eventual
reconciliation. There is always something immediate in
Keats's response—call it sensual, call it luxurious—to men
and to things which, unlike Shelley's rarefied emotion,
never fails to sustain him.[42] More remarkable is the fact
that he manages never to lose sight of the paradox at the
core of the Romantic principle of imagination. Endymion
might fly away with his Diana, but there remains for him
some serious worldly business. Earlier, the hero had shown
a glimpse of this tenacity:

> No, No, I'm sure,
> My restless spirit never could endure
> To brood so long upon one luxury,
> Unless it did, though fearfully, espy
> A hope beyond the shadow of a dream.
> (I.853–857)

His journey toward that hope was to begin immediately
after he finished the poem: ". . . at once it struck me,
what quality went to form a Man of Achievement especially in Literature & which Shakespeare possessed so
enormously—I mean *Negative Capability,* that is when
man is capable of being in uncertainties, Mysteries, doubts,

without any irritable reaching after fact & reason. . . ." [43]
Also, there is about this time frequent mention in his
letters of the need to go beyond the tautology of self,
against the "egotistical sublime" and be more the "came-
lion Poet," the poet of "no Identity." [44] It would seem
the pendulum had swung too far from *Endymion*, but
balance was soon restored. In a letter to George and
Georgiana written during the spring of 1819, he tries
to map out his identity, which he calls his "vale of soul-
making." Everyone is provided with the divine spark of
intelligence, but this will not become a soul unless he
develops his "identity" through joining his mind and his
heart to the sufferings of the world:

> I will call the *world* a School instituted for the
> purpose of teaching little children to read—I will call
> the *human heart* the *horn Book* used in that School—
> and I will call the *Child able to read, the Soul* made
> from that *school* and its *hornbook*. Do you not see
> how necessary a World of Pains and troubles is to
> school an Intelligence and make it a soul? A Place
> where the heart must feel, and suffer in a thousand
> diverse ways! Not merely is the Heart a Hornbook,
> It is the Mind's Bible, it is the Minds experience, it
> is the teat from which the Mind or intelligence sucks
> its identity. . . . [45]

Keats is here groping for words, and mixing his metaphor, but the drift is plain. Suffering and disillusionment alone can actualize hopes and ideals, and through
the recognition of sorrow as a type of wisdom, sorrow
itself is transformed into happiness, and the self, bridg-
ing the gulf between experience and the ideal, is unified.

The man who had referred to his own mind rather

bitterly as "a pack of scattered cards" [46] was about that same time one for whom the resolution of the Romantic paradox had become the foremost concern and whose poetry was well along toward resolving it. "La Belle Dame Sans Merci," a very Gothic poem with its vampire theme and use of the double identity, represents plainly the two contradictory attitudes toward the imagination, the one that would attribute reality to it, and the one that would deny it, while committing itself as a poem to neither.[47] In *Lamia* Keats dramatized his quest through Lycius, unable to choose between Lamia's beauty and passion and Apollonius' intellect.[48] Although here again one may really be baffled about where Keats stands, this question may be of no great consequence finally, for the poem is quite complicated enough to move it away from the purely personal focus. If the "Nightingale" also closes on a recognition of the gap between the imagination and reality, the "Ode on a Grecian Urn" veritably triumphs in its assertion of the unity. In his final ode, "To Autumn," Keats's work seems to have reached its destination. Here, life and death, youth and age, imagination and experience—all are resolved in what Kenneth Burke has called a "mystic oxymoron" of precise unsentimental description of what is and the calm untroubled acceptance of it. Unfortunately, Keats was unable to finish *The Fall of Hyperion*. Our regret that he could not is somehow more acute than it would be with Byron or Shelley.[49]

V

Frankenstein (1818) was of course planned as a Gothic romance.[50] All the familiar Gothic features—the terror and brutality, the lightning on the bones and on

the hideous visage of the Monster, the shrieking and
the vows of revenge—are carefully built into the story,
and, more important, both Frankenstein and the Monster share many of the characteristics of the villain-
heroes of an earlier time. Frankenstein's guilt derives
from his not disclosing the circumstances of his awful
experiment until the Monster has done away with five
people, and as a consequence his anxiety and remorse
drive him to melancholy, and eventually to a "deep, dark,
deathlike solitude." The Monster, by contrast, is an outcast from the start, one "born with a different face." As
he himself acknowledges, even "Satan had his companions, fellow-devils, to admire and encourage him." But
he is "solitary and abhorred." [51] Despite his determination to destroy his creator Frankenstein, the heart of this
monster, too, is "poisoned with remorse" (Walton's last
letter, p. 238).

The Faustian theme of thirst for knowledge is expressed particularly in the use of the laboratory. Not only
Frankenstein but Captain Walton as well is engaged in
scientific experiment. Walton's expedition parallels Frankenstein's Fausto-Promethean adventures. Nor is the Monster any different in this respect: His long tale within a
tale, covering six chapters (eleventh to sixteenth), might
well be called "The Education of a 'Natural' Man" (albeit
an "artificial" natural man), the author's assumption being
man's innate goodness and, voicing Godwin and Shelley,
the failure of existing institutions to sustain him. With
the Monster, too, it is an insatiable thirst for knowledge—
in particular, knowledge of his origin and identity—
that motivates him: "Who was I? What was I? Whence
did I come? What was my destination?" (Chapter 15, p.
134).

Godwin's daughter moved freely in the circle of the

foremost poets and writers of the time, and it was unlikely that she could allow *Frankenstein* to become just
another horror story. As a small child, she had heard
"The Ancient Mariner" recited by Coleridge himself,
and by the time she had finished her own story in May
of 1817, she had come to know Thomas Peacock, "Monk"
Lewis, Leigh Hunt, Byron, and, of course, Shelley. With
this background, *Frankenstein* could scarcely avoid reflecting a great many serious concerns of the Romantics:
the dualism of poetry and science, of the individual and
society, and of faith and humanistic rationalism.

The story opens with Walton's rescue of Frankenstein. Sensing somewhere in the dark gloom of his bearing a "double existence," composed of great suffering and
great glory too, Walton understands Frankenstein's dreams
of retiring within, where he can preside "like a celestial
spirit" (Letter IV, p. 18), for Walton, too, is pulled between his thirst for "a more intimate sympathy with a
fellow mind" and his longing for more inward "knowledge and wisdom" (Letter IV, p. 19). The two immediately recognize these poles in each other. At the end of
the story, when the ship is halted by mountains of ice
on all sides, the crew urge the captain to sacrifice the
expedition and return home straightaway with the first
sign of the thaw. However, the dying Frankenstein,
wanting desperately to track down his Monster, insists they
push on. There is here a remarkable resemblance to
Conrad's *The Secret Sharer,* in which Leggatt and the
captain meet and become by their identical quest indistinguishable. In *Frankenstein,* the encounter functions
as more than a mere narrative convention, acting to rein-
force the Faustian theme by mirroring it—Frankenstein
in Walton and vice versa—and in a paradoxical way uni-
versalizing their common solitude. There are hints here

too of the Mariner's meeting with the Wedding Guest, although comparison with Coleridge's poem brings out something else of interest. For a while, the Frankenstein-Mariner parallel is strongly suggested at several points. Walton, too, resembles the Coleridge hero (for example, "I am going to unexplored regions, to 'the land of mist and snow'; but I shall kill no albatross . . ." [Letter II, p. 10]). It is only after Walton decides to terminate the voyage that Frankenstein, released at last from his monomaniacal chase, dies. Walton, then, is a kind of other possibility for Frankenstein, a life which he might have had, and it is with this in mind that the Faustian motive should be looked into.

Against this, it would be natural to insist that Frankenstein's friendship with Clerval anticipates the later one with Walton. However there the relationship was not one of identity, but of contrast; Clerval was "a being formed in the 'very poetry of nature' " (Chapter 2, p. 28), and occupied with "the moral relations of things" (Chapter 2, p. 29). Frankenstein with his scientific interests, Clerval with his poetry, the two complemented each other: "Harmony was the soul of [their] companionship" (Chapter 2, p. 27). Had this balance prevailed, there would have been no Frankenstein creation and consequently no tragedy to tell. However, in the world of this work, friction and discord prevail. In Frankenstein's career, first science and then poetry occupies his interest, until the possibility of either is destroyed by the Monster's vengeful reappearance.[52]

The subtitle, *Or, The Modern Prometheus,* certainly suggests it is Frankenstein who in the creation of life has defied God and become Prometheus, but it is nonetheless the Monster's rebellion that dominates the story. The epitaph taken from *Paradise Lost*—"Did I request thee, Maker, from clay / To mould me man? Did I solicit thee / From darkness to promote me?" [53]—points to the essential identity between Monster and maker. They are both Promethean figures and both finally return to that one clay that was their common origin.

If we treated Frankenstein's life experiment purely as the outgrowth of his rationalistic obsession the Monster would fit well into the pattern of a being who is, rather limitedly, "reason in isolation." [54] As it happens he does not develop so straightforwardly as an embodiment of rational man. Faustian, yes, but his initial thrust of existence is toward development of his total being, moral and emotional as well as intellectual. From the De Laceys and his readings in Milton, Plutarch, and Goethe, he forms the notion, for one, of service to humanity. But there is no response to his earnest and generous efforts; on the contrary, people are horrified with his appearance and fear and hate him. He reasons that a child might be different, that he might mold a little one into a friend, but it turns out badly. The boy—Frankenstein's little brother—abuses him for his hideous appearance and the Monster strangles him. The period of Frankenstein's mastery is over; the Monster, discovering that he, too, can "create desolation," becomes a second Frankenstein. As he says to the scientist, recalling the ambiguous Master-Slave relationship so well understood by Hegel, "You are my creator, but I am your master" (Chapter 20, p. 179).

At the same time, Frankenstein's enormous creative effort seems to have completely exhausted him. Henceforth rejecting his scientific pursuits, he devotes himself to Clerval's world of poetry and emotion. "A serene sky and verdant fields filled me with ecstasy. The present season was indeed divine; the flowers of spring bloomed in the hedges, while those of summer were already in bud. I was undisturbed by thoughts which during the preceding year had pressed upon me, notwithstanding my endeavors to throw them off, with an invincible burden" (Chapter 6, pp. 66–67). Frankenstein the intellectual purges the intellect through Nature.

Only with the reappearance of the Monster in his life, with his program of revenge and destruction, is this balance shaken. He can no longer take delight in the beauties of Nature and is driven back once again to a tormenting sense of his great guilt. Like many of the Gothic heroes, he is utterly at a loss over what course to take next, and his indecisiveness, which, in a sense, allows the murder of Justine, Clerval, Elizabeth, and M. Frankenstein himself, only intensifies his remorse unbearably. The disintegration of his personality is now complete.

As though to mirror his creator's cycle of guilt and remorse, the Monster too finds himself agonized. The two voice an identical feeling of bearing a "hell within" them (Chapter 8, p. 88; Chapter 16, p. 143). The Monster has certainly systematically destroyed Frankenstein's family in retribution for not having been provided with a spouse. However, it may not be too far afield to propose that these murders are at the same time a projection of Frankenstein's own suppressed urge to destroy what he loves—a negative impulse lurking in the depths of rationalism. Indeed, it is only the absence of a carefully conceived plan that distinguishes Frankenstein's creation of the Monster from Dr. Jekyll's of Mr. Hyde, who is turned loose solely as a means by which the creator realizes his secret and abominable desires. The common error of calling the Monster "Frankenstein" has considerable justification. He is the scientist's deviant self.

The essential oneness of the two is manifest in still another way. Frankenstein and the Monster, engrossed with each other, are soon completely inseparable in their mutual hatred and common misery. The facts surrounding the Monster's origin, existence, and subsequent culpability are too strange to be believed, and as a result people around them lose interest in the two and their far-ranging wanderings—pursuer and pursued, creator and creature, maker and destroyer, trekking over Europe from the Alps to the Mediterranean, and from there to the North Sea. In a narrative recalling aspects of her father's *Caleb Williams*,[55] Mary Shelley unfolds this tale of a great chase which, with society receding in significance, gradually takes on the only meaning, the only existence even, for both pursuer and pursued. We see the fugitive posting a landmark here and there that the search might continue, and when death claims the hunter, the fugitive too must die—the chase has been his life.

The Monster is an all too real nightmare for his maker, yet there is some semblance here of the *Alastor* Poet's visionary quest. In this tale, as in the Shelley poem, there is a projection or reproduction of the self; nor is a reunion of the two ultimately possible, for the pursuit ends only with the death of the pursuer. For this reason primarily, the story is a commentary on Romantic alienation, although, like her husband, Mary Shelley is finally quite ambivalent toward the Romantic quest. Frankenstein dies a defeated man, but sublimely, in the style of the Poet.

To go back to Shelley for a moment, it was in the Preface of 1817 that he recapitulated the principle of the romance first set down by Walpole: "I have thus endeavored to preserve the truth of the elementary principles of human nature, while I have not scrupled to innovate upon their combinations. The *Iliad*, the tragic poetry of Greece—Shakespeare, in the *Tempest* and *Midsummer*

Night's Dream—and most especially Milton, in *Paradise Lost*, conform to this rule. . . ." What he means by "the truth of the elementary principles of human nature" and his innovations on various combinations of same should be clear in the light of his references to the epics and romances: simply, the ordinary and the marvelous. The romance tradition, blending the two, continues right into the nineteenth century and later. However, what is remarkable about this is not so much the continuity of the tradition, but its continual absorption of elements not yet utilized in the early romances. For instance, in *Frankenstein* the main vehicle of Gothic fantasy is no longer the conventional supernatural. Its author, writing in an age of increasing scientism when the old Gothic mysteries had lost much of their appeal, took instead as her theme this same new science whose role M. Krempe had defined as limited to "annihilation" of the old fantasies, and in effect annihilated it as a humane pursuit by demonstrating its possible monstrous results. Despite the many lines of correspondence to the ghosts and devils of the conventional romances,[56] science, with its growing prestige, can generate a totally new species of terror. If scientific man is a kind of God, his scientific method becomes a new supernaturalism, a contemporary witchdoctoring of frightening potential.[57]

However, what is more, oxymoron being a prominent feature of science fiction, contradictory demands are made on the tone and style of the work. To convince his reader, the writer must delineate objects and events in the story very clearly and completely. At the same time, fantasy requires that he surround these objects and events with an atmosphere of wonder and at least the suggestion of the supernatural. For the first, neither Beckford's whimsy and irony, Mrs. Radcliffe's misty landscapes and characterizations, nor Godwin's rhetoric would be appropriate. Instead, Mrs. Shelley borrows the realistic type of scene, event, and character from the by then fully developed orthodox novel of Maria Edgeworth, Jane Austen, and some aspects of Sir Walter Scott. Her description of the De Lacey family, for example, is straight out of the domestic novel, and her physical delineation of the Monster is quite un-Gothic in its graphic clarity:

> His limbs were in proportion, and I had selected his features as beautiful. Beautiful!—Great God! His yellow skin scarcely covered the work of muscles and arteries beneath; his hair was of a lustrous black, and flowing; his teeth of a pearly whiteness; but these luxuriances only formed a more horrid contrast with his watery eyes, that seemed almost of the same color as the dun white sockets in which they were set, his shrivelled complexion and straight black lips (Chapter V, p. 51).

The second requirement is met as much by ample infusions of the Romantic poets, mainly Wordsworth and Coleridge, as by the conventional Gothicisms. Mary Shelley quotes liberally from "Tintern Abbey" and "The Ancient Mariner," and the Alps, so important to these poets, are here exploited to heighten the feelings of solitude and awe in the two major characters. However, "The Ancient Mariner" is perhaps the most important of these Romantic influences, as we can see from the resemblance that the extensive wanderings of Frankenstein and Walton bear to the Mariner's voyage of atonement. Especially striking in its reference to Coleridge is the final scene:

Immense and rugged mountains of ice often barred up my passage, and I often heard the thunder of the ground sea which threatened my destruction. But again the frost came and made the paths of the sea secure (Chapter 24, p. 224).

September 9th, the ice began to move, and roarings like thunder were heard at a distance as the islands split and cracked in every direction (Walton's last letter, p. 234).

Here is the Coleridge:

And through the drifts the snowy clifts
Did send a dismal sheen:
Nor shapes of men nor beasts we ken—
The ice was all between.

The ice was here, the ice was there,
The ice was all around:
It cracked and growled, and roared and howled,
Like noises in a swound!

(55–62)

Mrs. Shelley has not fully worked out the symbolic potential of the scene. The term "mountains of ice," nowhere varied or made any more specific, is nowhere strongly referential either; we miss the full sense in it of their dead damp whiteness against the impenetrable night. However, if she has not conquered those particular mountains, others have. Take the way she concludes her tale of Fausto-Promethean defiance—flames that devour the Monster rising to the dark skies above the stark white icebergs—a scene strikingly anticipating Poe who ended his

Arthur Gordon Pym with just such components as Mrs. Shelley's, but with considerably greater awareness of their possibilities. With Poe, the romance tradition would take on new visual variety and symbolic depth, qualities not lost on other highly gifted romancers such as Hawthorne and Melville, and indeed Dickens.

IV

Scottish religious fanaticism is the material of another powerful story involving the dual personality, *The Private Memoirs and Confessions of a Justified Sinner* (1824), by James Hogg (the Ettrick Shepherd). The devil of this story, unlike those guardian angels of the Romantics, Satan and Mephistopheles, more properly belongs to the native tradition of Lindsay and Burns, and Scottish ballads and folklore.[58] Hogg himself attests to the local origin of his imaginative stock:

> I hae nae doubt, sir, that had I read *Udolpho* and her ither romances in my boyish days, that my hair would hae stood on end like that o' ither folk. . . . But afore her volumes fell into my hauns, my soul had been frichtened by a' kinds of traditionary terrors, and mony hunder times hae I maist swarfed wi' fear in lonesome spats in muirs and woods, at midnicht. . . .[59]

This is not to say that the self-instructed country boy was ignorant of the Romantics. He was a regular contributor to *Blackwood's* and *Fraser's* and had already become a kind of Boswell to the great Walter Scott. A "boozing buffoon" in certain quarters, he was nonetheless a valued intimate of the learned *Blackwood* men Lockhart and

John Wilson. He was known to Wordsworth, Southey, and Byron, and was in fact lionized by the London literati during a visit there in 1832—while his wife back home fretted lest the great Londoners' interest in him should grow as threadbare as his old coat. However Scottish his imagination and materials, his claim to membership in the English Romantic movement is not to be denied. Internationalizing him even further, one historian has suggested that the *Justified Sinner* was inspired by Goethe's *Faust*.[60]

The story in brief is this: A free-and-easy, fun-loving young man, George Colwan, marries a straightlaced Presbyterian, a union predictably disastrous from the outset. The husband retires to a separate apartment, taking his infant son with him. A year later a second boy is born to Mrs. Colwan, but when Colwan refuses to acknowledge him, she names him after her chaplain and guardian, the fanatic Antinomian, Robert Wringhim. (That this Reverend Wringhim and young Wringhim are natural father and son is strongly suggested, though the point is never made explicit.) The half-brothers are separately brought up, remaining complete strangers to one another. On his seventeenth birthday, young Wringhim is advised by the Reverend Wringhim that he is now ready for admission into the "society of *the just made perfect*," [61] that is, he is now a "justified person" whose covenant of salvation is eternally sealed, and who is predestined to sanctification regardless of future moral conduct. "To the wicked, all things are wicked; but to the just, all things are just and right" (p. 24). Before long, Wringhim makes friends with a certain young man who strangely looks exactly like him. Doppelgängers, shadows of each other, they both believe in predestination and are one in their program of purging the earth of sin and sinful men. Wringhim blindly believes that his friend Gil-Martin is in reality a great prince, whose murderous acts are solely for the greater glory of God. After their elimination of his half-brother and the death of the elder Colwan, Wringhim takes over Dalcastle. However, just about this time he is accused of several crimes he has no memory of having committed—the seduction of an innocent girl, the girl's murder, and at last the murder of his own mother. Not knowing whether he had done such deeds in an unconscious state or whether they are the work of his illustrious friend, Wringhim becomes confused and leaves home. Only then, too late, does he suspect that his mentor might be the devil. Unable to escape his devilish double, the exhausted Wringhim hangs himself.

An outline is of course quite unjust to the structure of a work which, resembling *The Ring and the Book* in certain ways, presents many points of view and manages an obliqueness unmatched by any other romance. The book has three main parts: the "Editor's Narrative"; the "Private Memoirs and Confessions of a Sinner," which is Wringhim's memoir; and the "Editor's Narrative" again. In the second section, Wringhim's absurd self-justification is enough to indicate his disordered mind. However, the discrepancies between his telling of the story and the editor's account not only clearly establish his monomania but focus attention on his interweaving of the factual and the fanciful and his gradually developing horror at some of the implications of his blind determinism. The imaginary "editor" who in the last section caricatures the actual author, James Hogg (Hogg probably wanted to forestall charges of heresy), playfully calls the whole story "either dreaming or madness; or . . . a religious parable" (p. 229), which then further pushes the work toward an obscurity that only the author's deliberate plan can adequately explain.

The Justified Sinner is plainly aimed at religious fanaticism, particularly the form of it bred by Antinomianism. But however fascinating Hogg may have found the specifics of the eighteenth-century Auchterarder Creed (in which, interestingly, a James Hogg, probably not related, was involved),[62] the many possibilities of broader significance in the doctrine of absolute predetermination obviate the mere local history frame of the story. To holders of the doctrine, absolute predetermination assures the elect that they will be saved regardless of how they behave themselves; because this election by God can in no way be verified or told in advance, the claim of the elect to salvation rests solely on his own assertion of the claim. Contradictions abound, such as that justice is irrelevant to justification, or morality to sanctity. With the end guaranteed, any means may be justified; with such certainty, proof is unnecessary. To secularize Wringhim's fanatic theology, where man is perfect his conduct is necessarily good. It is a familiar solipsism, this confusion of essence and existence, and it is readily manifest in many different ways, as moral hypocrisy, as political anarchy, even as artistic expressionism. Wringhim at one point wants to find out if his friend's foot is not cloven into two hoofs. "It was the foot of a gentleman in every respect, so far as appearances went, but the form of his counsels was somewhat equivocal, and, if not double, they were amazingly crooked" (p. 185). According to the view argued here which powerfully challenges these perplexities, solipsism, whether Antinomian, or Romantic, is more than "somewhat equivocal"; it is dualistic to the core.

Hogg's devil is hardly unique to this romance, for

many of his other tales borrow liberally from folklore and balladry [63] in which devil figures are prominent. However, in *The Justified Sinner* he is not brought on in a manner calculated to satisfy the requirements of a mere conventional superstition; instead, the presentation quite deliberately obscures the fine line between the devil as a supernatural being and the devil as a product of Wringhim's diseased imagination. In the first section Gil-Martin is reported as having been seen by several people, whose description tended to confirm Wringhim's description of his friend in the second section; however, one of these people, indeed a chief witness, is unable to distinguish Wringhim from his friend, feeling strongly that "they are one and the same being," or at least that "the one [is] a prototype of the other" (p. 83). As another case of Hogg's deliberate obscurantism, the last section includes a letter published in *Blackwood's* by a "James Hogg" [64] which gives the legendary explanation of Wringhim's suicide as having been assisted by the devil. Here again, the editor denies what he has just put forth and discredits the letter with the suggestion that it is probably nothing more than an ingenious hoax. Nor is Wringhim's confession in the second section of any help: There are such bewildering inconsistencies in his account, for one thing, and, more important, he is quite patently out of his mind. The supernaturalism of this romance, then, is not such a simple one that would demand of the reader only the suspension of his incredulity and subsequent relaxation but is based on a very elaborate technique that would force him first to cooperate quite fully and consciously, then, *volte face*, to discredit all extraordinary events and superstitious explanations of peculiar happenings, with the net effect of greatly strengthening credibility. The book's big achievement is to have struck a balance between myth, the devil theme, and a psychological interpretation of myth. Gide rather overstated the same case in his essay on Hogg:

> The personification of the Demon in Hogg's book is among the most ingenious ever invented, for the power that sets him in action is always of a psychological nature; in other words—always admissible, even by unbelievers. It is the exteriorized development of our own desires, of our pride, of our most secret thoughts. . . . Hence the profound teaching of this strange book, the fantastic part of which (except in the last pages) is always psychologically explicable, without having recourse to the supernatural. . . .[65]

Gil-Martin's ambivalence—as much real supernatural being as he is Wringhim's hallucination—refers immediately to the moral ambiguity of the work. If Gil-Martin is the devil, Wringhim is only in a remote or theological sense accountable for his atrocities. That is, he is accountable for having been at some earlier time evil enough to have invited Satan's attention, yet for all subsequent deeds committed at the devil's instigation, he is himself a mere instrument. If, on the other hand, Gil-Martin is a projection of Wringhim's psychological state, his guilt, if guilt it is, is more pathological than moral. Either way, it is a tale beginning as a satire against the Antinomian's perversion of good and evil which is soon transformed into a fairly sympathetic examination of disintegrating faith and values. The terror for the reader is the same that Wringhim experiences with this Satanic figure, whether it dwells within or without.

Wringhim's disintegration is described with remarkable psychological insight. On the very day he is received into the "society of *the just made perfect*" (p. 105) he meets the man who is "the same being as myself," a man looking like his "second self" (pp. 106–107). It is as if his confirmation released part of him as an independent being. This double, the incarnation of his Antinomian fanaticism, is thus his Frankenstein Monster, and the encounter between them, like that between the scientist and his creation, brings about both a division and a duplication of Wringhim's selfhood. The two join forces to exterminate all the damned of this earth, but as the campaign mounts, Wringhim gradually becomes frightened of him and separates himself from Gil-Martin. The dominant feeling is not one of alienation from a friend, but rather that he himself is split into two: "I generally conceived myself to be two people" (p. 139). Soon, whatever action performed in the name of Wringhim is carried out by the double or by that part of himself over which he, as a whole man, has no control at all. The sense of an integral true self is gone, and Wringhim as an identifiable person is reduced to a helpless observer. Worse, *he* no longer knows who he is, and as he loses his memory and sense of time he becomes an utter stranger to himself: "Either I had a second self, who transacted business in my likeness, or else my body was at times possessed by a spirit over which it had no control, and of whose actions my own soul was wholly unconscious" (p. 165). Wringhim knows repair of the self is out of the question: He is "amalgamated," "consociated in one" (p. 172) with Gil-Martin. Almost more than life itself, he craves freedom from this double, yet he has lost the battle before engaging the enemy. As Dr. Jekyll was to discover at the end of the century, the embattled selves of such an unhappy man can be reconciled only in suicide.[66]

Notes

1. Godwin's characterization of *Caleb Williams* in the "Advertisement" attached to the 1831 edition of *St. Leon,* p. iii.
2. The ending is considerably softened in the 1842 version: People stay away out of sympathy for him. The hero's death on the gallows, incidentally, bears striking resemblance to Tess's in Hardy's novel.
3. *The Poetical Works of William Wordsworth,* 2nd ed., ed. E. de Selincourt and Helen Darbishire (London, 1952), I, p. 127. The word appears only in an early manuscript. The Gothic elements also are toned down in the later versions.
4. "[*The Borderers*] is, I suppose, unparalleled by any serious production of the human intellect for morbid and monstrous extravagance of horrible impossibility. Some invention perhaps might be recovered from the earliest and most frantic romances of Eugène Sue . . . which if set aside this young imagination of Wordsworth's might seem, in point of sheer moral monstrosity, to come as near it, as moonlight unto sunlight, or as water unto wine." "Wordsworth and Byron," *The Complete Works of Algernon Charles Swinburne,* ed. Sir Edmund Gosse and Thomas James Wise (London and New York, 1926), *Prose Works,* IV, p. 207.
5. Wordsworth's description in his essay on the play. *Works,* I, pp. 345, 346.
6. Basil Willey suggests that Wordsworth wrote the essay after realizing his failure to create a good dramatic character. See *The Eighteenth Century Background* (Boston, 1961), p. 268.
7. *The Prelude: Or, Growth of A Poet's Mind,* 2nd ed., ed. Ernest de Selincourt and Helen Darbishire (London, 1959), XII, pp. 376–377.
8. The romance sources, together with the autobiographical origin, of *The Borderers* and "Guilt and Sorrow" are persuasively explained by Oscar James Campbell and Paul Mueschke in their articles, " 'Guilt and Sorrow': A Study in the Genesis of Wordsworth's Aesthetics" and "*The Borderers* as a Document in the History of Wordsworth's Aesthetic Development," *MP,* XXIII (1926), pp. 293–306, 465–482. De Selincourt disagrees, proposing in his Oxford lecture that Shakespeare is the main influence. See "Wordsworth's Preface to '*The Borderers,*'" *Oxford Lectures on Poetry* (London, 1934), pp. 157–179. John Jones elaborates further on the play's Shakespearean traits in *The Egotistical Sublime: A History of Wordsworth's Imagination* (London, 1954).

See also Mary Moorman, *William Wordsworth: A Biography: The Early Years (1770–1803)* (London, 1957), pp. 301–308.

9. A letter to William Mathews dated November 7, 1794. *The Early Letters of William and Dorothy Wordsworth (1787–1805)*, ed. Ernest de Selincourt (London, 1935), p. 128.

10. *Collected Letters of Samuel Taylor Coleridge,* ed. Earl Leslie Griggs (London, 1956), I, p. 209.

11. Stephen Potter, finding Coleridge a man of dual personalities—"Jekyll and Hyde," or as he also calls him "Coleridge" and "S.T.C."—devotes a book to the subject. But to Potter the Coleridgean duality seems little more than a parallelism of great and petty *aspects* in the man, which hardly justifies the term. *Coleridge and S.T.C.* (London, 1935).

12. *Specimens of the Table Talk of the Late Samuel Taylor Coleridge* (London, 1835), I, p. 69.

13. *Coleridge's Shakespearean Criticism,* ed. T. M. Raysor (Cambridge, Mass., 1930), II, p. 273.

14. *Inquiring Spirit: A New Presentation of Coleridge from His Published and Unpublished Prose Writings,* ed. Kathleen Coburn (London, 1951), p. 37.

15. Coleridge, whose interests ranged very widely, explored many questions in what would now be treated in psychology, as well as mesmerism, visions, ghosts, and other occult topics. Treatment of Coleridge's ideas on the self would alone require a book. J. H. Muirhead's *Coleridge as Philosopher* (London and New York, 1930) has a chapter on the self, but it is too brief and limited in scope. The proper full-scale study of the author would involve establishing the extent of his debt to the philosophers and scientists of the time and would of course take into account his notebooks, Miss Coburn's monumental edition of which is near completion.

16. The one poem that has bearings on the theme is "The Ancient Mariner": the Mariner explores the deep regions of the self, and the wedding guest is the self of the actual world. A tension does exist between the two, but the poem is expressive, finally, of their coming to terms rather than their conflict.

17. For a fairly developed program for the Faustian drama, see *Table Talk,* II, pp. 108–118. Also, about the time Wordsworth wrote *The Borderers,* Coleridge was writing his Gothic play, *Osorio* (later called *Remorse*). Osorio's guilt, however, works redemptively—a departure from the usual romance vacillation. For a discussion of the Gothic drama in general, see Bertrand Evans, *Gothic Drama from Walpole to Shelley* (Berkeley and Los Angeles, 1947).

18. E. C. Mayne, *The Life and Letters of Anne Isabella Lady Noel Byron* . . . (New York, 1929), p. 447. Cited by Leslie Marchand, *Byron: A Biography* (New York, 1957), II, p. 483.
19. "Lord Byron," *The Spirit of the Age, Works,* XI, p. 78.
20. *John Bull's Letter to Byron,* ed. Alan Long Strout (Norman, Okla., 1947), p. 80.
21. See, for instance, William J. Calvert, *Byron: Romantic Paradox* (Chapel Hill, 1935).
22. This view is best represented by Ernest J. Lovell, Jr., *Byron: The Record of A Quest: Studies in a Poet's Concept and Treatment of Nature* (Austin, 1949).
23. The typical anti-Byronic view. Quoting from Trelawny, Douglas Bush censures Byron: "Yet even in these last days Byron still possessed the two pairs of lenses through which, according to his mood, he surveyed the world. 'If things are farcical, they will do for *Don Juan;* if heroical, you shall have another canto of *Childe Harold.'* " Seeing the poet's "two sides" in his *The Isles of Greece,* Bush writes, "Here passion kindles rhetoric into poetry, yet Byron is so afraid of being caught shedding manly tears that he puts the poem into a flippant frame." *Mythology and the Romantic Tradition in English Poetry* (New York, 1963), pp. 76–77.
24. More recent readers regard his comic vision with far more seriousness than did earlier generations. Perhaps the most imaginative is Paul West, *Byron and the Spoiler's Art* (London, 1960).
25. *The Works of Lord Byron, Letters and Journals,* ed. Rowland E. Prothero (London, 1898–1901), II, p. 66.
26. *The Works of Lord Byron, Poetry,* ed. Ernest Hartley Coleridge (London, 1898–1904), II, pp. 59–60. All Byron references are to this edition.
27. Byron was an avid reader of novels and romances. In an 1807 memorandum book he wrote how he had "read (to my regret at present) about four thousand novels." Thomas Moore, *Letters and Journals of Lord Byron with Notices of His Life* (London, 1830), I, p. 99. Lovell traces the "Zeluco theme" in the earlier romances, and Peter L. Thorslev, Jr. devotes a book, *The Byronic Hero: Types and Prototypes* (Minneapolis, 1962), to a thorough analysis of the genealogy of the Byronic hero.
28. There are many writers impersonating their myths toward the end of the century, as the last chapter of this study shows. Poe is a good example for an earlier period (see N. B. Fagin, *The Histrionic Mr. Poe*); Walt Whitman at midcentury, another (Leslie Fiedler makes this point in the essay written for *Leaves of Grass: One Hundred Years After*). Poe, of course, tried to cut a Byronic

figure in his youth, but he is indebted to Byron in other ways as well. His "William Wilson," a dual-personality story *par excellence,* was suggested, according to Edward H. Davidson, by "an article of Washington Irving, 'An Unwritten Drama of Lord Byron,' in *The Gifts* for 1836. Irving stated that he got the tale from Medwin, who had received it from Byron himself." *Selected Writings of Edgar Allan Poe* (Boston, 1956), p. 500.

29. From the World Classics Edition translated by Bayard Taylor (London, 1932), lines 1767–1774.

30. Samuel C. Chew insists that *Manfred* is a greater work than *Faust* because it is "the fullest expression of . . . the doctrine of the authoritative and reflective principle of conscience, the Categorical Imperative, the affirmation that 'Man's Conscience is the Oracle of God.'" *The Dramas of Lord Byron: A Critical Study* (Göttingen and Baltimore, 1915), p. 84. It is hard to see how Manfred, who defies God, can be an "Oracle of God," although this notion is upheld and argued by E. M. Butler in her study of the Goethe-Byron relationship. The book, *Byron and Goethe: Analysis of a Passion* (London, 1956), offers the most lucid discussion of the influence of *Faust* on *Manfred,* affirming Byron's essential independence.

31. *The Works of Percy Bysshe Shelley,* ed. Roger Ingpen and Walter E. Peck (London, 1928), V, p. 199. All Shelley references are to this edition.

32. "To ———" published together with *Alastor.* Mrs. Shelley identified this poem as one addressed to Coleridge, while others (Dobell, Rossetti, Dowden) have said that it is to himself.

33. Floyd Stovall's characterization. See his *Desire and Restraint in Shelley* (Durham, North Carolina, 1931), p. 147.

34. The hero of *Alastor* is simply called "Poet." This capitalized form throughout my discussion of course refers to the poetic hero, not to Shelley.

35. *Alastor* is the subject of one of the liveliest controversies in Shelleyan scholarship. Aside from the question of unity between the Preface and the poem, what the Poet-hero *signifies* had to be argued; some said Shelley, some said a "natural allegory," whereas others suggested Wordsworth or even Thomas Jefferson Hogg. The following items propose varying views on these issues: Raymond D. Havens, "Shelley's 'Alastor,'" *PMLA,* XLV (1930), pp. 1098–1115; M. C. Weir, "Shelley's *Alastor* Again," *PMLA,* XLVI (1931), pp. 947–950; Harold L. Hoffman, *An Odyssey of the Soul: Shelley's "Alastor"* (New York, 1933); Paul Mueschke and Earl L. Griggs, "Wordsworth as Prototype of the Poet in Shelley's *Alastor,*" *PMLA,* XLIX (1934), pp. 229–245; Arthur E. DuBois,

"Alastor: The Spirit of Solitude," *JEGP*, XXV (1936), pp. 530–545; Marcel Kessel, "The Poet in Shelley's *Alastor:* A Criticism and a Reply," *PMLA*, LI (1936), pp. 302–310; Evan K. Gibson, "Alastor: A Reinterpretation," *PMLA*, LXII (1947), pp. 1022–42; Carlos Baker, *Shelley's Major Poetry: The Fabric of a Vision* (Princeton, 1948); Albert Gerard, "Alastor, or the Spirit of Solipsism," *PQ*, XXXIII (1954), pp. 164–177.

36. In "On Love" Shelley defines the epipsyche as a self which is the "ideal prototype of every thing excellent or lovely that we are capable of conceiving as belonging to the nature of man." *Works*, VI, p. 202.

37. Carlos Baker, p. 54.

38. His definition of the imagination remains unchanged in *A Defence of Poetry*, written about the same time. "But poetry defeats the curse which binds us to be subjected to the accident of surrounding impressions." "[It] creates for us a being within our being. It makes us the inhabitants of a world to which the familiar world is a chaos." *Works*, VII, p. 137.

39. Craving union, the "I" localizes the possibilities for it everywhere: in "life" and in "death," in "Heaven" and in "Hell," in "immortality" and in "annihilation," as though he were anticipating its impossibility. A similar point is made by Harold Bloom in his *Shelley's Mythmaking* (New Haven, 1959), p. 219. See also his discussion of the poem in *The Visionary Company: A Reading of English Romantic Poetry* (Garden City, New York, 1963), pp. 352–359.

40. The fullest comparison of *Alastor* and *Endymion* may be found in Leonard Brown's "The Genesis, Growth, and Meaning of Endymion," *SP*, XXX (1933), pp. 618–653.

41. *The Poetical Works of John Keats*, 2nd ed., ed. H. W. Garrod (London, 1958), Book I, line 779. All Keats references are to this edition.

42. Keats's strategy of acceptance is best expressed in his remarks about his friend Dilke (quite similar to Arnold's about Clough a generation later): he is "a Man who cannot feel he has a personal identity unless he has made up his Mind about every thing. The only means of strengthening one's intellect," Keats believes, "is to make up ones mind about nothing—to let the mind be a thoroughfare for all thoughts." *The Letters of John Keats*, ed. Hyder Edward Rollins (Cambridge, Mass., 1958), II, p. 213.

43. To George and Tom Keats, *Letters*, I, 193.

44. To Richard Woodhouse, October 27, 1818. *Letters*, I, p. 387.

45. April 21, 1819. *Letters*, II, pp. 102–103.

46. August 16, 1820. *Letters*, II, p. 323.

47. Earl R. Wasserman calls the poem Keats's "Center of Indifference." See his *The Finer Tone: Keats' Major Poems* (Baltimore, 1953).

48. Walter Jackson Bate (*John Keats* [Cambridge, Mass., 1963]) interprets the split as between Lycius' view of Lamia and Apollonius'. See Chapter 20, especially pp. 556–559.

49. Douglas Bush, who has seen a "divided soul" in the Keatsian corpus, concludes his argument on Keats as follows:

> His house was, most of the time, divided against itself, but his consciousness of the fissure, his unceasing endeavor to solve the problem of sense and knowledge, art and humanity, are in themselves an index of his stature. No other English poet of the century had his poetic endowment, and no other strove so intensely to harmonize what may, without undue stretching of the terms, be called the Apollonian and the Faustian ideals of poetry. However high one's estimate of what he wrote, one may really think—to use an often meaningless cliché—that Keats was greater than his poems.

Mythology and the Romantic Tradition, pp. 127–128.

50. The legend of the "ghost story" contest held high in the Alps by Byron, Polidori, Shelley, and Mary has been attacked by James Rieger in his "Dr. Polidori and the Genesis of *Frankenstein,*" *SEL,* III (1963), pp. 461–472, as "an almost total fabrication." An examination of Polidori's diary, he believes, will help us "see this novel totally divorced from and unembarrassed by the Gothic tradition." However, we are not embarrassed: Whether the *Fantasmagoriana* and other Gothic stories were the immediate stimulus for her writing of *Frankenstein,* Mary Shelley, like the other contestants, was a great reader of these tales. Her work cannot help but be—and *Frankenstein* gives everywhere evidence of being—informed with the romance tradition. Between 1814 and 1816 Mary had read, among others, Beckford, Radcliffe, Lewis, Godwin, Maturin, and Charles Brockden Brown. See the "List of Books Read," *Mary Shelley's Journal,* ed. Frederick L. Jones (Norman, Oklahoma, 1947), pp. 32–33, 47–49, 71–73.

51. *Frankenstein* (London and New York: Everyman's Library, 1960), Chapter 15, p. 136. This edition is used throughout the discussion. Chapter reference as well as page number is given for identification of quoted passages.

52. Another opposing pair in the book are the two professors. M. Krempe, scorning alchemy, still investigates nothing but those "realities of little worth" (Chapter 3, p. 39). M. Waldman, in

contrast, though very much a modern scientist by virtue of his training and experience, has not entirely abandoned the spirit of Paracelsian miracle. It is Frankenstein's fate, of course, to serve the Faustian aspiration represented by M. Waldman.

53. This epigraph, which appears in the editions of 1818 and 1831, is omitted in the Everyman's edition.

54. ". . . Frankenstein's relationship to the Monster expresses itself in the paradox of identity and conflict—an anticipation of the Jekyll-and-Hyde theme—from which certain symbolic situations emerge. Frankenstein himself states: 'I considered the being whom I had cast among mankind . . . nearly in the light of my own vampire, my own spirit let loose from the grave, and forced to destroy all that was dear to me.' We may visualise Frankenstein's doppelgänger or Monster firstly as representing reason in isolation, since he is the creature of an obsessional rational effort." Muriel Spark, *Child of Light: A Reassessment of Mary Wollstonecraft Shelley* (Hadleigh, Essex, 1951), p. 137.

55. In his review of *Frankenstein* (not published till 1832) Shelley briefly compares it with *Caleb Williams,* emphasizing several similarities. *Works,* VI, pp. 263–264.

56. Brown should be mentioned here. According to Glynn Grylls, "Charles Brockden Brown, the American, whose novels Shelley admired, rationalized the terror element, and his *Wieland* may be considered a precursor of Frankenstein in this respect." *Mary Shelley: A Biography* (London, 1938), p. 320.

57. According to our best intelligence, Erasmus Darwin's experiment certainly seems to have given Shelley a new hope for man's future. But Mary Shelley was apparently not so minded, being skeptical of science and very much aware of its negative potential as mere superstition. Meanwhile, because the notion of Faustian curiosity as hubris is the main "moral" of *Frankenstein,* we have her husband's disclaimer in the Preface: "The opinions which naturally spring from the character and situation of the hero are by no means to be conceived as existing always in my own conviction, nor is any inference justly to be drawn from the following pages as prejudicing any philosophical doctrine of whatever kind."

58. For discussion of the Scottish character of the work, see Sir George Douglas, *James Hogg* (Edinburgh and London, 1899), p. 98; Louis Simpson, *James Hogg: A Critical Study* (New York, 1962), Chapter 8.

59. *Noctes Ambrosianae* (Edinburgh and London, 1855), I, p. 201.

60. E. A. Baker, *The History of the English Novel* (London, 1935), VI, p. 255.

61. The Cresset Press edition (London, 1947), p. 105, is used through-

out this discussion of the *Justified Sinner*. Because the book has no chapter divisions, only page references are given here.

62. For an account of the Auchterarder Creed and *Marrow* controversies, see John Cunningham, *The Church History of Scotland* (Edinburgh, 1882), II, pp. 247–256, and W. M. Hetherington, *History of the Church of Scotland* (New York, 1859), pp. 340–347. Louis Simpson's book has a brief explanation of the affair (pp. 170–173).

63. For example, *The Brownie of Bodsbeck*, "The Brownie of the Black Haggs," "The Cameronian Preacher's Tale," or "The Strange Letter of a Lunatic."

64. The letter printed in the third section is in fact an almost verbatim reproduction of the letter Hogg published in *Blackwood's* in August 1823. This invention of the "editor" and the circumstance of anonymous publication led many critics (including George Saintsbury and Andrew Lang) to the belief that the book was not by Hogg alone, but very much helped along by Lockhart, a view no longer current.

65. The Introduction to the Cresset Press edition, p. xv.

66. *The Justified Sinner* makes use of several of the typical symbolic images of Romantic poetry. A notable one is the Brocken Specter that frightens George Colwan with its projection of his brother's face on a cloud twenty times larger than life-size. Beginning with *Faust,* this atmospheric phenomenon was a favorite with the Romantics. DeQuincey and Tennyson refer to it, and later on Yeats, who was greatly excited by a George Russell drawing of the Brocken Specter, and who later used it in his poems and plays.

Part II
Life Against Art

3.

Will as Form:
1830

Victorian writers started life with the knowledge of the Romantic failure in self-discovery. How they lived with it is the story of their art. To their own great fear of Romantic indeterminacy, they responded with what is often called the "Victorian conversion," which, defining a moral view of art as of life, tries to put the divided self together and make it work. Imagination must be disciplined by the rational, play by the reality principle. Nor was the self-contradiction of this conversion merely theoretical. Often, where the "statement" of the poem asserted unity in the plainest way, the direction of the poem as an artistic totality was toward anarchy. Incoherent details were many times forcibly "resolved" by the overall scheme, leaving a painful cacophony. This will to cement the disparate parts of life by moral commitment is most noticeable in the works of the early Victorians, the young Tennyson and Browning, and in those of Carlyle. It was left to Arnold and Clough later on to realize the psychological inefficacy of this conversion, and by the eighteen-seventies Victorian moralism was challenged at the root, marking the end of that remarkable response.

While the typical Victorian poetic statement was perhaps the most noticeable aspect of the early Victorian literary product, the Gothic motifs and themes were the appropriate vehicles for the underground impulses of the Victorian mind. At first, as the poets and writers made every effort to suppress these impulses, there was little likelihood that many would disinterestedly scrutinize their self-division and its symptoms. They were too interested in the cure. The appearances of Gothicism around 1830 are thus limited to stock villains and heroes in works like Tennyson's *The Devil and the Lady*, Browning's *Paracelsus,* and Carlyle's *Sartor Resartus*. The full-fledged dual-personality novel had to wait on the subsidence of the fervor of conversion. Bulwer-Lytton worked the Godwinian romance vein, but his novels unfortunately open no new perspectives either for the novel or for Gothicism. Charles Dickens shows traces of Gothicism even in early works like *Pickwick Papers* (1836–37) and *Oliver Twist* (1837–38), but his concern with self-division is more intense in later works and is more profitably discussed in connection with his last novels.

I

Byron's death marked the close of a remarkable poetic era. Tennyson said later he had thought then that everything was "over and finished for every one—that nothing else mattered." [1] In fact, there followed some twenty "lethargic" years for poetry. It was a time Sir Harold Nicolson has called the "interregnum between the gospel of Rousseau and the gospel of Carlyle," [2] after which it was Tennyson himself who came forward to become the "institution" of his time.

In his earlier years, Tennyson was very much under Byron's spell, the great Romantic's material and mood being reflected most noticeably in such efforts as "I Wander in Darkness and Sorrow," "Persia," and "Remorse," all from *Poems by Two Brothers* (1827), a volume unashamedly imitative. However, beneath the Byronics there are signs here of the Tennysonian sobriety, a feature shared by *The Devil and the Lady,* which is of the same vintage. A sort of comedy of black humours, it is an amazingly sophisticated work for a boy of fifteen. His Magus is the usual Faustian type, perhaps a bit fatigued from long tours of duty in the Romantic theater. It is his Devil who is notably new, not at all Satanic or evil, not even much of a rebel. On the contrary, he is, as he himself tells us, "a moralizing devil, / Quite out o' my element." [3] Like Magus, he is something of a Faust, although he lacks the elemental Promethean curiosity. His inquiry resembles Hamlet's more than Cain's, and more the questions of a bright pupil of Berkeley and Hume than Hamlet's:

> O suns and spheres and stars and belts and systems,
> Are ye or are ye not?
> Are ye realities or semblances
> Of that which men call real?
> Are ye true substance?
>
> .   .   .   .
>
> I have some doubt if ye exist when none
> Are by to view ye; if your Being alone
> Be in the mind and the intelligence
> Of the created?
>   (II.i'

The Devil and the Lady is Tennyson's first serious consideration of reality, and it shows the sobriety with which the young man set about disciplining this prime Romantic theme to his own uses. The Devil's doubt is Tennyson's, too, and yet with Tennyson neither doubt nor Devil is ever glorified. The sublime Dark Powers hold no sway in Tennyson's world, for beneath the Byronic mask there is the emergent laureate, deeply committed, among other projects, to the conquest of all signs of despair.

Take another ambitious (though incomplete) poem called "Armageddon," written about 1825. It is just before Judgment Day, and the speaker, on a hill overlooking the "valley of destruction," [4] sees all sorts of horrible, formless things amid a wretched "dissonance / Of jarring confus'd voices" (p. 8). This ghastly landscape seems to divide him dreadfully between East, with its "ineffable" silver tents of heaven, and lurid West, with its snake coiled around a giant banner. Then a Seraph, joining him, suggests he open his eyes and see, and with this sudden new view he feels himself a part of "God's omniscience," and strangely detached, as though far away from the "hum of men" (p. 12). As in so much Romantic poetry, the person in the poem, alien to the world, experiences the absolute:

> I was a part of the Unchangeable,
> A scintillation of Eternal Mind,
> Remix'd and burning with its parent fire.
> Yes! in that hour I could have fallen down
> Before my own strong soul and worshipp'd it.

Despite the Romantic egotism of the young man, the Seraph had no intention of carrying him off to an exultant *O Altitudo!* of the imagination but only of warning him of imminent war between the two great kingdoms of heaven and hell. Whereas his Devil had interminably asked the great moral and epistemological questions, his Seraph here shows no interest whatever in moving him to pursue the Eternal. Tennyson thus backs away from committing himself to the dualism posed in the poem—between the self that is reality and the universe that is unreality—while managing nonetheless to externalize doubt and despair in a peculiarly awesome landscape. The Seraphic prophecy of God's ultimate victory is vaguely re-assuring, but it brings the young man no real joy, and he remains an impotent and unhappy spectator of the battle.

With the reworking of "Armageddon" in *Timbuctoo*,[5] Tennyson brings the universal antagonism down to earth by posing the spirit of myth and poetry against the force of science and invention. With the defeat of "Fable," "keen Discovery" strikes the gloomy note of the last line: "and all was dark." [6] Nor do the shadows lift noticeably in *Poems, Chiefly Lyrical* (1830), in which "Nothing Will Die" is set off against "All Things Will Die," with no attempt to join the disparate attitudes in the manner of the Blakean polarity. The " 'How' and 'Why' " jingle poses Tennyson's basic puzzle, for all its childish sentimentality. "The Mystic" depicts the alienated man as the "purified" soul ("Ye knew him not: he was not one of ye").[7] " 'Οἱ ῥεοντες" speaks despairingly of the Heraclitean world where "all things are as they seem to all, / And all things flow like a stream." At times, he will manage a true dialogue of the mind with itself ("Song: A Spirit Haunts the Year's Last Hours" and "A Character"), at others, escape altogether into the never-never land of "The Merman," "The Sea Fairies," and "The Kraken," anticipating Arnold's deep-sea dreams.

The doubt and the anguished loneliness are most

apparent in the poem exasperatingly titled "Supposed Confessions of a Secondrate Sensitive Mind Not in Unity with Itself," which also contains the clearest evidence of what can only be called, however paradoxically, Tennyson's positive despair, an agonizing sense of disunity joined to a persistent determination to make up his mind. Forsaken by his friends and no longer confident of his ability to do anything at all on his own, the speaker in this poem is an outcast, yet he yearns for the "common faith" of his society. He remembers his childhood and his mother's great piety, and believes that, if she were living now, she would bring him back to faith. He had thought it "man's privilege to doubt," and had fallen from faith. Now even pride is gone: "I am void, / Dark, formless, utterly destroyed." This probing into "things that seem" and "things that be," begun in *The Devil and the Lady*, brings no great findings to the surface until the "Supposed Confessions," where instead of analyzing away the problematic "double nature," the inquiring intellect on its quest for faith works itself irremediably into a trap which is neither belief nor doubt. Characteristically, the Tennysonian man is unable to stay long in such an uncomfortable position, and the more he struggles, the greater his confusion—and the greater his confusion of syntax: "I fear / All may not doubt, but everywhere / Some must clasp Idols. Yet, my God, / Whom call I Idol?"

Aside from its technique of distancing the speaker by making him an old man, the poem gives small evidence of formal control. Its long recapitulation of spiritual crisis —the futile try at resolving the "double nature" of intellect and faith—is overwritten and tortuous, and the ironic "Secondrate" in the title is a question-begging more applicable to the poem than to the persona. The "Supposed Confessions" is a bad poem, but a fascinating one, not the least for its manifest terror of free inquiry. Not that the flight response on this issue is peculiarly Tennyson's: all the Victorians experienced this fear, many of them supposedly conquering it simply through "conversion," which avoided the problem. Newman, for one, was to advise strongly against the analytic habit of the free intellect:

> Resolve to believe nothing, and you must prove your proofs and analyze your elements, sinking further and further, and finding "in the lowest depth a lower deep," till you come to the broad bosom of scepticism. . . . If we insist on proofs for everything, we shall never come to action: to act you must assume, and that assumption is faith.[8]

Newman is of course assuming a faith that, although finally an act of will, is well-grounded in the doctrinal tradition of the Church. However, for the speaker in the poem, the philosophical possibility of faith has little relevance to his religious hankering. "Christians" are by nature "happy," women "saint-like," that is the way the world is; the speaker alone despairs. A cultural and religious alienation of this kind means that the choice for faith be made by the will alone. The issue turns on psychological, not theological terms, and involves the poet's personal strategy for survival. "Oh damnéd vacillating state!" is thus more than a mere statement of the dilemma, expressing as it does the deep frustration at the wretched imposition of such a choice in life: accept-and-be-saved or reject-and-be-damned.

The Tennyson of the 1833 volume of *Poems* is a poet both "lyrical" and "didactic," tending on the one hand toward an "aesthetic and mystic abstraction" and on the other toward religious and moral interests. As man and as poet he is at once escapist and deliberately engagé.[9] It is true that the Cambridge Apostles had been after him ever since Hallam had grouped him together with Keats and Shelley as the "Poets of Sensation,"[10] and they had been bearing down especially hard on his "pure poetry," with its corollary exoticism and love of the past. The Apostles were full of moral fervor, despising the "Stumpfs,"[11] as they called their home-grown Philistines, and puffed themselves up as the sole thinking agents in the universe.[12] For them poetry was either prophecy or edification, nothing else. At the same time, Tennyson's own long worries over reality would argue against our exaggerating their influence. The gradual ascendancy of the moral perspective in his poetry is generated from his own paramount need for a new vision of life.

Still, the poems of this volume do vacillate almost unendingly. Their motifs of isolation and flight and the sensuality of their mythic isle and ivory tower appear in a Keatsian luxuriance of diction and imagery, even as the frame-device, indicative of Tennyson's habitual critical attitude on his own temperament, explicitly challenges both the poetic matter and the manner. This is true of "The Sea Fairies," "The Lotos-Eaters," and "Morte d'Arthur." Even in "The Hesperides," a poem that has been called his "most eloquent defense of a pure poetry,"[13] the fugitive songs of the sirens take on substance for being overheard by a real historical man, Zidonian Hanno,[14] the enterprising navigator of the fifth century B.C. The fantasy presented as fantasy is quite a different story from the fantasy presented as reality.[15]

In "The Lady of Shalott," for instance, art is first a weaving of the shadows of the world. When love breaks through, however, she finds herself dissatisfied with mere

shadowy reflections of things and decides to experience
the wonderland of the "real world" behind the mirror.
By this act, she is cursed. The mirror cracks and she dies,
floating down the river. Her name has meant little to the
"welfed wits" of Camelot: art, after all, may be quite
irrelevant to reality. Still, they are struck with fear on
hearing her swan song, and hurriedly bless themselves.
Furthermore, her death seems to break the curse, and she
boldly asserts her identity: "this is I, / The Lady of
Shalott." [16] Even in death art disquiets the world, like a
ghost haunting the murderer. Plato's banishment, always
in process, is never a *fait accompli*.

"The Palace of Art" is preceded by twenty lines
dedicated to his friend R. C. Trench, who had once said
to him, "Tennyson, we cannot live in art." Whatever
Trench meant by this—is it an "ultimatum" [17] against
Tennyson's "Art Heresy" or is he agreeing with the
poet? [18]—"The Palace of Art" is not the work of an aesthete.
Tennyson, impatient with his continuing war of the impulses, sides determinedly, in this poem, with his "moral"
self—a decision made only after long debate. In the poem
the poet builds himself a "lordly pleasurehouse" so that
his soul could "live alone unto herself." Unlike Coleridge's pleasure dome, the mansion stands starkly alone
in barren surroundings. The palace is described first at
a distance, then at close range, and finally the poet's eye
moves into the interior.[19] With ever narrowing scope, the
subjects of the arras on the walls are scrutinized, as are
all the "dark corners" of the rooms. Inevitably the soul's
dark consciousness is broken and searched. As in a long
film close-up, the poet dwells on these details to effect an
almost suffocating pressure. The soul, meanwhile, com-
munes with herself, celebrating her supernal isolation
and "perfect artifice." (In the revised version she even

claps her hands, anticipating Yeats's Byzantium voyager.) But her solitude begins to weigh upon her: " 'No voice breaks through the stillness of this world— / One deep, deep silence all.' " The palace is all at once a prison of despair.

> "Make me a cottage in the vale," she said,
> "Where I may mourn and pray.

LXXVI

> "Yet pull not down my palace towers, that are
> So lightly, beautifully built:
> Perchance I may return with others there
> When I have purged my guilt."

These concluding lines are all ambiguous as to the soul's true feelings. To leave hoping to return can hardly be construed as a sincere act of purgation. Further, her "serpent pride" seems still active in her plan to bring people back with her. On the other hand, does she mean to bring everyone and convert her palace into a public gallery? What else is expressed in "So lightly, beautifully built" than the tenderest feelings for that structure? Finally, isn't the humble secluded cottage a fairly good substitute, at least for a temporary retreat?

Tennyson does unequivocally define the "message" of the poem in the dedication. Unlike the framework of "The Hesperides" and "The Lotos-Eaters," which opens an ironic perspective on the poems, these lines plainly and emphatically insist on the allegorical intent of "The Palace of Art" which is to deny the notion of "Beauty only." However, their very plainness makes them no match for the ornate descriptions of the soul's pleasures in her palace, nor can they help us in resolving the ambiguity at the end of the poem. Is the Tennyson of this poem, then, really all that clear about his project, which was simply to dramatize his understanding of the poet in the world without involving his emotions as a poet in the world? [20] Further, is he really all that *effective* in locking himself out of "The Palace of Art"? Sheer will cannot forge a great art. Nor is the problem simply the conflict between the enjoyment of art and the moral condemnation of it. The soul's claustrophobia in her palace is an authentic experience, and had Tennyson worked with that motif to its natural conclusion—the soul unambiguously deserting the mansion—he would have made a proper poem. As the poem stands, his last lines equivocate and spoil it.

One thing that emerges clearly from this is that poetry for Tennyson is essentially a personal strategy, a way of orienting his life. The formal unity of a poem, requiring for its achievement the evaluation and resolution of antagonistic impulses and the renunciation of didacticism, is a discipline in negative capability, but Tennyson sees it first and foremost as antithetical to his true mission in life. As this new purpose will define his life, so will it operate his poetry. A new poetic unity is forged through moral commitment in the same way that the personal identity of poet or reader is assumed to be confirmed in moral assertion. Poetic achievement will not then be measured by craft, however carefully it joins the materials of insight, but by the imprints of moral certainty and fervor. For Tennyson, as for most of his contemporaries, life as it ought to be lived is the supreme end, not art as it is formed by insight and craft. It is the moral vision which regulates their work, not the converse, a poetic vision which fires their faith.

Tennyson continues in "The Two Voices, or

Thoughts of a Suicide" to trace the process of pulling himself together. In this poem, written during a period of great personal despair in 1833,[21] the dialogue of the mind with itself takes literally the form of a debate, with the "I" arguing with one or another of two inner voices: one, the "Still small voice" counseling him to do away with himself, and the other, the more hopeful one heard toward the end of the poem. These voices constitute the poles of despair and hope, and the "I" communing with each one in turn shows Tennyson's tenacity in examining both sides. It is the same desperate energy that had earlier damned his wretched vacillation.

The poem opens with the despairing voice asking the speaker "Were it not better not to be?" The voice argues for suicide and for a while the speaker's acute suffering makes the reasoning almost persuasive. Since life is miserable and his particular death of no significance to the rest of mankind, why should he not terminate his misery? He is defensive and apologetic for being alive, and shyly advances a counterargument to the voice's— his suicide will only be ridiculed and scorned by others. The answer is disdainful:

> "Sick art thou—a divided will
> Still heaping on the fear of ill
> The fear of men, a coward still.
>
> "Do men love thee? Art thou so bound
> To men, that how thy name may sound
> Will vex thee lying underground?"
> (106–111)

Unable to refute this, the speaker admits his indecisiveness. As in the "Supposed Confessions" he tells how his wretchedness originated in a hopeful search for "some hidden principle," but that doubt had swiftly overtaken him, unfooting him from firm belief. At that, the voice sees its own advantage and drives its point hard: However much he tries, all is in vain and he can never hope to solve the "riddle of the earth" (170) he struggles with. If knowledgeable men can only delude themselves, what hope is there for such a one as he, this "dreamer, deaf and blind" (175)? If human understanding is nothing but shadow, dream, why shouldn't we seek at least the certainty of death?

> "Shadows thou dost strike,
> Embracing cloud, Ixion-like;
>
> "And owning but a little more
> Than beasts, abidest lame and poor,
> Calling thyself a little lower
>
> "Than angels. Cease to wail and brawl!
> Why inch by inch to darkness crawl?
> There is one remedy for all."
>
> (194–201)

The young man looks then to history for evidence of that "joy that mixes man with Heaven" (210), while the voice adamantly insists that salvation lies only in the nothingness of death. Suddenly, a flaw is discovered in that apparently irrefutable logic:

> "If all be dark, vague voice," I said,
> "These things are wrapt in doubt and dread,
> Nor canst thou show the dead are dead."
>
> (265–267)

.   .   .   .

> "But thou canst answer not again.
> With thine own weapon art thou slain,
> Or thou wilt answer but in vain."
>
> > (293–312)

This brings him to the bedrock of the traditional onto-
logical proof: the assertion that the absolute does not
exist presupposes the absolute truth of the assertion and
hence is self-contradictory. In this everlasting yea, the
speaker takes up the offensive:

> "These words," I said, "are like the rest;
> No certain clearness, but at best
> A vague suspicion of the breast:"
>
> > (334–336)

And again,

> "But thou," said I, "hast missed thy mark,
> Who sought'st to wreck my mortal ark,
> By making all the horizon dark."
>
> > (388–390)

Vanquished, the skeptical voice tunes out, but not without one last sarcasm: "Behold, it is the Sabbath morn"
(402), upon which the speaker views from his window
a saintly trinity of manly husband, gentle wife, and their
little maiden walking along beside them, all "demure"
and "in their double love secure" (418–419).

The passage is an object of derision to twentieth-
century readers and is a sore point even for otherwise
sympathetic students. Basil Willey, interpreting the pious

little family as the main way by which the speaker might somehow conquer the negative voice, is clearly apologetic, and barely manages to defend the poem's "modulation into a new emotional key" as psychologically true.[22] This is clearly insufficient as an explanation. The "I" overcomes the voice much earlier in the argument and does so *by argument*. The pious little family is no inspiration for faith, but his symbol of acceptance of the here and now. The speaker is altogether convinced that he *must* adhere to the "common faith" or remain perturbed and unfulfilled. "More life, and fuller, that I want" (399). It is a case either of acceptance of this Sunday family—and of society in general—or of surrendering to isolation and ultimate incoherence. Poetic vision as well as personal psychology demanded this certitude. However, his acceptance was as much the result of self-persuasion, as delineated in this poem, as it was from fear of death and the void. By this reading, the second voice with its call of "Rejoice! Rejoice!" cannot be discounted as mere Sunday rhetoric.

More important to our understanding of this poem than either the alleged Apostolic influence or the hollow sentimentality of the conversion passage is the poem's single-minded theme. "The Two Voices" is bluntly logical and argumentative, and its metaphors, instead of opening an ironic perspective on reality, are totally subordinated to the statement of it. This predominance of argument, the poet's only remedy for a severe but amorphous spiritual crisis, is more and more noticeably a Tennysonian strategy. In this sense, "The Two Voices" is quite different from "The Ancient Mariner" which also ends with the hero's exhortation ("Walk together to the kirk / And all together pray"); Moral difficulties are not set forth in dramatic terms but rather "solved" by way of argument. This is to become the habit of the Victorian convert writers for whom poetic reality is defined by the precept, the precept itself becoming an article of faith.

Despite this trend, Tennyson is too various a poet to be programed exclusively to such an ideology. Nor is the program very successful. Just as his moral vision comes to define itself, something happens to blur it again—some small detail or something in the tempo of the work. One of the most curious poems of this kind is "Ulysses" published with "The Two Voices" in 1842. Victorian readers by and large took the poem simply in the light of its last line, "To strive, to seek, to find, and not to yield," and even nowadays the unwary will see it as a pronouncement of Victorian vitality and fortitude, a generalized colonialist manifesto. There are reasons for this: an indefatigable Ulysses defying age and impending death for just one more heroic adventure in this world—Ithaca left behind, in its way a Shalott; the oceans and the "newer world" still to be explored. So read, the poem leads inevitably to that most quotable last line. It is this poem, Tennyson said, that expresses his "feeling about the need of going forward, and braving the struggle of life perhaps more simply than anything in 'In Memoriam.' " [23]

Certain details challenge this reading. For one, there is contempt in Ulysses' attitude toward his homeland, especially where he refers to it by the epithet "barren crags" and speaks of his countrymen as a "savage race," men whose laws are "unequal" and so by implication of no value whatever. Penelope is dismissed with the single description "aged." Throughout, the first person pronoun is used insistently with the effect that Ulysses comes across as much too self-centered to be the ideal hero. In fact, by his defiance of the gods and patronizing attitude toward Telemachus, he is practically a villain.[24] At the very least, he is a kind of Byronic egotist, on the order of Tennyson's Saint Simeon Stylites. Adding to the puzzle is the fact that Tennyson made another comment on the poem which seems to substantiate the second reading by linking his speaker to the Dantean Ulysses of the *Inferno*.[25] Like the Gestalt drawing which appears at once as a vase and two profiles, the poem is essentially ambiguous. The persona of Ulysses is there, looked at one way, but how this persona relates to the poet and to the readers of the poem cannot be determined. In this sense, the Tennysonian Ulysses, unlike the other protagonists in this discussion, is an impersonal portrait. Not, indeed, one with the sort of impersonality that many twentieth-century poets aspire to: The moral situation Ulysses faces is completely identifiable with the poet's own, and despite the poem's guise as a dramatic monologue its distance from the poet is not easily established. It is as though Tennyson, while understanding the issue and defining it for himself, does not know whether he ought to put the whole weight of his approval on the "message" of the poem. At the critical moment, he disengages entirely, leaving the poem with its fatal ambivalence.[26]

In "Locksley Hall" the treatment of conversion is quite similar to that in "The Two Voices," although *Sartor Resartus* with the same narrative framework is overall a better analogue.[27] Because life must be unified through action for Tennyson, as for the man in the poem, and because action springs from faith, the possibility of escape to the tropics is forcefully renounced: "I *know* my words are wild" (173), the speaker insists, and this knowledge infuses the poem, the persona once again solving the difficulties of life for the poet.

II

The time in the late fall of 1829 when the young men from the Cambridge Union went down to Oxford to debate the superiority of Shelley to Byron, they were not the favored side. Sunderland spoke first, then Hallam, followed by Oldham of Oxford, who "proceeded vigorously to pooh-pooh the pretensions of Shelley, of whom he knew absolutely nothing." In fact, none of the Oxford Byronists knew anything at all about this Shelley. Some thought the Cantabrigians must have been talking about Shenstone, famed for his poem beginning "My banks, they are furnished with bees." Others thought this Shelley "the man who drives the black ponies at Hyde Park." [28] There was, however, one talented youngster at this time —a nonstudent, as it happened—who had known Shelley's poems for years, was exceedingly jealous of him, but who adored him and only worried that he might not be the sole worshiper. This young man's earliest book, *Pauline: A Fragment of a Confession* (1833), seems at first glance suffused with the spirit of Shelley. Actually, the deep confusion in the work sets it worlds apart from the older poet.

Despite its near incoherence, *Pauline* is whole and complete. The confession addressed to the young lady comprises, roughly, three sections. The poet's unhappy retrospective journey to his earlier life falls principally in the middle section, and it is only in the third section that a faint glimmer of hope lights his dark mood. Throughout the poem it is the self, the "I," that generates plot, character, and action, and except in the long French footnote to line 811, and in those few passages that very roughly sketch her features, the lady of the poem scarcely exists, even as a silent confidante. It is Shelley instead who claims a long apostrophe in each part (141–229, 404–428, 1020–31), and so remains the constant Polaris for the "I."

In the first part, following a long eulogy to the "Sun treader," the "I" recalls the earliest emergence of his self-consciousness, which has provided "a centre to all things" (274).[29] Although he admits to "a need, a trust, a yearning after God" (295), he can never abandon the notion of the self as the real center of existence, a Romantic concept endemic among the poets of the generation before. His vestigial Romanticism is seen, too, in his subsequent description of his childhood and in the peculiarly exaggerated sense of guilt for which he says "remorse were vain" (349). At the same time, like the soul in Tennyson's "The Palace of Art," he also has to put down the wish for self-isolation.

> And first I sang, as I in dream have seen,
> Music wait on a lyrist for some thought,
> Yet singing to herself until it came.
> (377–379)

With the discovery of Shelley, he believes he is possessed of an utterly new and angelic knowledge, that he holds the very "key to life" (435). However, much as the Poet in *Alastor* was eventually forced to face others, this "I" in *Pauline*, for the first time seeing human beings in all their often inglorious actuality, finds his Shelleyan perfectibilism shattered. From this point, it is only a short step back to the old egotism, now aggravated by a deeper understanding of his guilt feelings. And since such blind self-worship cannot last, the speaker enters a period of violent fluctuation between elation and despair. It is during this time that he meets Pauline, although he is in no sense capable of love. Longing for pleasure he finds only pain. At the next stage, seeking out "abstractions" (608) everywhere, he closely observes this new-found "craving after knowledge" (621). But, whereas Byron's Cain had refused to make the choice between love and learning, Browning's hero at once decides against knowledge and comes to believe that an ignorance informed by love is preferable to a life of loneliness compensated only by that "sleepless harpy," knowledge (624). However, once he has acknowledged his inability to love, he recognizes the futility of his existence. He sees only the awful "chasm / 'Twixt what I am and all that I would be" (676–677).

In this state, he pleads with Pauline to go away with him. The verdant wood, which is evoked in one of the most gorgeous passages in all of Browning's poetry, is at once *Alastor's* quiet forest, the Paradise Island of *Epipsychidion,* the mystic gardens of Tennyson's "The Hesperides" and "The Lotos-Eaters," and, of course, Wordsworth's great Nature. Unlike Shelley, however, the young man is unable to sublimate his transcendental aspirations: "But my soul saddens when it looks beyond: / I cannot be immortal, taste all joy" (809–810).

Alongside these residual Romantic impulses are clear signs of the new Victorian posture of acceptance of the here and now. In a passage reminiscent of Mill's probing self-analysis in the *Autobiography,*[30] the "I" investigates a possible limit on the soul's capacity:

> The soul would never rule—
> It would be first in all things—it would have
> Its utmost pleasure filled,—but that complete
> Commanding for commanding sickens it.
>   (814–817)

Such reasoning had driven the young Mill to despair, but for Browning it points to resolution. Once cured of his colossal egotism, the poet is also able to purge himself of what he had once regarded as the "intensest life" (268), that "most clear ideal of consciousness / Of self" (269–270). At long last he is able to resolve the poem:

> I'll look within no more—
> I have too trusted to my own wild wants—
> Too trusted to myself—to intuition.
>
> (937–939)

There is then in *Pauline* a pattern of acceptance of reality much like Tennyson's early exercises. Pauline's friend, at the beginning all bewildered in matters of love and poetry and belief, gradually achieves confidence through the mediation of her love. What distinguishes this poem from those by Tennyson, however, is its greater degree of randomness and narrative confusion that makes the pattern of acceptance much harder to detect. First of all, despite many who have called *Pauline* "autobiographical" there is scarcely any reference to external events in the narrator's life, not to say Browning's. The action takes place only in the young man's view of himself, and there is no evidence that the curve of the poem parallels the chronology of his life. "Events" that appear in one part of the poem might have been put almost anywhere except the final passage without significantly altering the poem's shape. Second, and a corollary of the first, the tense-changes seem ill-considered and often unwarranted. The past is juxtaposed absent-mindedly with the present, as though he cannot distinguish memory ("a sad sick dream" [244]) from present awareness. Long-buried thoughts and feelings drift up to consciousness, a sequential frame arbitrarily imposed on these disordered happenings almost as an afterthought. Then there are those many weak connections between events made by the indiscriminate use of "then," "suddenly," "at length," "once more," etc. The locus of the poem is a boundless interior realm unmarked by spatial or temporal references, and the matter recorded belongs less to the speaker's conscious state or history than to the netherworld of an undifferentiated Id:

> I have felt this in dreams—in dreams in which
> I seemed the fate from which I fled; I felt
> A strange delight in causing my decay;
> I was a fiend, in darkness chained for ever
> Within some ocean-cave; and ages rolled,
> Till thro' the cleft rock, like a moonbeam, came
> A white swan to remain with me; and ages
> Rolled, yet I tired not of my first joy
> In gazing on the peace of its pure wings.
> And then I said, "It is most fair to me,
>
> .   .   .   .   .   .
>
> And then I was a young witch, whose blue eyes
> As she stood naked by the river springs,
> Drew down a god—I watched his radiant form
> Growing less radiant—and it gladdened me;
> Till one morn, as he sat in the sunshine
> Upon my knees, singing to me of heaven,
> He turned to look at me, ere I could lose
> The grin with which I viewed his perishing.
> And he shrieked and departed, and sat long
> By his deserted throne—but sunk at last,
> Murmuring, as I kissed his lips and curled
> Around him, "I am still a god—to thee."
>
> (96–123)

The dream-frame would seem an unnecessary device, at least in view of the several other tracts that are as unintelligible—occasionally to the pitch of nightmare—but which are not offered as dreams (see 469 ff.). It is not important that the lines point to his psychological state or to possible disturbances in his sexual life, but that they indicate the *depth* of irrationality at which the dialectic of *Pauline* operates. The young man's chronicle of his past so curiously confused with his present is a symptom of the great fears and anxieties currently besetting him.

Browning did seem aware of what he was about in the confession: "I have no confidence / So I will sing on —fast as fancies come / Rudely . . ." (257–259), "I will tell / My state as though 'twere none of mine" (585–586), and he has Pauline add the ironic footnote that supposedly discredits the poem. Her vagueness as a character and the uncertain form of the poem as a whole—is it a letter or a speech? [31]—are related problems. There is no identifiable center organizing the young man's "story."

And yet—and this is fairly important—the poem does trace some movement, however obscured to our view by the lack of temporal order. Pauline's friend insists he has been through a radical conversion and recovery. We do not necessarily believe him, nor Browning for that matter, as the young J. S. Mill would not when he read the poem.[32] In fact, his final declaration of being "free from doubt, / Or touch of fear" (1030–31) rings hollow. Still, the announcement "I'll look within no more" does put an authentic conclusion to the maddening search for the self. The indeterminacy of the unconscious, obliterating the clear shapes of things, actions, and concepts, has frightened the young man, who then "resolves"—at least tries very hard—to attend to life in the world. As we have seen, the consciously determined self that emerges from the poem by virtue of its imposition of a simple moral precept is not relevant to discussion of the organization of the poem but only to the poet's self-consciousness. And even there the psychological efficacy of such "resolution" is far from demonstrable. For Browning, as for so many of his contemporaries, the will runs his life and his poetry too, art for its own sake being pushed back behind the moral statement. In this sense, his "I'll look within no more" is practically interchangeable with Tennyson's "More life, and fuller, that I want."

Like Byron's Cain, Paracelsus (1835) rejects the choice between love and knowledge. However, each protagonist in this next poem starts with his exclusive commitment to one of the "Two Principles," the Faustian Paracelsus crying out, "God! Thou art mind!" [33] and Aprile asking to "love infinitely, and be loved" (II.385). The division cannot be maintained. Paracelsus, a renowned genius, is bitterly frustrated at his failure to attain absolute truth, and Aprile, disappointed in love, is about to die of a broken heart. Then, recognizing their complementary natures, Paracelsus implores him:

Die not, Aprile! We must never part.
Are we not halves of one dissevered world,
Whom this strange chance unites once more? Part? Never!
$$(II.633-635)$$

The poem might have closed on that understanding. With *Frankenstein,* not entirely incongruously, it would have said, rationality and impulse, head and heart, must be united. But in Part III the hero is shown deeply dis-

illusioned with both goals, after which there is still another cycle of aspiration and attainment (Parts IV and
V). Once having learned from Aprile to accept love, he
discovers that he can neither be another Aprile, nor can
he accept wholeheartedly his doctrine of love which bor-
ders the kind of aestheticism the young Tennyson was
battling about that time. (Aprile's pilgrimage of love
progresses from the more concrete to the more abstract,
and culminates in the prayer: "I have gone through /
The loveliness of life; create for me / If not for men,
or take me to thyself, / Eternal, infinite love!" [II.484–
487]). In a passage that recapitulates Tennyson's verdict
on the Palace of Art, Paracelsus comes to reject this
murky identification of love with beauty: "I cannot feed
on beauty for the sake / Of beauty only, nor can drink
in balm / From lovely objects for their loveliness"
(III. 701–703). But, in this attempt to unify them in his
own way, he begins to experience a breakdown of his
"general aims" (III.412), and mind is now felt to be
a "disease." He feels he has thrown his life away, and
that any further effort to put himself together again is
utterly futile.

Like the Empedocles in Arnold's poem, Paracelsus
sees that knowledge must be accompanied by "joy," although he himself is incapable of feeling it. And yet,
unlike the Arnoldian sage, he does at the end pull himself up and away from despair. His aspiration this time
does not come by rekindling the Faustian desire itself.
Earlier, poet and scientist each believed himself alone
to be elect, and in the light of this absolute covenant with
God, their projects were carried on without involving
their fellow men. To Paracelsus in his egotism people
were fools. Aprile, too, was a Shelleyan soul for whom
humanity was essentially irrelevant. But Paracelsus' sec-

ond aspiration underplays this transcendental egotism.[34] Hearing of Michal's death, he seems to grasp something of that ultimate limit of life. Paradoxically, it is this very understanding that releases him from his commitment to knowledge, and offers a belief in a life-after-this-life. Michal is dead, but her humble and genuine love is very much alive in him. Perhaps this love which he still feels is her soul transcending death, and if science cannot cope with such a phenomenon, then there must be found a new, truly absolute knowledge, in which love and knowledge can be reconciled.

Paracelsus' final unification of his two selves is thus no mere reenactment of his meeting with Aprile in Part II. Deepened knowledge in a new Paracelsus must be complemented by a deeper love in a new Aprile, and this is what takes place in the final death scene. The dying Paracelsus believes, in his delirium, that he is embracing Aprile, his old half-self. His long speech that opens with an address to the "emptiness of fame" quickly gathers to a Shelleyan frenzy:

> Cruel! I seek her now—I kneel—I shriek—
> I clasp her vesture—but she fades, still fades;
> And she is gone. . . .
>
> (V.213–215)

Waking up, he finds his old friend Festus there where he had watched Aprile dying, but the roots of his error go deeper than delirium. When he himself approaches death, he finally comes to realize that Festus *is* Aprile. Hidden from his self-focused sight, the truth and love he has been searching have been embodied all the while in the humble person of Festus. Festus, together with his wife Michal, has been voicing the message of true love throughout the poem, having always been skeptical of youthful Paracelsian aspiration. At the beginning of the final scene, though unknown to the dying physician, he utters *his* creed, "God! thou art love!" In his last moments Paracelsus is able to view his life undistorted by introspection and to recognize love for what it is. It is in this spirit, therefore, and hand in hand with Festus that he finally "attains" his goal.

The poem is dramatic in appearance, with its division into five "acts," its occasional "stage" directions, and its cast of characters. Paracelsus, furthermore, is usually on stage with another character who differs with him, providing some dialectic development. But, as Browning insists, it is "a poem, not a drama," being all speech and utterly devoid of dramatic action. World events crowding the life of the historical Paracelsus are merely alluded to, and the hero's interior happenings dominate the work. The purpose, as Browning understands it, is to "display somewhat minutely the mood itself in its rise and progress" (Preface). For the author of *Pauline* to continue in this poem to subordinate action and incident completely to "mood" or the "phenomena of the mind or the passions" is not really so surprising. As *Pauline* deals with the poet's anxieties and terrors and works toward their alleviation, so *Paracelsus* must examine those foremost concerns of the poet's present life and find some way of accommodating them to each other. Dramatic action would only get in the way of such purpose.

Despite this underlying structure, there is a quality in the poem related to its dramatic facade. *Pauline,* as we saw, is a thoroughly confessional soliloquy, but the hero in *Paracelsus,* while every bit as self-preoccupied, nonetheless addresses himself to other characters. Thus, while recording his introspective search, the young man must choose his words and align his arguments so that other people can understand him and either agree with him or disagree. To communicate clearly is a social imperative. For *Paracelsus,* the consequence of this clarity is that the poem tends to break up into a series of separate discussions which are argumentative and literal rather than dramatic.

It is the argumentativeness of *Paracelsus* that most distinguishes it from *Pauline.* Where nightmare prevailed in the earlier poem, there is here a compulsive adherence to the rational. It is the same realm to be explored, and a very similar crisis in that realm, but the perspective on it is very different. One is quite clear about a crisis that has passed.

The theme of the divided self remains conspicuous in *Sordello* (1840). Started immediately after Browning completed *Pauline* in 1833,[35] by 1840 it had overgrown to a great tangle of historical irrelevancies. Once extricated, this story of the "development of a soul" is seen to be remarkably similar to that of *Pauline* and *Paracelsus.* This hero's failure, however, is the failure of an enfeebled Hamlet more than a Faust, especially in his uneasy conjunction of the "Man-portion" and the "Poet-half."

Even as a child, Sordello amused himself with dreams and fancies, seeing himself as "Half minstrel and half emperor" (I.888).[36] After his victory over a rival poet, he thinks himself superior to his fellows and already beyond their influence. However, such self-aggrandizement is not supported by his audience, who see only a "mere singer, ugly, stunted, weak" (II.629). He can find his real being only in his imagination:

Weeks, months, years went by,
And lo, Sordello vanished utterly,
Sundered in twain; each spectral part at strife
With each; one jarred against another life;
The Poet thwarting hopelessly the Man—
Who, fooled no longer, free in fancy ran
Here, there: let slip no opportunities
As pitiful, forsooth, beside the prize
To drop on him some no-time and acquit
His constant faith (the Poet-half's to wit—
That waiving any compromise between
No joy and all joy kept the hunger keen
Beyond most methods)—of incurring scoff
From the Man-portion—not to be put off
With self-reflectings by the Poet's scheme,
Though ne'er so bright.
                                    (II.655–670)

But the springs of his imagination dry up. Renouncing his life at court, he decides to return home and
recover himself in Nature. He finds no cure there, however, and the dialogue of the separated selves continues
ceaselessly:

But all is changed the moment you descry
Mankind as half yourself,—then fancy's trade
Ends once and always: how may half evade
The other half? men are found half of you.

       .   .   .   .

        then, while one half lolls aloof
I' the vines, completing Rome to the tip-top—
See if, for that, your other half will stop
A tear, begin a smile!
                                    (V.250–261)

In this state, even his backbone of Victorian "earnestness" collapses. In the final book Sordello, for the first time able to get what he really desires, has only himself to answer for his choice: world's future or his present, the Guelfs or the Ghibellines, mankind or self, power or justice, warrior or poet. Even with this opportunity, he is rooted in indecision:

> "Why must a single of the sides be right?
> What bids choose this and leave the opposite?
> Where's abstract Right for me?"
>
> (VI.445–447)

He at long last does reach a decision, but it is by then too late and he dies by his "flesh-half's break-up" (VI. 467).

To extract a story line in this way is, of course, to distort the poem—even if it happens to be one in which the "development of a soul" is all important and the rest mere "historical decoration" (Dedicatory Letter). For no matter how Browning may have come to regard it twenty-five years later, *Sordello* is anything but a sharply focused study of the hero's coming of age. We hear time and again how Jane Carlyle, having read it through once, was unable to make out if Sordello was "a man, a city, or a book," [37] and that Tennyson could understand only the first and last lines of the poem, "Who will, may hear Sordello's story told" and "Who would has heard Sordello's story told," and thought them both lies. The poem's obscurities arise from several sources. First, the many irrelevant incidents, comments, and details throughout the narrative are quite distracting. Second, the style of *Sordello* (Browning called it "brother's speech") [38] is so boldly experimental as to be almost unintelligible: so many ellipses in conjunctions, prepositions, relative pronouns; the rugged diction; and alliteration and cacophony to jar on the ear. Third, his discourses on topics such as mind, matter, will, and poetry clutter the poem with a verbal profusion very hard to follow.[39] Another, perhaps greater, problem is the peculiarly vague conception of the central character: Just who is this Sordello? What is his place in the poem? What does his failure mean in the context of the poem?

Just as in the earlier poems, the hero struggles to attain the here and now, and his difficulties are almost identical with those faced by his predecessors. The "resolution," however, never occurs. The doomed poet-hero labors along, the narrator disdainfully keeping an unsympathetic distance. Furthermore it is clear from the long poetic theory the narrator interpolates in Book III that the narrator's views mirror the author's own aesthetics, whereas Sordello's is throughout hopelessly amorphous. The narrator's jeers and sarcasms at the hero are hardly subtle: See his asides, for example, "(For here the Chief immeasurably yawned)" (V.559). It is as if he no longer had a great deal to say about those youthful spiritual crises that were once quite real to him. He is impatient with them and more than a trifle bored.

Sordello's problems stem from his failure to bleed a little reality into imagination, to graft his existence onto essence. Moreover, these same deficiencies are noticeable in the very making of the poem. Determined to write an historical (that is, impersonal) poem, Browning did research on Sordello. Then, unable to extricate himself from the materials he had accumulated over seven years, Browning had to commit himself to a character who had in that time become uninteresting to him. Sordello's split is thus apparent in the author as well—between "him who felt and him who spoke" (V.334). He found himself no longer able to flesh out a poetic form to fit Sordello's spirit, and the poem became a burden to him, an empty enormity that had to be force-fed and fattened. And his fussing with style is attributable to the same long delay in composition. Sordello's personal failure has, at any rate, little to do with Browning, whose emotional climate at the time is far better represented by the "barefoot rosy child" and the central role of Pippa in his next work.[40]

III

Unlike *Sordello, Sartor Resartus* (1833–34) is a masterpiece of voice manipulation, a quality not universally appreciated. Emerson, occasionally wrong-headed in literary matters, wrote Carlyle about his "theory of rhetoric": "I comprehend not why you should lavish in that spendthrift style of yours Celestial truths. . . . I look for the hour with impatience . . . when your words will be one with things." [41] Carlyle's "spendthrift style," with its varieties of tone and attitude ordered in a structure of great complexity, makes for a very subtle and comprehensive exploration of the modern self and ultimately a remarkable equilibrium among its many points of view. As for its "rhetoric," there is that passage early in the book in which the Editor recommends Teufelsdröckh's Philosophy of Clothes under the banner of the "free flight of Thought." [42] Grand challenges of this kind, masking the true purpose of proselytizing for a specific creed, are of course a common rhetorical device, but here it also sounds the note on which the dramatic movement of the book develops: Teufelsdröckh's conversion is, thanks to this maneuver, no mere accident and the more readily available for generalization. There is then, too, an authorial dividend in that the universality of his hero's pilgrimage will prove—at least to the extent that it does indeed involve Carlyle's—the "rightness" of his own spiritual choice.

If *Sartor* is an elaborate fiction, Diogenes Teufelsdröckh is also fictitious, outrageously so in the full romance tradition: With his mysterious origin (he calls himself "God-born Devil's Dung") and evil eye, he is the complete Byronic figure, a Cain and a Wandering Jew as well. Alienated from his fellowman, he suffers an agonizing loneliness. Like so many of his Gothic predecessors, he notes a "strange contradiction" in himself: he "as yet knew not the solution of it; knew not that spiritual music can spring only from discords set in harmony; that but for Evil there were no Good, as victory is only possible by battle" (II,iv, p. 126). It is these warring elements—love of mankind and withdrawal from it, for instance—that make him seem at once "a very Seraph" and a "Mephistopheles" (I,iv, p. 32). Teufelsdröckh's job in the book is to work toward resolving this self-division.

However, *Sartor Resartus* involves Carlyle's personal life and thought to a much greater degree than is usual in any straightforward fiction, and Teufelsdröckh is in this sense less a novelistic character than an expedient projection of Thomas Carlyle.[43] The choice of the Byronic-Satanic archetype is a good one, offering the author many opportunities for now revealing, now hiding his own identity.[44] Because he can assume that the reader knows the type, he need not waste words filling in the usual narrative details. He can also take for granted a certain amount of sympathy for his hero. Finally, his hero

embodies for him a deep disaffection with his own fragmented identity.

   The type is not new to Carlyle. There is an earlier,
unfinished work, *Wotton Reinfred,* in which he presents
a similar account of a lovelorn Werther's despair. However, there it is done in a more plainly fictional and conventionally novelistic mode, despite the handicap that
the Carlylean ideas—a few of which are repeated verbatim in *Sartor*—must be put forth in the mode of specific
events, while the Carlylean interest in describing such
life particulars is never so strong as it is in the speculative.
Lacking some general or symbolic reference, the mere
concrete incident required by the novel of verisimilitude
will fail to stir Carlyle's imagination. This is apparent
even without first examining the man's explicit statements
on fiction which had changed radically at that time from
a kind of reserved tolerance to absolute contempt.[45] To
read *Wotton Reinfred* is to see clearly the main limitations of Carlyle's fictional powers. The Wotton-Jane Mon-
tagu romance—paralleling the Teufelsdröckh-Blumine
affair later—comes awfully close to straight domestic melodrama with its soldier-seducer, mysterious golden locket,
and inexplicable forest rendezvous. At intervals in this
narrative, Carlyle interpolates the many opinions and
creeds that he feels constitute the sole *raison d'être* of
fiction: instruction. The Aristotelian dictum, "The end
of man is an action, not a thought," [46] must be put in a
letter read to the hero by his cousin, and the Carlylean
metaphysics that will be central in the Professor's book
on the Philosophy of Clothes is put forth in a leisurely
conversation that rather quickly deteriorates into a series
of monologues with no dramatic continuity whatever.
When, with the melodramatic reunion of Wotton and
Jane, the story finally catches up with the philosophy, the

novel immediately turns into a long soliloquy by Jane
who retraces the details of her life as though she had
never before had a single opportunity to talk with her
love. In such passages the author's distance from his fictional framework is imperceptible.

Fiction, certainly, is not Carlyle's métier. However,
his more purely expository writing also suffers, if for
different reasons. In order to see more clearly Carlyle's
art of self-definition at work, it will be helpful to consider the ways in which the undefined border between
fiction and nonfiction is relevant to this purpose. "Signs
of the Times" (1829) is one of his more successful essays,
and it is full of verve and force. Its eloquence no doubt
appeals strongly to those who share its opinions and
recommendations. But it is doubtful whether it can hold
its own as a piece of rational discourse—defining, analyzing,
synthesizing, and persuading:

> Were we required to characterize this age of ours by
> any single epithet, we should be tempted to call it, not
> an Heroical, Devotional, Philosophical, or Moral Age,
> but, above all others, the Mechanical Age. It is the
> Age of Machinery, in every outward and inward sense
> of that word; the age which, with its whole undivided
> might, forwards, teaches and practices the great art of
> adapting means to ends. Nothing is now done directly,
> or by hand; all is by rule and calculated contrivance.
> For the simplest operation, some helps and accompani-
> ments, some cunning abbreviating process is in readi-
> ness. Our old molds of exertion are all discredited, and
> thrown aside. On every hand, the living artisan is
> driven from his workshop, to make room for a speed-
> ier, inanimate one. The shuttle drops from the fingers
> of the weaver, and falls into iron fingers that ply it
> faster. The sailor furls his sail, and lays down his oar;

and bids a strong, unwearied servant, on vaporous
wings, bear him through the waters. Men have crossed
oceans by steam; the Birmingham Fireking has visited
the fabulous East; and the genius of the Cape, were
there any Camoens now to sing it, has again been
alarmed, and with far stronger thunders than Gamas.
There is no end to machinery. . . .[47]

The axiomatic first assertion here is not developed but
merely repeated. The second sentence advances the argument not at all, the phrase "Mechanical Age" being
altered, with little effect, to "the Age of Machinery." The
relative clause that explains the "age" contains a phrase
for emphasis, a redundant catalog, and a *non sequitur*.
Emphases abound throughout the passage, and phrases
such as "directly, or by hand," as against "by rule and
calculated contrivance" cannot be said to contrast a mechanical age with old times adequately but are purely expressive of the author's disapproval. The second part of
the passage manages to instance the mechanization process, but even here, once the pattern is set, the essay only
repeats the pattern, presenting one "sign" after another
which Carlyle assumes will be accepted matters of fact.
The technique is the same throughout—instead of documentation and analysis, emphasis and repetition. In almost every paragraph there is a sentence exactly reproduc-
ing the thesis sentence of the passage quoted above:
"Not the external and physical alone is now managed by
machinery, but the internal and spiritual also" (p. 60);
"Philosophy, Science, Art, Literature, all depend on machinery" (p. 61); "Men are grown mechanical in head
and in heart, as well as in hand" (p. 63). Midpoint in
the essay, "dynamic" and "invisible" are introduced as
counterterms to "mechanical" and as applicable to the

things and qualities regrettably now gone. The essay swiftly skims over all elements of civilization, and the argument, too impatient to build a coherent structure, must rely on the flow of often powerful sentences, the frequent emotive assertions, and the hypnotic effect of repetition for its persuasiveness.

As rhetorical devices, neither Carlyle's single-minded assertiveness nor his repetitiveness are effective. Both of these habits of style suggest that he might have had a few misgivings about the simplistic diagnosis of his age put forth in the essay. However, the irresistible current of his argument does not allow him pause to look at the thesis from new vantages. Too eager to judge, not quite critical enough to make the fine discrimination, he protests too much. The "desperado," [48] which Matthew Arnold saw later on in Carlyle, is much too prominent in this essay.

At the frontier of fiction and life, Carlyle seems to have found the only way he could to document as he knew it the contemporary condition of man divided. If Carlyle fails as a novelist and fumbles as an essayist, he eminently succeeds in *Sartor Resartus* with its mixed bag of tricks. First, the double-faced Teufelsdröckhian mask, apocalyptic prophet one moment and comical eccentric the next, gives an elasticity to the handling of the argument that would not be available to an undisguised philosophical pronouncement. The "Reminiscences" chapter shows the advantages of this form over either novel or straightforward essay: The reader is warned against uncritical acceptance of each and every oracle; and whatever defects he might note in them he can attribute to Teufelsdröckh rather than to Carlyle—the author's personal endorsement of the professor not being expected at every point. Second, the device of the unidentified Editor, who transmits Teufelsdröckh's Philosophy of Clothes, adds to the effectiveness of the technique of indirection, for he too is not always a reliable narrator and commentator. Third, the presence of the false hero-worshiper, Hofrath Heuschrecke, still another narrator in the process of Carlylean expression, further complicates the irony without which Teufelsdröckh's beliefs would be mere assertions.

Of these three, the most important device is that of the Editor. This intelligent and enlightened English critic, never hesitating to express his astonishment at Teufelsdröckh's eccentric statements, anticipates and modifies the reader's possible hostility to the unfamiliar ideas Carlyle assigns to the German philosopher. The Editor approaches Teufelsdröckh initially with an open-minded caution, and as he begins to arrange the Volume, his numerous editorial comments, often mildly ironic and at times openly sarcastic, keep him at a pleasant distance from his master. Although their relationship is never fully dramatized, the Editor does show somewhat increasing sympathy and support, which suggests he is gradually being converted.

Carlyle has his reservations about the Clothes Philosophy. If the prophet in him demands the German professor, the critic in him has to provide the English Editor. Carlyle searches vigorously for his new metaphysics, but only after carefully reserving some portion of his intelligence. The tension between the two energies saves him both from despair and too much zeal. If the division of himself into two personae reminds us of the speaker's in "The Two Voices," there is in *Sartor* nothing of the stultifying moroseness of that poem. On the contrary, the most attractive thing about the work is its vigor in maintaining the balance of the double vision, not allowing either to be sacrificed to the other. In *Sartor Re-*

sartus Carlyle puts into effect one of his own dicta: "Few men have the secret of being at once determinate *(bestimmt)* and open; of knowing what they do know, and yet lying ready for farther knowledge." [49]

Carlyle's double vision is evident in still another structural feature of *Sartor Resartus*—its division into the parts called "Volume" and "Life." Superficially, it would seem the fusion of biographical narrative and philosophical discourse would mitigate the probable tediousness of the book's continual assertions and repetitions. This is partly true, but there is more to the device than that. Whereas the Volume sections generalize, the Life sections individualize, and the relationship between these two ways of treating identical problems points to a peculiarity of Carlylean thought. No matter what Teufelsdröckh's philosophy is or may be, it is presented here not as abstract speculation, but as a generalized account of his own experience. Any discourse is finally traceable to man's experience, but there is this difference with *Sartor:* Experience, not the universal laws of thought, tests the validity of argument. Also, the experiential quality of Carlyle's thought—despite the fact that Teufelsdröckh's biographical accounts mainly consist of arguments—is indicated by this narrative device which in Kenneth Burke's terms "temporizes essence." [50] What is involved here is the widespread post-Enlightenment retreat to experience as the only basis for certitude in an age when traditional values and systems were disintegrating. However, Carlyle does not let "experience" become solipsism; instead, he universalizes it by translating the "Life" terms into the "Volume" terms. The Editor urges open-mindedness, and personal experience must be founded again on the unassailable impersonality of argument. Ideas such as "Me and Not-Me," or "Transcendental-Descendentalism," therefore, should not be considered merely speculative terms borrowed from the Germans, but rather as approximations of psychological events Carlyle had actually experienced. The dramatic climax of *Sartor,* the three central chapters treating Teufelsdröckh's conversion, is the core of Carlylean thought *and* life.

If in the Volume parts of *Sartor* Carlyle at once reveals and conceals, in the Life sections he mingles fact and fiction, presenting them in varicolored lights of humor, irony, satire, and an occasional lyricism and sentimentality to achieve his double effects. The child Teufelsdröckh has a normal and happy boyhood until the time when he begins to experience a painful collision of "Freewill" and "Necessity." He temporarily resolves this problem through an "obedience" which anticipates his later conversion:

> Obedience is our universal duty and destiny; wherein whoso will not bend must break: too early and too thoroughly we cannot be trained to know that Would, in this world of ours, is as mere zero to Should, and for most part as the smallest of fractions even to Shall.
>
> (II,ii, pp. 98–99)

His maturation takes him beyond the pleasure principle. He is still a student when his foster father dies and he is told the mysterious circumstance of his adoption, a discovery which breaks his slender hold on his identity. He vacillates between elation and depression and suffers an acute sense of alienation. His love for Blumine, meanwhile, develops into one of those angelic affairs where the "young Forlorn" searches for "Light," "Form," and "Soul," like the Psyche seeking the Epipsyche. To Teufelsdröckh the search is "a discerning of the Infinite in the

Finite, of the Idea made Real" (II,v, p. 141). With the inevitable Romantic failure, he tends to see himself "through the ruins as of a shivered Universe" . . . "falling, falling, towards the Abyss" (II,v, p. 146).

The broken-hearted youth rejects Satanic poetry, Bedlam, and suicide, and chooses instead another Romantic escape—wandering. But Nature, which had earlier offered its healing powers to the poets and their heroes, is no longer available to him: He finds that "Viewhunting" appeals to him about as much as the plague. Religious faith which seems to him "the one thing needful" (II,vii, p. 159)—a phrase Matthew Arnold was to assail in *Culture and Anarchy*—is also on the wane. (Looking back on this crisis, Teufelsdröckh was to decide that doubting God's existence is not entirely negative after all, but a necessary step toward belief. Besides, like Pauline's friend, he had always felt a "certain aftershine [Nachschein] of Christianity" [II.vii, p. 165].) In profound despair, Teufelsdröckh finally confronts the ultimate spirit of denial, the Everlasting No, and answers the challenge with the "whole Me":

> Thus had the Everlasting No (*das ewige Nein*) pealed authoritatively through all the recesses of my Being, of my Me; and then was it that my whole Me stood up, in native God-created majesty, and with emphasis recorded its Protest. Such a Protest, the most important transaction in Life, may that same Indignation and Defiance, in a psychological point of view, be fitly called. The Everlasting No had said: "Behold, thou art fatherless, outcast, and the Universe is mine (the Devil's)"; to which my whole Me now made answer: "*I* am not thine, but Free, and forever hate thee!"
>
> (II,vii, pp. 167–168)

This fire-baptism is another case of Victorian negation of negation and the resultant assertion of a unified self. Almost identical with that of "The Two Voices" and *Pauline*, Teufelsdröckh's ascent to affirmation begins at once. No longer a "Spectre," he is now a "Spectre-queller" (II,viii, p. 170). The "whole Me," confirmed in the denial of nothingness, is ready now to search out the "Not-Me" —the world—for its nourishment. There, at the Center of Indifference, he recognizes the nothingness of himself, and in his self-isolation he prepares for acceptance of the universe.

The "first preliminary moral Act," says Teufelsdröckh in a grand Hegelian gesture, is "Annihilation of Self (*Selbsttödtung*)." [51] What Carlyle seems to be getting at is a rejection of the body and a simultaneous identification of the spirit with universal intelligence. To borrow the sartorial metaphor, the self is a vesture of the Me, the "celestial Me," the "divine Me." So, when Teufelsdröckh translates the Everlasting Yea as the imperative "Love not pleasure; love God" in whom "all contradiction is solved" (II,ix, p. 192), he is avoiding his Victorian reality. As with Tennyson and Browning the contradiction of spirit and matter is not so much resolved in the Yea as it is repressed and for the time being forgotten. Whether or not this repression is psychologically plausible is not even touched on. [52]

But the transcendental definition of man's existence is not allowed to glide for long in the metaphysical ether. Because belief is "worthless till it convert itself into Conduct" (II,ix, p. 195), the "celestial Me" must be brought down to earth. Duty here and now is the highway of Descendentalism: " '*Do the Duty which lies nearest thee,*' which thou knowest to be a Duty! Thy second Duty will already have become clearer" (II,ix,

p. 196). The circle is drawn: In the name of the Ideal, the actual—restricted by time and space—must be ignored; but the Ideal can only be discovered in the actual— "America is here and nowhere." The paradox of Transcendental-Descendentalism is, of course, not new. In fact, it is as old as the Incarnation with its notion of the timeless working through time. However, it is curious to see the Everlasting Yea convert immediately into the principle of work, as expressed so succinctly in the famous imperatives "Up! Up!" and "Produce! Produce!" To work, to produce—to *really* exist—is for Teufelsdröckh to root himself deeply in the here and now in order, paradoxically, to transcend time and space. Because he shows no transition from existence to production, the two categories appear as identical in the argument. This is indeed a curious twist: The Teufelsdröckhian epistemology, which is largely sustained by intuition, is here embracing the rationale and implications of work and production which are based on anti-intuitional, Utilitarian doctrines. One wonders why his insistence on the ascendancy of the unconscious over the conscious in *Sartor* and elsewhere [53] did not suggest to him a parallel eminence of a poetic, "irrational" world, organized on the contemplative and sensuous primitivism of a Rousseau or a Thoreau over the work-oriented life dedicated to the reality principle. In this context, of course, the words "work" and "produce" do not refer strictly to the mechanical-industrial concept of work and output, but rather to a much more general notion of work. As Dr. Arnold indoctrinated his children, " 'Work.' Not, work at this or that—but, Work." [54] To the Victorian, work in this process sense, if not in the compulsion sense, is the fulfillment of man's moral mission, a psychologically beneficial act of creation. Yet it seems clear, in view of the Carlylean message to the Captains of Industry in *Past and Present* and other works that follow *Sartor,* that in his Puritan way he was unable to distinguish between the moral and psychological satisfactions of work and the economic rewards which follow on it. Indeed, in *Past and Present,* Teufelsdröckh's work-philosophy approximates the evangel of exploitation: "All these, all virtues, in wrestling with the dim brute Powers of Fact, in ordering of thy fellows in such wrestle, there and elsewhere not at all, thou wilt continually learn." [55]

That the satisfaction of having done one's work temporarily brings an accord among conflicting impulses is a psychological truism. Although modern men are often aware of the void underlying such makeshift accords, the more they apply themselves to their tasks the more the compulsion to work appropriates the energy of "destructive" self-divisive impulses. Taken seriously, so inelastic and incomplete a theory of life is bound to deprive man of joy and warmth, as the next generation of Victorians were to discover—often at the cost of their creativity. And yet, this narrowing down of human life—to such terms as faith or work—was the common response of the early Victorians to the Romantic tragedy. Inheriting the Hegelian dialectic, Marx will soon put forth his diagnosis and prescription for man's alienation from his fellowman, from his work, and from himself—leaving the task of a radical reassessment of work for those in our time who have come to enjoy the terror of not having to.[56]

Teufelsdröckh's oracle of work, abstracted from the understructure of *Sartor,* amounts to an almost pathetically barren and contradictory proposal. And yet one remembers, too, that at this point Carlyle clearly understood the need to examine the common spiritual crisis of his age from many points of view and did so: *Sartor Resartus* is fully clothed. Shuttling to and fro between the universal and the particular, from exploratory maneuvers to standing pat, and around again, using now the confessional, now the suasive tone, the book weaves its cloth, styling the fabric precisely to suit itself.[57] As for the material of *Sartor* ("material" corresponding to Emerson's "spirit" and "things" as against "vehicle" and "words"), it demonstrates a rhetorical technique of retailoring the tailor himself, reconstructing the self by a kind of Victorian psychoanalysis. The apparent confusion in form reflects the difficulties of the matter.

In the final unity of the work, Carlyle managed to achieve a very balanced perception of the world and human existence. At the end of *Sartor,* Herr Diogenes Teufelsdröckh disappears from Weissnichtwo. In Carlyle's own career, it is rather the Editor whose presence is increasingly missed as Carlyle more and more takes on the role of the prophetic professor. In this book, however, art conquers philosophy—and this, despite Carlyle's great contempt for the art of fiction.

Notes

1. Anne Thackeray Ritchie, *Records of Tennyson, Ruskin, Browning* (New York, 1892), p. 12.
2. *Tennyson: Aspects of His Life: Character and Poetry* (New York, 1962), p. 19.
3. Ed. Charles Tennyson (London, 1930), Act I, Scene v.
4. *Unpublished Early Poems,* ed. Charles Tennyson (London, 1931), p. 6.
5. The poem won the Chancellor's Medal in 1829. Interestingly enough, Arthur Hallam, who was one of the unsuccessful competitors, admits the influence of *Alastor* on his (Hallam's) *Timbuctoo.* See *The Writings of Arthur Hallam,* ed. T. H. Vail Motter (New York, 1943), p. 40.

6. References are to the text of the first edition of *Timbuctoo* (Cambridge, 1829).

7. For this discussion of *Poems, Chiefly Lyrical,* I have used the text of the first edition (London, 1830).

8. "The Tamworth Reading Rooms," *Essays and Sketches,* ed. Charles Frederick Harrold (London, 1948), II, p. 206.

9. See Harold Nicolson, *Tennyson,* pp. 27–28; Sir Charles Tennyson, *Alfred Tennyson* (New York, 1949), p. 313; E. D. H. Johnson, *The Alien Vision of Victorian Poetry* (Princeton, 1952), p. 4; Jerome Buckley, *The Victorian Temper: A Study in Literary Culture* (Cambridge, Mass., 1951), Chapter IV, and *Tennyson: The Growth of a Poet* (Cambridge, Mass., 1961), Chapters II and III.

10. This characterization, together with Hallam's exaggerated eulogy on Tennyson, aroused such rancor in John Wilson and John Wilson Croker that they blasted Tennyson into his "ten years silence." Wilson was actually attacking Hallam primarily, but his and Croker's reviews together established the myth of Tennyson as pure poet not only among Tennyson's foes but among his friends. Hallam's review was praised by Yeats later on, but its argument on the role of the artist is conventionally moral, and his assessment of Tennyson incomplete and one-sided. It would have been better all around if he had not written it. For an incisive discussion of what the review did to Tennyson's reputation, see Edgar Finley Shannon, *Tennyson and the Reviewers: A Study of His Literary Reputation and of the Influence of the Critics upon His Poetry* (Cambridge, Mass., 1952). Hallam's review (published in August 1831 in the *Englishman's Magazine*) is reprinted in the *Writings.*

11. Thomas R. Lounsbury, *The Life and Times of Tennyson* (New York, 1962), p. 71.

12. As John Mitchell Kemble said about this time, "The world is one great thought, and I am thinking it." Lounsbury, p. 70.

13. Buckley, *Tennyson,* p. 47.

14. I used the first edition of the 1833 *Poems* (London, 1833).

15. G. Robert Stange, "Tennyson's Garden of Art: A Study of *The Hesperides,*" first published in *PMLA* in 1952 and later reprinted in the *Critical Essays on the Poetry of Tennyson,* ed. John Killham (New York, 1960). The essay interprets the Zidonian Hanno prologue as the "familiar framework of vision poetry" (p. 100), and consequently the poem as a whole as a "statement of what 'the people's poet' came to feel was the devil's side" in the conflict of social engagement and pure art (p. 111).

16. The revised version of the poem published in 1842 is undoubt-

edly superior both for its tighter control of detail and its ironic ending, although the 1833 version manages a more convincing identity for the lady.

17. Arthur J. Carr, "Tennyson as a Modern Poet," first published in *UTQ* in 1950 and reprinted in *Victorian Literature: Modern Essays in Criticism*, ed. Austin Wright (New York, 1961), p. 313.

18. There is no direct record of the circumstances in which this oft-quoted remark was made. Our main document is Hallam Tennyson's *Memoir* (London, 1897), in which he writes, "In 1890 he [Alfred Tennyson] wrote the following notes: 'Trench said to me, when we were at Trinity together, "Tennyson, we cannot live in art" ' " (I, p. 118). But curiously, Hallam makes a remark earlier in the same memoir which suggests that Trench was relatively unacquainted with Tennyson: "Hallam said to Trench in 1832: 'Alfred's mind is what it always was, or rather, brighter, and more vigorous. I regret, with you, that you have never had the opportunity of knowing more of him' " (I, p. 35). There is another recollection by Aubrey de Vere: "I remember a legend about it ["The Palace of Art"], whether authentic or not. Alfred Tennyson and Richard Chenevix Trench had been friends at Cambridge, and had a common love of poetry. Soon after his ordination the future Archbishop paid a visit to the future Laureate. He spoke about the new heresy which substituted Art for Faith and Beauty for Sanctity. His brother-poet, it is said, contested nothing, but simply listened, occasionally replenishing his pipe. When Trench had taken his departure the auditor took up his pen, and the single thought became a poem." "The Reception of the Early Poetry," printed in Hallam Tennyson, *Memoir*, I, pp. 505–506. If this "legend" is the true version, Trench's remark cannot have been an "ultimatum" to Tennyson.

19. This ordering of the descriptions—from exterior to interior—is much more carefully wrought in the far superior revised version published in 1842.

20. For recent discussion on this issue, see Valerie Pitt, *Tennyson Laureate* (London, 1962), pp. 63–65, and Clyde de L. Ryals, *Theme and Symbol in Tennyson's Poems to 1850* (Philadelphia, 1964), pp. 82–86.

21. Tennyson told his son, "When I wrote 'The Two Voices,' I was so utterly miserable, a burden to myself and to my family, that I said, 'Is life worth anything?' " *Memoir*, I, p. 193.

22. *More Nineteenth Century Studies: A Group of Honest Doubters* (London, 1956), pp. 68–69. Buckley, at least in *The Victorian Temper*, is unconvinced about the speaker's conquest of doubt. See page 76. To at least one Victorian reviewer this is the best

part of the poem: "The best part is where the disputing voices have ceased to talk, where the poet throws open the window, and sees every one going to church in the summer morning." Stopford A. Brooke, *Tennyson* (London, 1894), p. 106.

23. *Memoir,* I, p. 196. A similar remark he made on the poem is recorded by W. J. Rolfe in his notes in the Cambridge Edition (Boston, 1898), p. 808. According to Buckley, the first draft, as it appears in Tennyson's notebook, "shows no condescension to the blameless round of common duties." *Tennyson,* p. 60. Perhaps Ulysses is more the ideal hero there—without the conspicuous blemishes discussed below.

24. This view is very forcefully presented by E. J. Chiasson in his "Tennyson's 'Ulysses'—A Re-Interpretation," first published in *UTQ* and reprinted in Killham's collection. John Pettigrew further elaborates on the ambiguity of "Ulysses," arguing that the figure of Ulysses is a precise "correlative not for one simple feeling but for a complexity of feelings, a unified product of a divided sensibility"—a view I am not wholly in agreement with. See his "Tennyson's Ulysses: A Reconciliation of Opposites," *VP,* I (1963), pp. 27–45.

25. "Yes, there is an echo of Dante in it," *Memoir,* II, p. 70. Also, see Tennyson's note in the Eversley Edition, referring to *Inferno,* xxvi.

26. Tennyson's pairing of the poem with "Tithonus" does not help to clarify the issue. See Chiasson's discussion, pp. 172–173.

27. W. D. Templeman argues that Tennyson is indebted to Carlyle for the narrative line. This is probably an overstatement. See "Tennyson's *Locksley Hall* and Thomas Carlyle," printed in *Booker Memorial Studies: Eight Essays on Victorian Literature in Memory of John Manning Booker* (Chapel Hill, 1950).

28. Lounsbury, pp. 154–157. Although the Cantabrigian version of the report is warmly protested by Sir Harold, an Oxonian (see page 75 of his *Tennyson*), Sylva Norman (neutral on this issue) gives essentially Lounsbury's version in *Flight of the Skylark: The Development of Shelley's Reputation* (Norman, Okla., 1954), p. 218.

29. The text used here is that of the first edition (London, 1833) which is reproduced by N. Hardy Wallis (London, 1931).

30. "In this frame of mind it occurred to me to put the question directly to my self: 'Suppose that all your objects in life were realized . . . would this be a great joy and happiness to you?' And an irrepressible self-consciousness distinctly answered, 'No!' At this my heart sank within me: the whole foundation on which my life was constructed fell down. . . . I seemed to have nothing

left to live for" (*Autobiography of John Stuart Mill* [New York, 1944], p. 94). Mill evidently missed the point of this passage in Browning, since he drew a line through it from line 811 to line 821.

31. *Pauline* as "an absolute failure" formalistically is succinctly discussed by Park Honan in his *Browning's Characters: A Study in Poetic Technique* (New Haven and London, 1961), pp. 11–17, especially p. 16.

32. See my article on the Mill-Browning relationship, "Mill and 'Pauline': The Myth and Some Facts," *VS*, IX (1965), pp. 154–163, part of which is incorporated into this discussion.

33. It happens that textual variations in *Paracelsus* are relatively insignificant. Because the first edition has no line numbers, the Florentine Edition, eds. Charlotte Porter and Helen A. Clarke (New York, 1910), is used here. II, p. 229.

34. In "Browning's Conception of Love as Represented in *Paracelsus*," William O. Raymond argues: ". . . both [Paracelsus and Aprile] are idealists and transcendentalists, with a thirst for the absolute, an unquenchable desire to surpass all finite limitations, a vision of perfection which forbids them to rest content with any finite attainment. As Paracelsus aspires and fails, so Aprile aspires and fails." *The Infinite Moment and Other Essays in Robert Browning*, 2nd ed. (Toronto, 1965), p. 168. For other helpful treatments, see E. D. H. Johnson, *The Alien Vision*, pp. 73–77, and F. E. L. Priestley, "The Ironic Pattern of Browning's *Paracelsus*," *UTQ*, XXXIV (1964), pp. 68–81.

35. In connection with her discussion of *Sordello*, Betty Miller cites the self-division in Browning himself that so impressed Eliza Flower: "It was the inexplicable division of a once unified nature that puzzled her most. 'If he had not got the habit of talking of head and heart as two independent existences, one would say he was born without a heart,' she wrote. The words carry their own echo. For is not this precisely Sordello's 'accustomed fault of breaking yoke, Disjointing him who felt from him who spoke'?" *Robert Browning: A Portrait* (London, 1952), p. 44.

36. For this discussion of *Sordello*, Charlotte Porter and Helen A. Clarke's Florentine Edition is used.

37. William Clyde DeVane, *A Browning Handbook*, 2nd ed. (New York, 1955), p. 85.

38. Quoted by Stewart W. Holmes in his "Browning: Semantic Stutterer," *PMLA*, LX (1945), p. 247.

39. Though awkwardly handled and insufficiently developed, Holmes's article points up the interesting matter of Browning's verbal uncertainty in his early career.

40. Lacking, apparently, broad understanding of other Victorians and their experiences of self-division, Stewart W. Holmes compares *Sordello* with certain notions in Jung's *Modern Man in Search of a Soul*. See "Browning's *Sordello* and Jung: Browning's *Sordello* in the Light of Jung's Theory of Types," *PMLA*, LVI (1941), pp. 758–796.

41. *The Correspondence of Emerson and Carlyle*, ed. Joseph Slater (New York and London, 1964), p. 99.

42. I,i, p. 7. The text cited is Charles Frederick Harrold's edition (New York, 1937).

43. Innumerable studies have been published on this subject. One of the most recent and comprehensive is *Sartor Called Resartus: The Genesis, Structure, and Style of Thomas Carlyle's First Major Work* (Princeton, 1965), by G. B. Tennyson.

44. In this section more than others, I am indebted to the work of other scholars, particularly the following: "Thomas Carlyle and Fiction: 1822–1834" by Carlisle Moore in the *Nineteenth-Century Studies*, eds. Herbert Davis, William C. DeVane, and R. C. Bald (Ithaca, 1940), pp. 131–177; Leonard W. Deen, "Irrational Form in *Sartor Resartus*," *Texas Studies in Literature and Language*, V (1963), pp. 438–451; and George Levine, "'Sartor Resartus' and the Balance of Fiction," *VS*, VIII (1964), pp. 131–160. Mr. Levine's article is one of the very best I have come across in Victorian studies.

45. The best treatment of this change is in the article by Carlisle Moore cited above.

46. *Wotton Reinfred: A Romance* in *The Last Words of Thomas Carlyle* (New York, 1892), p. 13.

47. *Critical and Miscellaneous Essays*, II, Centenary Edition (New York, 1899), pp. 59–60.

48. *The Letters of Matthew Arnold to Arthur Hugh Clough*, ed. Howard Foster Lowry (London and New York, 1932), p. 111.

49. *Two Note Books of Thomas Carlyle: From 23d March 1822 to 16th May 1832*, ed. Charles Eliot Norton (New York, 1898), pp. 77–78. The passage appears in the entry dated December 5, 1826.

50. *A Grammar of Motives* (New York, 1954), pp. 430–440.

51. For an authoritative discussion of Carlyle's sources in German philosophical systems, see Charles Frederick Harrold's *Carlyle and German Thought: 1819–1834* (New Haven, 1934), IV, 4, "Nature: *Ich bestimme die Welt*," pp. 95–103, and VIII, 4, "Renunciation: *durch welche der eigentliche Eintritt ins Leben denkbar ist*," pp. 214–230.

52. It would be unfair to hold Carlyle responsible for affirming the Everlasting Yea the rest of his life. Naturally he had his doubts

and suffered all his life from a debilitating self-consciousness. Carlisle Moore traces the post-*Sartor* history of Carlyle's struggles in "The Persistence of Carlyle's 'Everlasting Yea,'" *MP*, LIV (1957), pp. 187–196.

53. See III,iii, "Symbols." Unconsciousness is the central theme of his essay "Characteristics."

54. Thomas Arnold the Younger, *Passages in a Wandering Life* (London, 1900), p. vi, quoted by Walter E. Houghton in his most helpful section on "Work," in *The Victorian Frame of Mind: 1830–1870*, p. 243. The influence of Goethe on Carlyle's notion of work is discussed in Harrold, VIII, 3, pp. 208–214.

55. Centenary Edition (New York, 1897), III,xi, p. 198.

56. I have in mind here the post-Freudian reinterpretation of work in Herbert Marcuse's *Eros and Civilization: A Philosophical Inquiry into Freud* (Boston, 1955).

57. To Leonard W. Deen, in the article cited above, the Carlylean style is an "irrational form."

To thine own self be true, the wise man says.
Are then my fears myself? O double self!
And I untrue to both.

Dipsychus

4.

The Colloquy of the Self:
1850

There is an apparent calm in the religious poems written by Tennyson and Browning at midcentury. But while the mere abstract of a poem like *In Memoriam* seems to "resolve" the crisis of the self for the poet, its music paces the more difficult course of a painful experience. It is only over the whole length of the work that Tennyson's self-torment and division is folded into the steady ascension of the stated hope and faith. With Browning the poetic statement is still dominant over the poetic experience, as the poet still determinedly insists on a rationale of faith. His apologia in *Christmas-Eve and Easter-Day* is thus a syllabus for moral commitment and not in any sense a phenomenology of moral experience.

While these two statesmen of poetry are now secure in their explicit doctrine, younger men still had to work theirs out. The predicament, however, for a Clough or an Arnold is a different one. "Conversion" for the older poets meant a clear "should" and "will" and any irrational impulse a "should not" and "will not," whereas the younger poets are not quite so sure about the efficacy of this strict moral commitment. Dipsychus' "conversion," which has been compared to Teufelsdröckh's, comes at the very end of Clough's poem, where his eternal yea amounts only to a conviction about the conduct of daily life. Arnold has a temperamental preference, too, for the figurative shoreline where his two "territories," land and sea, touch but are in no sense involved in each other. The dialogue of the mind with itself intricately spelling out the dilemmas of experience is carefully attended to and recorded in their poems and correspondence, despite an occasional incoherence in argument or syntax. Furthermore their "solutions," when discovered, are of quite a different composition than those of the older poets. Clough's self-ironic spirit often seems to remove him to a safe distance from the wearying struggle, and Arnold follows his wiry intelligence as it leads away from his youthful infatuation with personal difficulties as poetic material. This evasion of the either-or by wit and irony and a pose of disinterestedness opens new horizons later on in his prose writing where he deftly parries the dilemma of personal identity as though it were the dialectical maneuvering of society as a whole.

Gothicism, that passion for the irrational, appears now in the Faust theme of the most ambitious poems of both these poets, although, interestingly, it is Arnold's rejection of "Empedocles on Etna"—his *Hamlet* and his *Faust*—that is crucial for the definition of terms in his crisis of self-division. However, the Gothic is also in evidence in the poetry of the so-called "Spasmodic School," consisting mostly of minor or insignificant poems, with the notable exception of Tennyson's *Maud*. In the prose of the period, of course, Gothicism is fully revived by the

Brontë sisters. Both *Jane Eyre* and *Wuthering Heights,* in their uninhibited style, typical Gothic symbols, and the Gothic personalities of the characters, are thoroughly informed with the romance spirit. Here too, however, the drift toward wildness, toward self-indulgence, is fenced in by "reason" and civilization. This urgency to impose an order, a rational "solution" on the identity problem is indicated in Charlotte's over-structuring of her book, whereas Emily's great work ends on a very subtle ambivalence: *Wuthering Heights* never can finally choose order over disorder, civilization over eros, self-control over ecstasy.

I

When Arthur Hugh Clough entered Balliol College in 1837, the Oxford Movement was at its height. W. G. Ward, his mathematics tutor, was an eager follower of Newman, and soon the young Clough was deeply involved in the Newmanist arguments on the Apostolic authority of the English Church, the validity of the Thirty-Nine Articles, the Catholicity of the Roman Church. This best pupil of Dr. Arnold had been instilled at Rugby with the earnestness that condemns moral indifference, and he could no more ignore the moral and theological dilemmas of his time than he could make up his mind on them. As Bagehot saw Clough's problem: "Too easily one great teacher inculcated a remarkable creed; then another great teacher took it away; then this second teacher made him believe for a time some of his own artificial faith; then it would not do." [1]

Thomas Arnold and Newman represent polarized traditions in the intellectual life of Clough's England, both of which, as it happens, are traceable to Coleridge. For Dr. Arnold, *The Constitution of Church and State* was the foundation for his broad-church program: religion would concern itself with moral, social, and practical matters. His passion at this time lay in his plans for reorganizing England—along the lines of his brilliant reorganization of Rugby School. Thus, the Oxford Movement was an "old error," and the Newmanites idolators and "malignants": "When we look at the condition of our country; at the poverty and wretchedness," he wrote, "can any Christian doubt that here is the work for the Church of Christ to do . . . ?[2] For Newman, of course, Dr. Arnold is simply not a Christian in any sense. Newman traces his own justification of faith to Coleridge, for whom faith was a total "commitment of the will to the insights of Reason."[3] Moreover, his concepts of faith and reason closely parallel the Coleridgean Imagination and Understanding, for, however sublime his intellect and dogmatic his theology, Newman's search for the foundations of Christian faith springs ultimately from the transcendental will, not the intellect. In *The Idea of a University* he sharply distinguishes intellectual excellence and moral excellence, and in *A Grammar of Assent,* "notional assent" from "real assent."[4] To the extent that Newman's concern is transcendental, it fastens on *that* world, not *this;* and to the extent that he is unconcerned with this world, he is aloof from it, guilty of a sacred egotism.

By the time the Oxford Convocation met in 1845 to condemn Ward and Newman, Clough was out of immediate range of the two great forces: Dr. Arnold had been dead for two years, Ward's too-intense friendship with Clough was about over, and Newman had been away a great deal at his parish at Littlemore. Not that

Clough would ever be able to make up his mind and take a position. At one period he seemed to hold Carlyle responsible for this pass, telling Emerson how "Carlyle has led us all out into the desert, and he has left us there." [5] He could see his way only to wait it out among the shifting sands of doctrine.[6]

Clough's inability to commit himself to one or another theological position is already apparent in the poems written during his Oxford years which he later contributed to *Ambarvalia* (1849). "When Israel Came Out of Egypt," for one, although it concludes on an adjuration to believe, hovers closely for the greater part over the no-man's-land between acceptance and rejection:

> No God, it saith; ah, wait in faith
> God's self-completing plan;
> Receive it not, but leave it not,
> And wait it out, O Man! [7]

This suspension of belief and disbelief, the holding off from a clear yes or no marks the whole course of his poetic career. But like Byron, Clough was virtuoso enough to sing more than one tune: he could indulge himself in his unhappy state, or he could take a playful, ironic view of it. "ἐπὶ Λάτμῳ," also in *Ambarvalia,* is an early example of his satiric spirit. A recent biographer has called it Clough's "personal love poem," [8] but it can scarcely be read as autobiography. Yet "ἐπὶ Λάτμῳ," drawn up as an answer to the great Romantics, in particular that poet whose hero met his Ideal Beauty on Latmos, quite tellingly illustrates the difference a generation put between the two poets. In the later work, the hero, having given up completely on life and on women, goes to find his true goddess in a secluded wood much like that of Keats's hero, only to discover she is not, after all, that Higher Reality that the Romantic poets, those shapers of the universe, would create out of Nature. This is a very sober Endymion who knows that his goddess is only his own creation and that inevitably she will be decomposed, "dis-created." The last stanza is a brilliant parody of the finale of Shelley's *Epipsychidion.*

> 'Twas the vapour of the perfume
> Of the presence that should be,
> That enwrapt me!
> O my Goddess, O my Queen!
> And I turn
> At thy feet to fall before thee;
> And thou wilt not:
> At thy feet to kneel and reach and kiss thy finger-tips;
> And thou wilt not:
> And I feel thine arms that stay me,
> And I feel—
> O mine own, mine own, mine own,
> I am thine, and thou art mine!

Only because this vision is created *by* the self *out of* the self can she be real *to* the self, while at the same time, it is ironically implied, she is unreal to everyone else. As with the Byron of the comic poems, the whole Romantic vision is the object of Clough's satire.

There is also a common subject matter linking Clough and Byron, the Cain and Abel story, although in Clough's version the first murderer is not the God-defiant villain that Byron makes him out to be in his *Cain: A Mystery,* nor is he the sole protagonist. In Clough's *The Mystery of the Fall,* the main characters, Cain and Adam, represent the poet's own dilemma. The central conflict of Clough's play has been seen as that between Adam and Eve, "between his liberal ethical philosophy and her

Christian orthodoxy." ⁹ This polarity is there, certainly,
and is even reinforced by the parallel conflict of Cain and
Abel. Of greater interest, however, is the disparity between the son's desperate need to do something to assert
himself in the world and the old Adam's determination to
wait the world out. Through these opposing voices,
Clough seems once more to be alternating between the
claims of action and inertia, though Adam's lines at the
end of the play suggest that the poet finally favors the
old man's stoicism:

> Yes, in despite of all disquietudes
> For Eve, for you, for Abel, which indeed
> Impelled in me that gaiety of soul—
> Without your fears I had listened to my own—
> In spite of doubt, despondency, and death,
> Though lacking knowledge alway, lacking faith
> Sometimes, and hope; with no sure trust in ought
> Except a kind of impetus within,
> Whose sole credentials were that trust itself;
> Yet, in despite of much, in lack of more,
> Life has been beautiful to me, my son,
> And if they call me, I will come again.
>   (XIV.37–48)

A speech of this sort makes it easy to see why Clough
has often been dismissed as a sort of agonized Hamlet
mourning for a lost identity. For, high-minded though it
is, there is a kind of brooding sentimentality about it.
Eventually, Adam's habit—and the poet's—of allowing his
mind to fold back on itself would have quite put out
that "gaiety of soul" which alone had warmed his life.

What we have come to understand about Clough is
that although he was hardly ever self-forgetful, he was
often capable of standing at a distance and looking at this
self with a light-hearted irony and sense of fun, as in "Sa

Majesté très Chrétienne." The poem is a monologue
meant to resemble Browning's.[10] In the confessional the
king insists that God intended him to remain a "little
quiet harmless acolyte," yet he knows that little children
—even princes—must grow up and come to grips with suffering. Ordinary people may choose to retire from the
world and seek solace in Mother Church (about the time
of Clough's writing of the poem the Tractarian movement had just subsided, leaving hordes of "verts" in its
wake), but the king is urged by the Church to take an
active role in the world. Then the question is how any
action can be chosen—indeed, why is choice even necessary
—in this "perplexing labyrinth" where "all are like, and
each each other meets." The king reminds us he is not
an English Protestant:

> Yes, holy Father, I am thankful for it;
> Most thankful I am not, as other men,
> A lonely Lutheran English Heretic;
> If I had so by God's despite been born,
> Alas, methinks I had but passed my life
> In sitting motionless beside the fire,
> Not daring to remove the once-placed chair,
> Nor stir my foot for fear it should be sin.
>   (80–87)

But the fact is, as a Catholic he is scarcely different:

> Ah, well a day!
> Would I were out in quiet Paraguay,
> Mending the Jesuits' shoes!—
>   (101–103)

The poem makes the point that between Oxford "malignants" and Protestant "infidels" there is hardly any room

for choice, but at the same time it lampoons Clough's own inability to choose even if there were sound and urgent reasons for doing so.[11]

After *The Bothie of Tober-na-Vuolich* (1848), an unusually happy poem (for once, almost oblivious of the self), the poet in *Amours de Voyage* returns to the old self-consciousness. "Easter Day" and "Easter Day II" place him on theological dead center again, this time between "Christ is not risen" and "Christ is yet risen." It is in *Dipsychus,* of course—the convention of the divided self being the perfect vehicle for Clough's self-satire—that the poet's irony achieves its finest expression.

Despite its name, the poem is not about a simple dualism. In the poem proper, Dipsychus, already a divided personality, discloses the part-self identified as the "Spirit," though the hero sometimes calls him "Mephistopheles" or simply "Mephisto."[12] As in many other poems of this time, one self watches another self, which in turn watches and analyzes another, the poem in effect like a series of Chinese boxes, one inside another, inside another, ad infinitum. Related to this is the fact that the poem is all argument, and that it is only through the hero's soliloquies and his "dialogues" with the Spirit that we can piece together the rudiments of a plot. We learn of his abortive flirtation after which he apparently is challenged to a duel by the girl's lover, takes fright, and runs away. Then toward the end we hear how, with much effort, Mephisto finally succeeds in sealing his compact with the young man.

There is nothing particularly devilish about this Mephisto.[13] Far from being the "Enemy," the "hateful unto God,"[14] or even the "voice of the worldly philosophy" assaulting Dipsychus the "Idealist," Mephisto is a rather helpful and sagacious soul intent on goading a morally and emotionally sick young man to decision and commitment, to that "more life, and fuller," as the speaker in "The Two Voices" would call it. Also, far from being unable to comprehend Dipsychus' "sublimities," Mephisto has a nearly perfect insight into the hero's disabling sentimentalism. As for the devil-compact—traditionally, the basis of his business with men—it hardly constitutes a bargain for Dipsychus. In no sense a fair exchange of the hero's soul for Satan's extraordinary gifts, it is a one-sided arrangement by which only the hero must agree to throw aside his "scruples" and engage himself in the here and now; the Spirit gets off scot-free.

Not that Dipsychus does not complain:

> What is this persecuting voice that haunts me?
> What? whence? of whom? How am I to detect?
> Myself or not myself?
>
> (II.17–19)

He would find any voice a torment that urged him to action of any sort—even flirting. Throughout the poem, this desire for sexual experience and simultaneous fear of it provide important dramatic poles. The Spirit pokes fun at his fastidiousness and then takes him to task for his failure even to act on his professed respect for the "matrimonial sanctities":

> Well, well—if you must stick perforce
> Unto the ancient holy course,
> And map your life out on the plan
> Of the connubial puritan,
> For God's sake carry out your creed,
> Go home and marry—and be d——d,
> I'll help you.
>
> (IIA.88–94)

When the hero at long last makes up his mind to visit one of those alluring "Venetian pets," he very nearly accomplishes his mission, and then withdraws. The Spirit knows all too well how it is with his young friend, and it is not implausible that he is here effecting a *double entendre* at the hero's expense:

> You feel yourself—to shrink and yet be fain,
> And still to move and still draw back again,
> Is a proceeding wholly without end.
>
> (III.12–14)

Dipsychus, now an admitted failure in love, wants only that solitude so congenial to the Romantics. He has hardly settled in his hideaway when he is discovered by the perspicacious Mephisto, who would use any argument to lure him out again. He cites the glories of "the classic mind" (IV.211), but Dipsychus slips away again, this time losing himself in the loveliness of the Venice night, which is just so much Wordsworthian "moonshine" [15] for the Hellenic Spirit. Dipsychus is fooled out of his Wordsworth only to hurry along to the Lido, where the mood of a worldly-wise and naughty Byron overtakes him:

> Ting, ting, there is no God; ting, ting—
> Dong, there is no God; dong,
> There is no God; dong, dong!
>
> (V.13–15)

At this, even the liberal Spirit feels his young charge has gone too far. In the guise of a genial Anglican, he chides Dipsychus for this sort of unbelief, but the sermon only moves him to an alternate Byronic role, that of the Childe Harold of Canto IV:

> Aha! come, come—great waters, roll!
> Accept me, take me, body and soul!—Aha!
> (V.220–221)

The Spirit shrewdly detects that in immersing himself the hero is merely enacting a baptism—a highly senti-mentalized one at that—and he simply will not let him get away with it.

In the next scene Dipsychus is presented with a clear-cut situation demanding action (he has been challenged to a duel by the angry lover), so when he runs away, he is hard-put to justify himself to the sharp-tongued devil:

> I am not quite in union with myself
> On this strange matter. I must needs confess
> Instinct turns instinct in and out; and thought
> Wheels round on thought.
> (VI.123–126)

Mephisto is as mercilessly argumentative as ever:

> What is your logic? What's your theology?
> Is it or is it not neology?
> That's a great fault; you're this and that,
> And here and there, and nothing flat.
>
> .   .   .   .
>
> You think half-showing, half-concealing,
> Is God's own method of revealing.
> (VII.18–21, 27–28)

The Spirit thereafter only intensifies his efforts to make Dipsychus seal the agreement, requiring only that he come to terms with the here and now. It is this which still seems to Dipsychus formidably beyond his ability. Much less would this agonized Hamlet be able to take some of the consequences of the deal—falling in love, marrying, choosing a profession, supporting a family. "Action, that staggers me," he cries at one point (IX.38). Long doubt and indecisiveness seem to have atrophied his will:

> No, no;
> The age of instinct has, it seems, gone by,
> And will not be forced back. And to live now
> I must sluice out myself into canals,
> And lose all force in ducts. The modern Hotspur
> Shrills not his trumpet of "To Horse, To Horse!"
> But consults columns in a railway guide;
> A demigod of figures; an Achilles
> Of computation. . . .
>   (IX.104–112)

It is a pitiless look at one's own impotence—social, political, as well as sexual—very close to the Eliot of *The Four Quartets* almost a century later, though without his bitterness:

> . . . all go into the dark,
> And dark the Sun and Moon, and the Almanach de Gotha
> And the Stock Exchange Gazette, the Directory of
>   Directors,
> And cold the sense and lost the motive of action.[16]

And there is the "Prufrock" of "Do I dare / Disturb the universe? . . . I have measured out my life with coffee spoons" in Clough's bureaucrat:

We ask Action,
And dream of arms and conflict; and string up
All self-devotion's muscles; and are set
To fold up papers.

(IX.131–134)

And "Prufrock's" "ragged claws" image in *Dipsychus'*
"coral-worm":

But I must slave, a meagre coral-worm,
To build beneath the tide with excrement
What one day will be island, or be reef,
And will feed men, or wreck them. Well, well, well.

(IX.142–145)

It is a far cry from the Carlylean view of work as sac-
ramental, this perceptive Freudian understanding of labor
and civilization as excremental. It is unlike "Prufrock,"
of course, in that Dipsychus makes some progress, as indicated by the Spirit's command to "Submit, submit," now
arising, we are told, *"from within"* the hero. Just as a few
years back Tennyson and Carlyle finally came to deny the
transcendental reality and embrace the here and now of
England, Dipsychus must, so the Spirit urges, "see things
simply as they are"—a phrase that was soon to play a key
role in Arnold's work. (In this sense, Clough's Dipsychus-
Spirit antithesis anticipates Arnold's Hebraism-Hellen-
ism.) For Dipsychus, the here and now is attainable by
none other than the old familiar common sense. "Action"
is no longer identifiable with the search for the absolute
ground of faith (Newman) nor with a program for reconstructing the English nation (Dr. Arnold). It consists
simply in the engagement of oneself in the daily business

of life, simply in saying a clear aye or no to each new life situation. Yet even this, as Dipsychus had discovered, was very close to impossible:

> To do anything,
> Distinct on any one thing to decide,
> To leave the habitual and the old, and quit
> The easy-chair of use and wont, seems crime.

For his final offensive, in Scene XI, the Spirit is at his most diabolical:

> Or will you write about philosophy?
> For a waste far-off *maybe* overlooking
>
> The fruitful *is* close by, live in metaphysic,
> We cannot act without assuming x,
> Schematise joy, effigiate meat and drink;
> Or, let me see, a mighty Work, a Volume,
> The Complemental of the inferior Kant,
> The Critic of Pure Practic, based upon
> With transcendental logic fill your stomach,
> The Antinomies of the Moral Sense: for, look you,
> And at the same time y, its contradictory;
> Ergo, to act. People will buy that, doubtless.
> $\qquad\qquad$ (XI.152–163)

> $\qquad$ Will you go on thus
> Until death end you? if indeed it does.
> For what it does, none knows. Yet as for you,
> You'll hardly have the courage to die outright;
> You'll somehow halve even it. Methinks I see you,
> Through everlasting limbos of void time,
> Twirling and twiddling ineffectively,
> And indeterminately swaying for ever.
> $\qquad\qquad$ (XI.182–189)

The High Victorian Credo has thus been undermined for Dipsychus by his nagging awareness of the alternative to faith, the "proofs" advanced by the skeptics. Thus, between the wish to believe and the recognition of the inadequacies of belief, action is precluded.

Dipsychus' last stand against the wisdom of the Spirit is his futile and delightfully childish plot to save out a tenth of himself from the bargain "to doubt with, / Just to pause, think, and look about with" (XIII.16–17). Mephisto is no dupe, of course, and at long last the hero, cajoled if not cudgeled into one hundred per cent surrender, bids farewell to his "dreams," and goes forth to welcome the world.[17]

Through its various personae, *Dipsychus* reflects many aspects of its author: the Dipsychus gripping his armchair for fear of sin or doctrinal error if he leaves it is Clough's neurasthenic aspect; Mephisto, who sees things as they are, reflects his healthy outgoing self; the poet, who is shown in the Prologue and Epilogue seeking to resolve the conflict between "the tender conscience and the world" in the unity of art, this is Clough the poet, of course; and the uncle, for whom the younger generation is "a sort of hobbadi-hoy cherub, too big to be innocent, and too simple for anything else"—and who is convinced in any case that "it's all Arnold's doing"—he is Clough's commonsense rather conservative streak. Certainly, identifying Clough with his hero in a one-to-one relation is as absurd as calling Mr. Eliot "Prufrock." For one thing, Clough is remarkably saner and stronger than the enfeebled Dipsychus, and for another, much less robust than Mephisto. The poet's characteristic skepticism is as agonized as ever,[18] but he has gained significantly in intellect, wit, and irony, and an enormously attractive humor, all of which have

gone most noticeably into the blood and bones of Mephisto.

What Henry Sidgwick said of Clough in 1869, that
he was "in a literal sense before his age," [19] we see now
was not exactly the case. In 1850, a good ten years before
the full effect of the new spirit was felt, the cultural life
of the nation was already in turmoil. The Oxford Movement was still adding members, when the Higher Criticism
rose to challenge the foundations of Christian faith. Mary
Ann Evans' translation of Strauss' *Leben Jesu* appeared in
1846; J. A. Froude's *Shadows of the Clouds* in 1847 and
Nemesis of Faith in 1849, and Francis Newman's *The Soul*
in 1849 and *Phases of Faith* in 1850. In 1848 Rossetti and
his friends organized the Pre-Raphaelite Brotherhood,
publishing *The Germ* to propagate their doctrines. A new
style of sensibility began to form along with the new religious attitude, and the doubt troubling Clough was ener-
vating many young Britons, among them Clough's best
friend, Matthew Arnold. There were Europeans and
Americans, too, infected by that sickness unto death:
Melville's Bartleby would "prefer not" to be bothered
with anything at all; for Goncharov's Oblomov, there is
nothing in the world to compare with the appeal of his
warm bed, and he refuses to climb out; Baudelaire, meanwhile, drones on in his monotone, *c'est l'ennui, c'est
l'ennui.*

The difference with Clough was that after a brilliant
diagnosis of his spiritual malaise he pulled himself together, administering the simple but for that time radical therapy of laughing the symptoms away. Adam's
longed-for "gaiety of soul" became Clough's own achievement, and the means by which *Dipsychus*—not at all the
feeble *Hamlet* or mere inferior *Faust* that Arnold would

have criticized—came into its own as a wise and worldly minor masterpiece.

II

With Dr. Arnold's death in 1842 Clough became more and more of an older brother to Matthew Arnold, as his letters of that time show.[20] Arnold struck the pose of dandy, a "chanson of Beranger's on his lips," [21] but under the mask of insouciance, there was that other Arnold hard by his studies of himself and the troubles of his age—like Giacopone's bride, who, falling to her death, reveals under her glowing garments "A robe of sackcloth next the smooth, white skin." [22]

And he scrutinized Clough. In a letter written in December 1847 he accuses Clough of despising the joys of the imagination and trying too hard to "*solve* the Universe," an attempt he finds "as irritating as Tennyson's dawdling with [his] painted shell is fatiguing." [23] Such recognition of the need for a joyous art, anticipating his later theory that poetry must "inspirit and rejoice the reader," [24] is a main theme in his correspondence with Clough. In line with this he often attacks his friend for the "deficiency of the *beautiful*" in his poems, arguing that contemporary poets such as Bailey and Novalis, like Clough, ignore beauty because they are too concerned with the "rhetorical, devotional or metaphysical." They are not artists but, with their "passion for truth" (*Letters to Clough*, p. 66), would perhaps make great scientists. The idea Arnold so clearly formulated in the 1853 Preface puts in another early appearance in the famous passage of the November 1848 letter to Clough:

—I have been at Oxford the last two days and hearing Sellar and the rest of that clique who know neither life nor themselves rave about your poem gave me a strong almost bitter feeling with respect to them, the age, the poem, even you. Yes I said to myself something tells me I can, if need be, at last dispense with them all, even with him: better that, than be sucked for an hour even into the Time Stream in which they and he plunge and bellow. I became calm in spirit, but uncompromising, almost stern. More English than European, I said finally, more American than English: and took up Obermann, and refuged myself with him in his forest against your Zeit Geist.

(Letters to Clough, p. 95)

The feverish search for a theoretical solution for everything in life, the "American" style, is thus contrasted to the "European" tradition of established institutions, which require no further justification than that they have always existed. To escape from the "American" *Zeitgeist* would demand the suspension of that ceaselessly inquiring intellect operating continually on things that change and which in turn effects change, until completely exhausting itself. It goes without saying that *The Mystery of the Fall* was quite repugnant to Arnold.[25]

When *Ambarvalia* was published in 1849, Arnold again wrote his friend emphasizing beauty and pleasure, what he called "naturalness . . . of form," and the need to avoid too much philosophizing in poetry. "The trying to go into and to the bottom of an object instead of grouping *objects* is . . . fatal to the sensuousness of poetry. . . . 'Not deep the Poet sees, but wide'" (*Letters to Clough,* p. 99). In this *"unpoetical* age," he believes,

Clough and certain other poets are not determined enough to make beautiful poems; they are merely thinking aloud in poetry. "My dearest Clough these are damned times," Arnold writes a few months later, "everything is against one"—even "our own selves"—"but for God's sake let us neither be fanatics nor yet chaff blown by the wind . . ." (*Letters to Clough,* p. 111). The poet's "sickening consciousness of [his] difficulties" is bound to produce an "aridity" (*Letters to Clough,* p. 131) in poetry which then requires a camouflage by those "exquisite bits and images" (*Letters to Clough,* p. 124). In their place he prescribes acceptance:

> You ask me in what I think or have thought you going wrong: in this: that you would never take your assiette as something determined final and unchangeable for you and proceed to work away on the basis of that: but were always poking and patching and cobbling at the assiette itself—could never finally, as it seemed—"resolve to be thyself"—but were looking for this and that experience, and doubting whether you ought not to adopt this or that mode of being of persons qui ne vous valaient pas because it might possibly be nearer the truth than your own: you had no reason for thinking it *was,* but it *might* be—and so you would try to adapt yourself to it. You have I am convinced lost infinite time in this way: it is what I call your morbid conscientiousness—you are the most conscientious man I ever knew: but on some lines morbidly so, and it spoils your action.
>
> (*Letters to Clough,* p. 130)

This is strong criticism; perhaps Arnold could so fully express himself only because Clough was uninhibited in return. Although most of Clough's answers have disappeared, an indirect one survives in "Recent English Poetry," an article published in the *North American Review* in July 1853. In his discussion of Alexander Smith's *A Life Drama* [26] there is a long paragraph, the gist of which is the question: Should literature treat modern subjects or ancient? His answer is characteristically equivocal, but finally his choice of the "actual, palpable things" over wandering "into the pleasant field of Greek or Latin mythology" [27] does come through. A novel like *Vanity Fair* or *Bleak House* may be discarded tomorrow, but is "devoured" today, and so, the implication goes, poetry like the novel should treat modern subjects. "We are, unhappily," writes Clough, as if in answer to Arnold, "not gods, nor even marble statues" (p. 145).

Interestingly enough, Clough's discussion of his friend reads like a sketch of himself. Even Empedocles emerges in Clough's eyes as a darker version of his own Dipsychus: "weary of misdirected effort, weary of imperfect thought, impatient of a life which appears to him a miserable failure, and incapable, as he conceives, of doing anything that shall be true to that proper interior self, 'Being one with which we are one with the whole world'" (p. 153). Similarly, the "morals and meanings" of "Tristram and Iseult" are, among others, "the difficulty of living at all, the impossibility of doing any thing" (p. 159).

Clough feels he must even pass judgment on these traits, take a stand on them. Against Smith's call to action, Arnold's inertia must be examined. "How is it," he asks, "we find ourselves here, reflecting, pondering, hesitating, musing, complaining, with 'A' [?]" In dead earnest he stalls for over a page trying to decide which of the two to favor. Must he choose one, or should he suspend choice and "adore in sacred doubt the Supreme

Bifurcation" (p. 162)? When he finally makes up his mind, Smith gets the nod—although, here again, the verdict is obscured by excessive qualification:

> Nevertheless, upon the whole, for the present age, the lessons of reflectiveness and the maxims of caution do not appear to be more needful or more appropriate than exhortations to steady courage and calls to action. There is something certainly of an over-educated weakness of purpose in Western Europe—not in Germany only, or France, but also in more busy England. There is a disposition to press too far the finer and subtler intellectual and moral susceptibilities; to insist upon following out, as they say, to their logical consequences, the notices of some single organ of the spiritual nature; a proceeding which perhaps is hardly more sensible in the grown man than it would be in the infant to refuse to correct the sensations of sight by those of the touch. Upon the whole, we are disposed to follow out, if we must follow out at all, the analogy of the bodily senses; we are inclined to accept rather than investigate; and to put our confidence less in arithmetic and antinomies than in "A few strong instincts and a few plain rules" (p. 163).

That Clough, the creator of Mephisto, the Spirit of Action, should advocate "courage" and reprimand "caution" is in itself not surprising. What is remarkable is that he should also advocate and reprimand, in reference to Arnold (who had been saying very nearly the same thing for years): Resolve to be thyself, accept your assiette.

There is agreement between the friends even on matters of style. Clough condemns, for example, Smith's way of coining metaphors and similes. A poet should concentrate on his outline *"simplex et unum,"* but

Smith tends to get lost in his "Chinese boxes" of simile. The "happy, unimpeded 'sequence" is often undiscovered even by the most attentive reader (pp. 166–167). We have the Elizabethans and Romantics to blame for this promotion of "Texture" over "Structure" in modern poetry—a judgment that Arnold will make a few months later in his Preface.

Between Clough and Arnold, however, there is one basic difference in their aesthetics pointing to a fundamental disagreement in their philosophy of life. For Clough, poetry should fully engage itself with modern questions; for Arnold, it must ignore the *Zeitgeist*. The divergence soon becomes explicit. Arnold wrote his friend on August 25, "They think here that your article on me is obscure and peu favorable—I do not myself think either of these things" (*Letters to Clough*, p. 140). A more complete answer was to follow shortly: "The Preface is done" (*Letters to Clough*, p. 144).

The ostensible purpose of Arnold's 1853 Preface was to account for his not having included "Empedocles on Etna" in the volume. However, the Preface should be looked at not only for its program against Romantic lyricism, but for Arnold's personal statement on the merits of action in life as well as "action" in poetry. At the time of the historical Empedocles, the remarkable serenity of the Greek spirit had been severely undermined by an increasingly persistent and unproductive "dialogue of the mind with itself." It was a time, like Arnold's, of doubt and discouragement, a time of "Hamlet and of Faust" (p. xvii). For these reasons, an accurate historical representation of Empedocles and his times is of great interest to us, says Arnold, but poetry must do more than interest its readers. Modern poetry, like "Empedocles on Etna," is overpreoccupied with those situations "in which the suffering finds no vent in action . . . in which there is everything to be endured, nothing to be done" (p. xviii). But Arnold does not merely present the dialogue of the mind with itself as a literary problem, for he also writes how, when it occurs in everyday life, it is "painful, not tragic." His discussion of action, too, has this double reference. It can mean an Aristotelian "action"—that is to say, the event imitated in the plot: "All depends upon the subject," he writes, following Aristotle, "choose a fitting action, penetrate yourself with the feeling of its situations; this done, everything else will follow" (p. xxiii). But there is also "action" in the sense of man's conduct of life, so often in modern times crippled by the division of his will. This is the "action" to which the Spirit in *Dipsychus* tried to stir the hero, and it is only possible where the assiette of the self is accepted. Therefore, when Arnold talks about that "multitude of voices counselling different things bewildering" (p. xxiv), he is not only reviewing an impersonal literary situation but also worrying personally about charting the right course through the many contrary and contradictory opinions and dispositions [28] that swirl and foam in and about himself.

Arnold's long devotion to the ancients as models for life as for art should be looked at in this connection. The study of the ancients will produce, he believes, "a steadying and composing effect upon [people's] judgment, *not of literary works only, but of men and events in general*" (p. xxviii, italics added). Those who habitually traffic with the ancients

wish neither to applaud nor to revile their age: they wish to know what it is, what it can give them, and whether this is what they want. What they want, they know very well; *they want to educe and cultivate what is best and noblest in themselves.* . . . They do not talk of their mission, nor of interpreting their age, nor of the coming Poet; *all this, they know, is the mere delirium of vanity;* their business is not to praise their age, but to afford to the men who live in it *the highest pleasure which they are capable of feeling.* . . . They are told that it is an era of progress, an age commissioned to carry out the great ideas of industrial development and social amelioration. They reply that with all this they can do nothing; that the elements they need for the exercise of their art are great actions, calculated powerfully and delightfully to affect *what is permanent in the human soul;* that so far as the present age can supply such actions, they will gladly make use of them; but that an age wanting in moral grandeur can with difficulty supply such, and an age of spiritual discomfort with difficulty be powerfully and delightfully affected by them.

(pp. xxviii–xxix, italics added)

The argument is carried in terms of literature's general effects on the reader, and, further, in terms of what those men of "strongest head" and "widest culture" (p. xxix) will do and will be—in short, in terms of the total psychological and cultural context. In line with his earlier attack on the *Zeitgeist,* he insists here that people should not be overwhelmed by "the pretension of [the] age" (p. xxix). One should make a constant effort to clear the mind of all contradiction, irritation, and impatience.

Read as a literary manifesto the Preface is theoretically weak, and as a practical literary program it does not work, as the poems of this volume show.[29] But the Preface is significant as a reading of both the spiritual disorders experienced at that time and Arnold's prescription for the cure. Appearing fifteen years before *Culture and Anarchy*, it anticipates many of the ideas of that great essay: culture, disinterestedness, Hellenism, contradiction, division, the arid irritability of the age, and its delirious vanity—all these notions would later be focused in his recommendation for sweetness and light as the remedy for the acerbity of personal and cultural existence.

Clough apparently did not have much to say about the Preface. In regard to his friend's reception of "Sohrab and Rustum," the poem supposed to best exemplify the theory, Arnold wrote John Blackett, "Clough, as usual, remained in suspense whether he liked it or no." [30] Arnold did not seem overly concerned. Perhaps he did not really care all that much about Clough's reaction. Despite the many attitudes in common between Clough's *NAR* article and Arnold's Preface, their essential divergence by this time is unmistakable. Clough, like Dipsychus, would soon get a job and marry, perhaps in an effort to alleviate some of the boredom of interminable inaction and indecision; also, he would write virtually nothing of importance the whole last decade of his life. Arnold (also wed and working now) would stoically accept his assiette, still searching for his model for the untroubled self among the distant ancients. The more tenacious of the two, he refused to be beaten by his failure to achieve the desired classical effect in his poetry. Instead, he applied his reading of the classics ever more assiduously to his criticism of literature, culture, and religion. "You are too content to *fluctuate*," Arnold wrote in the fall of 1853, "to be ever learning, never coming to the knowledge of the truth. This is why, with you, I feel it necessary to stiffen myself—hold fast my rudder" (*Letters to Clough*, p. 146). This, his last important letter to Clough, would be his spiritual valediction and declaration of independence from his friend.

III

The Arnold of the poems is only imperfectly reconciled with the critic determined to see his age *sub specie aeternitatis*. The poet who believes that the "passion for truth" has no place in poetry nonetheless philosophizes; the critic who finds disease in the modern dialogue of the mind with itself endlessly talks to himself. When he banished "Empedocles on Etna" from the 1853 volume, he failed to exile him from his poetic self, and when he finally did succeed in exorcising that haunting spirit, the ancient philosopher avenged himself by stealing Arnold's Muses. In any case, his poetry hardly expresses a unified sensibility. Arnold himself understood this: "Fret not yourself to make my poems square in all their parts, but like what you can . . . my poems are fragments . . . I am fragments." [31] Moving back and forth between solitude and the world, his longing for the past and hope for the future, his poems try both to transcend his time and to live deeply in it.

The central Arnoldian conflict is explicit in his first volume, *The Strayed Reveller, and Other Poems* (1849), particularly in its contradictory attitudes toward man and Nature. In "In Harmony with Nature" the speaker declares that "Man must begin . . . where Nature ends," asserting the primacy of man over the physical world, and in "Quiet Work," Nature is the hero, silently perfecting its works despite man's noisy disturbances. The two poems are not juxtaposed in the volume, nor is the inconsistency between them made prominent in any other way.[32] Yet a close look at them reveals a still subtler discord in the young poet. "In Harmony with Nature," supposedly addressing itself to an "independent preacher," is at once too strident ("Restless fool," he exclaims) and too diffuse (Nature is described only in general terms like "cruel," "stubborn," and "fickle," among others) to be a convincing argument against acquiescence to Nature. Only the urgency of his feeling comes through. In contrast, "Quiet Work" seeks "tranquility," which the speaker sees permeating Nature; yet in this poem, too, he is not concerned with the purpose of Nature's steady performance. In both poems the speaker proclaims a view he is not really convinced of, a feature pointing to the lack of conviction in the early Arnold.

The suspension of any effort to resolve divisive feelings or outright contradictions becomes a favorite poetic technique with Arnold. The sonnet "Written in Butler's Sermons" denounces those who would break down "God's harmonious whole" into "a thousand shreds" as they analyze man's nature. Presumably, man's indivisible unity exists somewhere—either "under the sea" or over the "cluster'd peaks." And yet this notion is undercut by the curious qualification that man's identity "sits alone" "where none may see." His desire for wholeness is thus poised against the impossibility of his ever experiencing it. The tension provided by this paradox is disquieting, however ironic. What is more, the striking imagery of sea and mountain peaks in the sestet is unfair competition for the jarring nouns describing man's disunity and the speaker's railing against the analytic approach. There is a wistfulness in his desire for wholeness, but the unbalance in the poem underlines the contradiction of its own explicit statement.

The speaker in "Resignation" devises a way out of the conflict, but the voice advising resignation is unsteady and betrays its misgivings. Instead of struggling for the sole purpose of reaching the goal, he tells his sister "Fausta," she should be more like the resigned traveler whom "an unblamed serenity / Hath freed from passions." This "milder" pilgrim is then explained through a detailed recounting of his excursion a decade earlier for the sole purpose of pleasure in the trip itself. However, unlike the speaker in "Tintern Abbey," with which the poem has been contrasted,[33] the "I" in this poem takes no real pleasure in Nature. The gypsies he sees along the way suggest detachment and disinterestedness. If their resignation is merely "hereditary," the poet's will involve an active effort at detachment. The tangled syntax makes for obscurity in the passage describing the poet's way, as though Arnold himself is groping toward a clear sense of it, but he apparently means to suggest that the poet can achieve resignation by identifying himself with the "general life" of humanity. The speaker's confidence in his own counsel begins to flag. The most he can hope for after all from this stoic resolution is only a "sad lucidity of soul." When he detects the retort in Fausta's smile, he does not so much answer her skepticism as his own, trying hard to persuade himself that the temporal world that we all experience will somehow outlast his personal life.

If this were his true conviction on the matter, the last stanza of the poem would be peculiarly anticlimactic. To begin with, the argument of the first sentence "if a life . . . , Though bearable, seem hardly worth [the pain], Yet . . . [Nature] . . . Seem[s] to bear rather than rejoice" is not a reasonable one. The "bearableness" of one's life is hardly increased by a Nature that simply endures, and the imagery of "mute" turf, "sol-emn" hills, and "strange-scrawl'd" rocks only intensifies the unbearable loneliness of one's existence, quite the contrary of the poem's presumed intention. And despite reference to a deity, there is no assurance that resignation now will bring final joy later. There is instead only a half-hearted wish that man's "intemperate" prayer might "pierce Fate's *impenetrable* ear" (italics added). All his willful resoluteness to the contrary, his poem offers no solace or hope as it registers the speaker's numb knowledge that he is every bit as hopelessly "in action's dizzying eddy whirled" as his Faustian sister.

Whereas the earlier Victorians could use their poems as a way of sounding out their convictions, often at the expense of poetic form, Arnold and Clough can no longer sustain even the thematic consistency of their poems. As they formulate one doctrine, a second thought at once challenges it; and frequently the muddled syntax, the dissident tonalities, and even the palpable contradictions of the argument break up the poetic matter as well. This is true not only of their "philosophical" poems, but of much of the narrative and dramatic poetry, which often defies the reader to follow it. One such puzzle is "The Strayed Reveller," the title poem of his first volume. The concept of the poet in this "reveller" who wanders into Circe's temple and drinks too much raises many questions. What sort of poet is he? Is he a Keats whom Arnold elsewhere condemns, a parody of the Romantic poet? [34] Or, is he one who has simply "strayed from the world of revelry into the world of poetry"? [35] In sum, does he represent the poetic views Arnold holds, or the ones he attacks? Actually there seem to be at least four different poets and seers in the poem.

There are the Gods who from their great height on

Olympus see the world as totally happy and content, and there are the bards, whose vision has been granted by the Gods on condition that they identify themselves with human suffering: "such a price / The Gods exact for song / To become what we sing." [36] Their poems as the youthful reveller recites them are quite serene and have little of that morbid introspectiveness Arnold attacks in his aesthetics. All in all, their assumption of other identities, recalling Keats's doctrine of negative capability,[37] seems to suggest that theirs is the ideal way of poetic creation. Then there is the reveller himself, who stands for still another attitude toward poetic creation. Thanks to Circe's wine, he sees in the Dionysian ecstasy all that the bards can see, and more, but without their suffering. It is especially hard to know Arnold's attitude toward this young man, although there is one passage—the youth's meeting with Ulysses—that would seem to shed some light on it. Ulysses, the fourth seer, is an experienced man of action who has known great suffering in his lifetime. The youth asks him if he is in truth the "wise Ulysses," and the proud, if "travel-tarnished," voyager asks him in turn, sarcastically: "And thou, *too,* sleeper?" (italics added). With that "too" Ulysses challenges the reveller to compare his dreams with Ulysses' real heroic achievements. Arnold is ironic here toward the great hero, who, by his condescension to the youth and the bards, betrays his ignorance. "Sleeper" though he may be, the reveller has observed well and understood a great deal. With his energy and freshness of poetic vision, he has become in his own way a kind of hero. Arnold is here less concerned with a particular poetry, such as Romanticism, than with a general concept of poetry as it relates to action. The three ways of seeing —absolute detachment, merging of self with others, and

Dionysian immediacy—are all ways of the Arnoldian poet. "Not deep the poet sees, but wide" from his distance on the world of action that would, were he part of it, destroy his joy and serenity.

This reading, certainly, does not preempt other possibilities of interpretation. It is still possible to argue, for instance, that the Gods are classical, the bards Romantic, and the reveller an inarticulate but "poetic" young man, and that Arnold finally sides with one of the three. And why Arnold assigned Circe as his reveller's Muse is not really clear. The poem, after all debate is done, remains disturbingly obscure, the only explanation for this being the ambivalence of Arnold's feelings about the role of the poet.

"Mycerinus" and "The Forsaken Merman" show the essential Arnoldian ambivalence much more clearly. In "Mycerinus," the young king accuses the gods of injustice. He argues how his father had "loved injustice," and lived to a ripe age, while he himself who has "loved the good" is now given only six years to live. In the second half, a third-person narrator tells how the king fled to the mountains and, to double his remaining years, lit a hundred lamps so he could revel night and day. The final passage is heavy with qualifications ("It may be . . . sometimes . . . Might . . . half . . ."), indefinite comparisons ("like a guilty man . . ." and "as some pale shape . . ."), and negatives ("not less . . . not . . . Nor . . . Nor . . . No, nor . . ."), all of which serve to deepen the mystery of this Byronic king's last spiritual condition. The outward gaiety only masking his inner turmoil, it is probable that even his fellow revellers remain in the dark as to his true feelings. And, of course, his subjects below—like the readers of this fable—can only conjecture about him from sounds that would sometimes drift down from his kingdom in exile. The outcome—whether the Romantic hero was finally able to make his point and reconcile with the gods or not— is carefully concealed.

In "The Forsaken Merman," Margaret must choose between her merman family in their "sandstrewn cavern, cool and deep" and her human kinfolk in their bleak, white-washed, pious village. As we have seen, Tennyson's poems on this theme always make clear that the poet's rational consent is to the world of social and moral action, whereas Arnold's only bring to the theme an increasing anxiety over the arid landlubber's life and an intense longing for the tranquility and beauty of the life of the deep—a conflict which might be interpreted, variously, as between rationality and the irrational, morality and art, responsibility and freedom, or for that matter, civilization and eros.

Arnold's pursuit of self-discovery gathers momentum in his next volume, *Empedocles on Etna, and Other Poems* (1852), where his conflicts continue to be told through dissident voices in such poems as "Self-Dependence," "Human Life," "A Summer Night," and "The Buried Life."

The man in "Self-Dependence" can only wish he were, as he voyages on the sea of life:

> Weary of myself, and sick of asking
> What I am, and what I ought to be,
> At this vessel's prow I stand, which bears me
> Forwards, forwards, o'er the starlit sea.

To one exhausted by self-consciousness, the stars and the sea offer a refreshing other consciousness to hear him and perhaps to heal him. In the advice of the "air-born" voice ("Live as [the stars and sea]"), the speaker recognizes the resolution he once made: "Resolve to be thyself; and know that he, / Who finds himself, loses his misery!"—a counsel Arnold had so persistently imposed on Clough. But there are some serious problems here: The "I" who is weary and the "self" that seems to be causing this weariness are not reconciled anywhere in the poem. The voice in his heart adds still another self that tells him to be "thyself." But how can the "I" be "[him]self" when he does not know where, among these selves, his true being lies? To find himself he must resolve to be himself, but of course to be himself he must first find himself. This vicious circle is very tiring.

The more impersonal "Human Life" again makes man the voyager on "life's incognizable sea," and again, too, unable to locate his "inly-written chart." He sails the sea of life "by night," sensing all the while that he is circumscribed by "unknown Powers." However, his advice to us all—"Let us not fret and fear to miss our aim" —does not help very much. Whatever his destiny might be, man can never glimpse the ultimate and must make his choice in the dark every moment of his voyage. As he delivers his oracle, his voice takes on an increasingly melancholy tone. We leave behind our "homes," our "joys," our "friends," but we are not at all sure we will ever reach a new harbor.

The landscape of "A Summer Night" is a deserted street. The only comfort for the speaker here is his recollection of a moonlit beach he had once known. It is the familiar polarity of land and sea, but here the "I" belongs to neither. Eternally equivocating, he is unlike all other men, who either resign themselves to meaningless mundane activities or ignore them and sail out on the sea of freedom only to meet disaster. Between these two courses, either of "madman" or "slave," there is no

real choice, and he does not know what he can do, what
he should be. Although the poem ends recommending
detachment—the clarity of the moon—the weight of the
poem hangs on the impressive passage describing those
awful alternatives neither of which he is able to accept.

"The Buried Life" addresses itself to the problem
of self-knowledge. The speaker in this dramatic monologue is talking to the woman he loves, but her response, more like Marguerite's than the woman's in "Dover
Beach," does not warm him enough. Very soon, as in the
Switzerland lyrics, he can no longer talk to her meaning-
fully, and his glance turns inward:

> I knew the mass of men conceal'd
> Their thoughts, for fear that if reveal'd
> They would by other men be met
> With blank indifference, or with blame reproved;
> I knew they lived and moved
> Trick'd in disguises, alien to the rest
> Of men, and alien to themselves.

While recognizing that alienation from others is only another aspect of self-alienation, he still believes in the
existence of that "unregarded river" of his true identity.
But can man discover the "buried stream" of this true
self? As in "A Summer Night" (the passage also recalls
"Tintern Abbey"), the speaker often experiences an uncontrollable urge to know his "true, original course." Not
that he holds much hope. Still, though infrequently, there
are moments when he can sense it:

And what we mean, we say, and what we would, we know.
A man becomes aware of his life's flow,
And hears its winding murmur; and he sees
The meadows where it glides, the sun, the breeze.

This self-knowledge is hardly absolute—he only "thinks he knows"—and yet the poem, unlike "A Summer Night" or "Dover Beach," ends on a somewhat positive note.

Exactly a year after Arnold wrote Clough that he had taken up *Obermann* to fight off the *Zeitgeist,* he bade a half-hearted farewell to Senancour in "Stanzas in Memory of the Author of 'Obermann': November, 1849." There, high in the Alps, he thinks of three poets, all of whom managed to see their way despite the turmoil of the times. But their way would not necessarily have to be his way. Wordsworth, now in his "grey old age," still refuses to see the darker side of life; and Goethe, though a "strong much-toiling sage" in later years, had at least that "tranquil world" of his youth to look back upon. And so, in this "hopeless tangle of our age" there is only Senancour to turn to. The author of *Obermann* felt this same dilemma of solitude and the world:

> Ah! two desires toss about
> The poet's feverish blood.
> One drives him to the world without,
> And one to solitude.

The poet considers retiring with him to the Alps where there are still the mountain air and "healing sights" of verdant slopes. Then suddenly, in a passage reminiscent of "Ode to a Nightingale" and "Locksley Hall," he wakes up:

> Away!

> Away the dreams that but deceive
> And thou, sad guide, adieu!
> I go, fate drives me. . . .

Not nearly so resolute as Tennyson's hero, he will leave, he tells Senancour, "Half of my life with you." With this half-heartedness he can hardly expect to be living fully "in the world."

Throughout the volume, Arnold's struggle with self-consciousness is recorded in almost unbroken prose argument. What little craft he employs may be seen in those memorable lines that document the important ideas of this time and in those passages where he successfully manipulates the many voices. As Arnold himself correctly diagnosed, whatever poetic impulse there was in him at the time was largely spent in articulating his understanding of his struggle, an effort which left little energy for shaping it into poetic form. Among the 1852 poems, perhaps "Tristram and Iseult" succeeds beyond a mere poetic diary of suffering and introspection. Even here, however, the "two desires" that divide the poet compose the basic structure of the poem: Iseult of Brittany standing for dull but durable affection and Iseult of Ireland for all-consuming passion. But his dilemma, as it happens, is fully translated into dramatic terms. The poem is really bigger than this statement of its contradiction theme suggests. By the intricacies of narrative form (dialogue, narration, and reverie), and the use of color,[38] flashback, and a variety of meters, it builds to an unusually complex and fulfilled poem.

The title poem of the volume, more typically Arnoldian with its heavy concern with the self, is much more ambitious than "Tristram and Iseult." Empedocles, the brilliant statesman, physician, and poet, is presented here as "half mad / With exile, and with brooding on his wrong" (I.i.23–24). He has with him one companion, Pausanias, whom he instructs on the ills of the age, and when he speaks to this disciple it is in his public voice, putting his true thoughts in other men's mouths and then attacking them. Some believe, he declaims, that man's soul is like a mirror the Gods have hung on a cord:

> Hither and thither spins
> The wind-borne, mirroring soul,
> A thousand glimpses wins,
> Looks once, and drives elsewhere, and leaves its last employ.
>
> The Gods laugh in their sleeve
> To watch man doubt and fear,
> Who knows not what to believe
> Since he sees nothing clear,
> And dares stamp nothing false where he finds nothing sure.
>   (I.ii.82–91)

With the soul's vision so fragmentary as to be unable to comprehend the whole—almost like Childe Harold's broken mirror—the very heavens appear to these people to war against the earth and men against themselves. In opposition to such views, Empedocles urges a stoic acceptance not unlike that practiced by the early Victorians. Instead of allowing the discrepancy between his actual behavior and his ideal behavior to torment him, man must learn, Empedocles warns, that he has absolutely "no *right* to bliss, / No title from the Gods to welfare and repose" (I.ii.160–161). The flatness and chill of his exhortation takes on interest with our realization that Empedocles is assaulting the errors "we," all of us, commit. The generic first person plural is left ambiguous so as to include Empedocles himself. There is consequently a fascinating tension set in motion each time a stanza describing "our" follies is interrupted by his attack on the "we," signaled by the vocative "Fools" (in

II.ii.347, 382, etc.), as if he needs to refocus his target from time to time.

Empedocles' long harangue, however, expresses only a side of himself. If he pontificates to Pausanias, there is still that part of him that, as he listens to the songs of Callicles, can admit his own doubt. In the last act his whole speech style changes, indicating that, because Pausanias has had his lesson, and the debt is paid, he now has only himself to lecture. Here, his public wisdom is irrelevant. Empedocles' torment is now more directly Arnoldian than ever:

> No, thou are come too late, Empedocles!
> And the world hath the day, and must break thee,
> Not thou the world. With men thou canst not live,
> Their thoughts, their ways, their wishes, are not thine;
> And being lonely thou are miserable,
> For something has impair'd thy spirit's strength,
> And dried its self-sufficing fount of joy.
> Thou canst not live with men nor with thyself—
> (II.16–23)

Here Callicles' song counterpoints such bleak considerations. Although this stripling bard's intentions are not easy to discover, he does seem bent on impressing the philosopher with the utter disinterest of the Gods in man and his sufferings. But to little avail. Empedocles pursues his own train of thought, which this time leads him straight to the summit of Mt. Etna, far above the city. He has pared down his spirit to a point where, like the soul in "The Palace of Art," he is almost suffocating.

But still he vacillates, now with another worry— that intellect and its abstractions might finally sever the last fragile hold he has on his soul, his "own only true,

deep-buried [self]" (II.371). Only in death can his en-
slavement to thought be redeemed, for only death can
return him to his wholeness. Speaking now to the universe ("O ye elements!"), he is able at the last to "breathe
free," and he leaps to his death triumphantly.

Aside from the character of Empedocles, Arnold
employs another obvious device which embodies his own
self-division: the contrast of poet and philosopher. We
remember how, at the beginning of Act I, Callicles is
shown alone enjoying the mountain morning. Act II, in
contrast, opens on Empedocles' twilight view of Etna's
"charr'd, blacken'd, melancholy waste." [39] Unlike *Paracelsus*, where the two aspects of the poet's character were
finally joined, no such union takes place in *Empedocles*.
Perhaps a closer parallel is to be found in *Sordello*, which
ends with the barefoot child singing as he races up the
hill to "beat / The lark, God's poet."

Empedocles made the irrevocable leap, but Arnold
survived his crisis,[40] saved undoubtedly by an ironic com-
prehension of his spiritual impasse. In the act of poetic
composition he understood that the dialogue of the mind
with itself can only be terminated in death. Without allowing himself "a hostile attitude" toward contemporary
life, he would at the same time take care not to be
"overwhelmed" (p. xxix) by it.[41] This program, as set
forth in the Preface, amounted to a *"volte-face,"* [42] as E.
D. H. Johnson calls it, in his poetic development. As it
turned out, he paid a high price—poetry—for his spiritual health, and it is a great irony that the famed document prescribing a new course for that art should fore-
cast his eventual farewell to the practice of it. Ultimately,
however, he did get full value: the few good poems
written after 1853 ("Stanzas from the Grand Chartreuse,"
"Rugby Chapel," "Thyrsis," "Obermann Once More,"

"Heine's Grave"), though still persisting in the dialogue, show a new serenity which leads, gradually, to a
new hopefulness.[43] Looking to the ancients, he found
that deepened sense of history that helped him see
his own age in a more variegated light. Paradoxically,
the flight from the *Zeitgeist* at this time cleared a way
for him to approach it again, a decade later,[44] with confidence in history and in himself, as we will see later on.

IV

In one of those charming gossipy letters of hers, Elizabeth Barrett Browning wrote Miss Mitford that she liked
Clough's *Bothie* and that both she and her husband
thought it "worth twenty of the other little book, with its
fragmentary, dislocated, unartistic character." [45] Clough's
Higher Criticism poems, "Epi-Strauss-ium," "Easter-Day,"
and "Easter-Day II," were not included in the "other
little book," although they were written about this time
(1849), and, if Clough did meet the Brownings in Florence that year,[46] it is reasonable to imagine that the talk
among the three at least touched on current pressing
questions of faith and conduct.

A very good case can be made for considering Browning's *Christmas-Eve and Easter-Day* (1850) an answer to
Clough's religious position. Although not quite the simple "R. B. a poem" which Elizabeth Barrett had once
wanted him to write,[47] it is a personal statement in the
sense that the views expressed in the poem are Browning's own. *Christmas-Eve* examines the beliefs that prevailed at the time—the Oxford Movement, German rationalism, Nature, and nonconformism—by having the
speaker visit various churches. Throughout his pilgrim-

age he is guided by the vision of God, and as he leaves the Göttingen lecture-hall, the last stop on his itinerary, he falls into the "genial mood" of "tolerance" (XIX.-1138):

> Let me enjoy my own conviction,
> Not watch my neighbor's faith with fretfulness,
> Still spying there some dereliction
> Of truth, perversity, forgetfulness!
> Better a mild indifferentism,
> Teaching that both our faiths (though duller
> His shine through a dull spirit's prism)
> Originally had one color!
>
> (XIX.1144–1151)

This is probably about as far as Browning would allow his Cloughian indecision to go, for just then the Lord becomes angry. Where He may remain above making such distinctions, man as a mere finite being must choose, discriminate. In the last section, the speaker is back again among the Dissenters, and his mind is made up. Sternly rejecting Rome, with all her "buffoonery," and "posturings and petticoatings," her "bloody orgies of drunk poltroonery," he also attacks the German professor for purveying flimsy "fable" and "myth" (XXII.1324 ff.).

Easter-Day, the second part of the poem, presents a debate between a skeptic and a believer finding it nonetheless "very hard to be a Christian." The dialogue is very much like that in "The Two Voices," [48] but neither debater here is a tortured soul. The skeptic, recognizing that scientific explanation is useless, "Frustrates the very end 't was meant / To serve" (VI.125–126), satisfies himself with thought of the "mere probability" of God's existence. He tells the believer how by this calculation the skeptic can manage to achieve a modicum of "trusting ease" (XI.326). Meanwhile, the believer keeps insisting on his Christian faith and hope based on the "human heart." The rest of the poem is a monologue by the believer, who, upset by the approach of Easter, wonders if he will be saved.

Certainly this poem is other than—or less than—a dramatization of the two selves warring over commitment versus "indifferentism." The poem lacks strikingly the dramaticity which might have saved it from becoming wholly an apologia. The *Christmas-Eve* part does begin as a "realistic" account of an actual experience. The shabby chapel is described with a frankness which is very rare in the poetry of this time. Here is a young mother in the congregation:

> Prompt in the wake of her, up-pattered
> On broken clogs, the many-tattered
> Little old-faced peaking sister-turned-mother
> Of the sickly babe she tried to smother
> Somehow up, with its spotted face,
> From the cold, on her breast, the one warm place;
> She too must stop, wring the poor ends dry
> Of a draggled shawl, and add thereby
> Her tribute to the door-mat, sopping
> Already from my own clothes' dropping,
> Which yet she seemed to grudge I should stand on:
>   (II.59–69)

Browning's eye is ruthless, unfolding a convincing novelistic scene in these startlingly ugly lines. Outside the chapel, however, the realistic mode is discarded. Not that the next event—his sight of the moon rainbow and then God—is "improbable," but the "dream vision" sequence does require a different narrative style. Sudden changes in the weather have nothing to do with meteorology but follow instead the poem's conceptual structure. Throughout the imaginary tour, the narrative is completely divorced from experience and dominated by argument. Of course, a dream poem must move within a conceptual framework, and the lack of authenticity in its scenes is not in itself bad. However, because the poem glosses four types of belief—rejecting three in the dream sequence and embracing finally the one presented realistically—the effect of the stylistic variation is to weaken rather than enhance his argument. The speaker recounts the events of the dream sequence without emotional involvement, and as a result they seem all the more arbitrary. The more the poem depends on such flat assertion of its notions, the less it persuades. In fact, *Easter-Day,* even more barren of episodes than *Christmas-Eve,* is a great chore for anyone not devoted to extracting Browning's official doctrine.

Browning's failure in the poem involves more than faulty poetic strategy. As he proceeds to apologize for faith in the manner his wife had prescribed for him,[49] he feels more and more constrained to make clear to himself the direction and style of the creed he will treat in his poem. To formulate the doctrine and to argue and defend it tire him to the point where he can no longer cope with the poem as poem. Instead of radiating a "pure white light," Browning gives us his "truth broken into prismatic hues." [50] Arnold's diagnosis proves correct again: Browning uses his poems to analyze and hopefully confirm his identity, and his grotesque, at times outright ugly, rhymes, rhythms, and diction hint of his misgivings that all may not be so "right with the world"—or with the poems—all his emphatic doctrines to the contrary.

Browning wrote *Christmas-Eve and Easter-Day* after many years of experimentation with dramatic works, and with the next book, *Men and Women* (1855), he finally caught on to his true form—the dramatic monologue. In these poems, each persona he speaks through both reveals something and conceals something of his own feelings. With so many masks to put on, the poet is not personally involved with any one of them. He is released from the struggle with doubt and belief, and can concentrate on form. The monologue is thus the one great poetic contribution of Browning and the Victorians. However, despite its lack of dramaticity, *Christmas-Eve and Easter-Day* is not totally without merit. Thanks to it, Browning had no need to write an "Easter-Day II."

In Memoriam (1850) is also a poem of pilgrimage. Tennyson called it "a kind of *Divina Commedia*," [51] a quest which takes the speaker through the agonies of Inferno, the doubts of Purgatorio, to the triumphant faith of Paradiso. In the earlier sections doubt and despair almost overwhelm him in his continual struggle toward hope and control. The temporary pause in Section XI, occasioned by the deepening of a lovely autumn and brought about by repeated use of long vowels ("calm," "deep," "peace," "fall," "heart," "sleep," [52] and so on) that drowse the movement, is interrupted in Section XII with the nervous staccato of lines like "Is this the end? Is this the end?" In the next section the extended widower simile again slows the tempo. These tempo and rhythmic modulations and rapid adjustments of pitch are second nature to the poet who was known to have "the finest ear of any English poet since Milton." [53]

In the section (LVI) closing the well-known "evolutionary" passage, there is a long interrogative sentence whose subject and predicate are separated by three stanzas. These intervening qualifying clauses, contrasting man with brute "Nature, red in tooth and claw," bring his terrible contradictory thoughts to a climax. And the question "shall [man] . . . Be blown about the desert dust, / Or seal'd within the iron hills?" is ignored in the last two stanzas of the section which, being mere ejaculatory fragments ("A monster then, a dream, / A discord"), show only the hero's inability to formulate a coherent thought. This latest crescendo to despair is again subdued in the next section describing his leave-taking from his friend's grave: "Peace; come away: the song of woe / Is after all an earthly song." These stanzas are meditative, with many pauses and short but deliberate sentences, and their vocal modulations perfectly objectify the psychological struggle as they carry the "argument" of the poem. Here again, the famous stanzaic form is so elastic as to be painfully monotonous at one moment and refreshingly alive the next.

Another passage that shows the power of the poet's music to dramatize wide swings of mood is the one (LXXI) telling of his dream reunion with his friend. His awareness here that he is merely running away from grief ("bring an opiate trebly strong, / Drug down the blindfold sense of wrong") is plain from the repetitions "talk/talk'd," "walking/walk'd," "breaker/breaking," redundancies which seem to point to the fruitlessness of his attempt to bring back the past. The dream is shattered in the next section in which he marks the first anniversary of his friend's death. This time, charged with frustrated indignation at his irretrievable loss, he is all the more bitter at having to recognize the futility of dreaming:

Risest thou thus, dim dawn, again,
   And howlest, issuing out of night,
   With blast that blow the poplar white,
And lash with storm the streaming pane?

The music of this section is stark, building its anger
with accents on the words "day" and "thou" and cul-
minating in the last stanza with the pointing at "thy
vault," "thy thick noon," "thy dull goal," "thy shame,"
and the memorable alliteration of "disastrous day."

Despite this vacillation, his moods are gradually
brought together into the poem's steady ascension toward
serenity. But his conversion does not suddenly happen
through any positive act, nor through intellectual conviction. There is no clear event to mark the conversion,[54]
nor does the "I" who endlessly argues in *In Memoriam*
ever really try to reconcile science and faith. The Prologue prefacing the main body of the poem warns that
"We have but faith: we cannot know"—a proposition
which, with some slight change in emphasis, is identical with the stand taken by the speaker at the beginning
of the poem. His conversion, then, is one of mood or
emotional attitude, not of belief, and his conquest of doubt
is, strangely, so passive as to be almost involuntary. Passivity in fact is probably the main feature of his recovery
and conversion. The earlier dream, the one he had deliberately invoked, ends in disillusionment, whereas the
important later dream-vision, in which he is able to achieve
a semimystical reunion with his dead friend, is only a
suggestion of a turning point in his pilgrimage. This
contradiction in Tennyson's attitude toward the hero's
dreams is often noted,[55] but there is a difference between
the two experiences that explains the poet's seeming inconsistency. The earlier dream encounters result from

the hero's conscious effort to invoke them, whereas the vision in CIII comes to him uninvited. A conscious plan to retreat into a dream world would deny the reality of his visionary reunion, whereas a passive experience would prove the trance as truly a higher reality. What measures the degree of his conversion is his growing disinclination to escape and concomitant desire simply to surrender to time.

Here we should consider the temporal framework of *In Memoriam,* the cycle of the years with their seasons and Christmases and anniversaries. As the poem slowly unfolds, with its speaker unendingly asking the great questions of life, he gradually realizes—not intellectually, but simply by living through his despair—that he is surviving. In time, he begins to notice his changing reactions to seasonal signposts and a corresponding diminuendo in his emotional fluctuations. Time kills, but it also revives; the timeless is gained and regained in time. This simple realization more than anything else restores his confidence in life. The ceaseless flow of identical stanzas— indeed the almost painful length of the poem—is Tennyson's way of objectifying the arduousness of living out day after day a life immobilized by a consuming grief.[56]

In Memoriam is immediately and inescapably powerful. In the ringing of the wild bells that bring to a close the sustained wavelike movement of the poem over its great length, there is the joyous celebration of certainty. Its religious and philosophical assertions may no longer convince, but its poetry persuades. The dissociated sensibility does not finally matter very much. Rather, the very disunity of thought and feeling—the curse of the modern sensibility—is superbly folded into the movement of the poem with its incredibly perceptive music. The speaker's beliefs concerning art, immortality, and society may not be valid in our time, for our experience, but the way he came to them, the manner and style of his convictions, is unfailingly appealing. Doubt and despair, as expressed in *In Memoriam,* nowhere reduce the self to the febrile dialogue of yes and no, nor do they puzzle him unduly. The speaker reflects darkly, and if head and heart conflict, the two voices are subsumed in the flow of time.[57]

Tennyson once thought of calling *Maud* "Madness," and another time referred to it as "a little Hamlet." [58] The hero is a Byronic-Spasmodic figure who undergoes violent alterations of mood—disappointment, love, passion, remorse—and finally goes insane. The poem's numerous metric forms are all well adapted to these rapid changes. A first-person "monodrama," the story is narrated mainly in the present tense, a feature which gives immediacy to incidents otherwise unordered by the temporal sequence of memory. The fusion of the melodramatic plot (chock-full of such events as a family feud, a Romeo-and-Juliet love affair, a murder, an exile, a commitment to a madhouse, and the Crimean War) with lyrical outpourings is highly experimental. Tennyson seems confident after the success of *In Memoriam* and is liberal with his social commentary. He explores imagery to the fullest [59] and even tries his hand at a bit of clinical psychology. Amazing performance though it is, the beauty of its details does not jibe with the overall movement of the plot. It is true the theme of war and madness run through the entire work, making the call to arms at the end less irrelevant than it might appear on casual reading; nor is the speaker's jingoism entirely indefensible. And yet one is drawn to dazzling details and not to the *Architectonicé* of the poem or even the character of the hero. In fact, his identity as a morbid Hamlet—"At war

with myself and a wretched race, / Sick, sick to the heart
of life, am I" (I.x.ii.364–365)—is better disclosed by the
very form of the poem's fragmented lyricism than by his
characterization as a tormented and self-divided young
man. His recovery process—here Tennyson is rather less
bold—is a familiar one, with social action resolving the
warring selves.

V

Kathleen Tillotson suggests that the newness of *Jane
Eyre* (1847) as a novel is tied to its profound exploration
of the "unlit gulf of the self," [60] and for this reason is
profitably looked at next to the poetry of the time as well
as the fiction. Angria was Charlotte's dark sea, deep
and strange enough for Clough's coral worms and Arnold's sad forsaken mermen. If passion runs unbridled
there, and blood and tears flood forth as in a Gothic
nightmare, Charlotte's "day dreams," [61] as the aging laureate called them, her "world below," [62] also had much of
that trancelike quality Clough and Arnold were struggling against in their work. For Oxford scholars and cler-
gyman's daughter alike, the self was a fascinating netherworld, if one that had to be left behind in their search
for life.

Charlotte Brontë wrote *The Professor* while she was
still in the "fifteen years war" [63] against her fantasy world.
When it met rejection from so many quarters, she decided to return to Angria for her next story and use its
atmosphere as a counterpoise to the type of bare realism
of *The Professor*. *Jane Eyre* is thus born from both Gothic
nightmare and Charlotte's everyday experience, and its
subtitle "An Autobiography," while it points to Charlotte's

experiences as pupil, governess, and mistress, must say something, too, of her own fundamentally Gothic temperament.

Jane Eyre, even as a child, is a full-blown Romantic. An exile "in double retirement," sitting "cross-legged, like a Turk," [64] she could take off, in a thrice, for the exotic places and landscapes described in her favorite book. And she is a passionate girl, answering with fury each and every injustice and cruelty she encounters. Her foster-mother comes to dislike her intensely, for a nine-year-old rebel and dreamer of this sort is quite impossible to live with. The child's search for identity begins when, after a particularly severe punishment, she looks at herself in the mirror and sees there a "strange little figure" gazing back at her, "Half fairy, half imp."

At school, her best friend is a girl named Helen Burns.[65] They are rather alike—both daydream, for one thing—but Helen has a strength Jane lacks. Under her influence, Jane learns self-control, especially control of her flaring *ressentiment*. This influence is so powerful that when she dies in Jane's arms her spirit seems almost to enter into the other girl. Jane will soon be ready for her encounter with the archetypal Romantic.

Rochester is a man of passion straight out of the Gothic-Byronic tales. A wanderer in search of ideal beauty, a villain-hero with a guilty past, he is cynical and eccentric. He has many mistresses abroad yet chooses to stay for long periods in his haunted house in England. Rochester has a longing for Jane's elfin, ethereal calm, so in contrast with his own temperament, but he also finds in her a likeness to himself, a tie more of substance than of love even: "I sometimes have a queer feeling with regard to you," he confides, "it is as if I had a string somewhere under my left ribs, tightly and inextricably knotted to a similar string situated in the corresponding quarter of your little frame" (II,16). The marriage of two so similar souls would be disastrous. In their common indifference to civilization, they would sink to the depths of passion. Their union must therefore be broken:

> It was not without a certain wild pleasure I ran before the wind delivering my trouble of mind to the measureless air-torrent thundering through space. Descending the laurel walk, I faced the wreck of the chestnut-tree; it stood up, black and riven: the trunk, split down the center, gaped ghastly. The cloven halves were not broken from each other, for the firm base and strong roots kept them unsundered below; though community of vitality was destroyed—the sap could flow no more; their great boughs on each side were dead, and next winter's tempests would be sure to fell one or both to earth: as yet, however, they might be said to form one tree—a ruin; but an entire ruin.
>
> (II,47–48)

With the implied castration [66] and the lovers' separation, there is still a warning from this shattered tree against the terrible division of the self into those extremes of reason and passion that spell ruin. In Rochester, whose feeling overwhelms reason, the loss of his vision and one limb demands a radical reconstitution of his character in which passion will be sharply abated. In Jane, it is reason which, having saved her from passion, now becomes the "tyrant" (II,76). "We are born to strive and endure," she tells Rochester, and indeed, after leaving Thornfield Hall, she strives and barely manages to endure hunger, exhaustion, and illness. At this low point, she meets her nemesis in St. John Rivers.

Where Rochester is Gothic, St. John is "classic" (II, 139); where he is fire, St. John is "ice" (II,211); and where Rochester is all passion, St. John is reason itself. But just as there is that substantial likeness between Rochester and Jane, between St. John and Jane too there is a tie: "She [Rosamond Oliver] said I was like Mr. Rivers" (II,171). Rochester loves Jane for her elfin quality, while St. John admires her fine "affections and sympathies" (II,154), wanting her as his comrade in the total service of God. This zealot has made a compact with the Absolute and gives no quarter.[67] Because he so desperately fears ordinary warmth and the fleshliness of everyday domestic life, his mission must be carried out some place far away from the familiar and repugnant world he knows. Conscience, morality, duty, and God's work—Jane spoke these words to the agonized Rochester just a short while before. Now it is Jane who is begging for gentleness, for some tolerance of human feelings: "Oh, St. John," she cries, "have some mercy!" (II,216). Yet she almost agrees to his demand for a loveless marriage: "I believe I must say, Yes—and yet I shudder," a situation which reverses, as in a mirror, the earlier one in which Jane said in effect "I must say, No—and yet I shudder." The shudder of horror and the shudder of passion have a strange affinity. The circle is complete: Jane, by this annihilating yes, is suddenly rekindled with feeling, and knows directly what she must do. Rochester meanwhile has accepted defeat ("I am no better than the old lightning-struck chestnut-tree in Thornfield orchard"). With this acceptance he can restore his vision, regain the lost garden. Passion and reason are reconciled in both, and together they come to accept the here and now of ordinary domesticity. *Jane Eyre* thus represents Charlotte's reapportionment of passion and reason in the make-up of the self, her descent from Latmos [68] to Victorian reality.

"The first duty of an author is . . . a faithful allegiance to Truth and Nature; his second, such a conscientious study of Art as shall enable him to interpret eloquently and effectively the oracles delivered by those two great deities." [69] This is as good a statement as any of Charlotte's aesthetics, but it falls short of her artistic practice. It has been said that *Jane Eyre* shares in the absurdity of *The Castle of Otranto.*[70] It certainly revives several Gothic character types—Rochester, Bertha Mason, and St. John Rivers. And of course the reason-passion dualism at the core of the work is Gothic. Then there are the familiar mechanisms—the ghost-haunted mansion, the thunder in the night, the supernatural interventions and mysterious voices.[71] By the rules of the probable ("Nature," we remember, is one of Charlotte's two great "deities"), many of the happenings and circumstances are simply preposterous. Despite her ponderous manifesto, it is her "Art" that redeems the work from its failure in what she regarded as her primary business in writing. First, the structure of *Jane Eyre.* Once compared to that of *Moll Flanders,* it is, if "nearly artless," [72] at least coherent. There are the five distinct locales, which suggest the five acts of a play, and more important there is the theme of Jane's self-discovery, which is a carefully wrought process indeed—from the domination first by passion, then by reason, all the way to a comfortable balance of the two. Hardly at any point is the line of argument lost, even where credulousness is strained. Far from being, as *Moll Flanders* often is, a haphazard recording of unordered episodes, it employs its incredible events to expedite the plot. As in many other Victorian novels, *Jane Eyre* vigorously asserts the author's moral vision. This asserted "Truth," anticipating Arnold's dichotomy of Hebraism and Hellenism, and Hardy's gloomier version in *Tess* later on, is of some historical interest. But, above all, it is the novel's quick pace and intense tone that hold the work together.

Second, the Gothic terror deepens the psychological insight. Often absurd in themselves, the tricks and paraphernalia nonetheless are good instruments for exploring the depths. The famed tree episode which tells so much is undoubtedly Gothic in inspiration, as is Rochester's "repression" of his libido in the person of Bertha Mason in the attic of the house.[73] This introduction of the Gothic into an everyday setting can become theatrical—an effect George Henry Lewes says "smack[s] of the circulating-library"; [74] Rochester's disguise as a gypsy fortune teller is an instance of this. And yet *Jane Eyre's* contribution to the English novel is precisely this element now dignified by such terms as "symbolism." This is what is meant by the "poetic" nature of this remarkable novel.

Wuthering Heights (1847) carries the Brontëan self-division of reason and feeling to an uncompromising extreme. In civilization's battle with Nature, it is the great vitality of Heathcliff and Cathy that keep the elemental forces alive in man against repressive attempts to name, define, and order that energy. To put it another way, in these two the Romantic aspiration clashes violently with Victorian control. In ordinary human terms, Heathcliff and Cathy are in love, but what to call this "love" eludes us. It is not specifically sexual (there is no evidence, for instance, of adultery), not even particularly sensual (Heathcliff is very much a Lawrencian hero; he detests Isabella's clinging desire), not by any means purely spiritual (they seem to require physical proximity), and, of course, it lacks the ethical-social basis of most human relationships. Yet the two insist on their oneness, their consubstantiality: "I *am* Heathcliff," [75] Cathy says, and for Heathcliff she is his "life" (191), his "soul" (192). They are independent, self-sufficient, and in that sufficiency irrelevant even to God. Together, they live in their own heaven; separate, in hell. This union is even more intense than that Shelley conceived for his psyche and epipsyche, for Heathcliff and Cathy are identical in being. Their union is not even one of two distinct personalities but more like two embodiments of the same element, an incest of river and ocean, of angry gale and raging tempest. It is only in such elemental terms that their relationship can be expressed.

Any discussion of *Wuthering Heights* that begins with the novelistic perspective must conclude with the symbolic, if only because the characters, convincingly "realistic" at the outset are soon inexplicable in terms of the ordinary. Heathcliff and Cathy are mythical figures, corresponding in their union to the oneness of what *is,* a oneness which remains single, undifferentiated until human consciousness begins to order and divide it in the name of civilized values and institutions.

With Cathy's move to Thrushcross Grange, the indefinable first confronts the defined. Cathy is attracted to the handsome Edgar Linton and through him to the charms of order and civilization. The girl who roamed the heather day and night must now be combed and groomed. She will give at least part of herself to the social and economic union which is marriage. However, her engagement to Edgar is an act of self-contradiction, self-betrayal: She abandons the heath and the storm— the stuff of herself, which is her common nature with

Heathcliff. The indefinable will be defined, the unnamable will be named. In his desire to be with Cathy and her new friends, Heathcliff, too, briefly makes peace with civilization. "Nelly," he cries, "make me decent. I'm going to be good" (63). But he is unable to cross the threshold: The ordered world of Thrushcross Grange treats him as an undesirable alien.

Cathy's relative happiness is immediately destroyed when Heathcliff returns. With his violent thrust into her delicately equilibrated life she is forced to recognize that next to this energy Edgar's order—call it "decency," or "duty," or even "humanity"—diminishes, as Heathcliff boasts, into something "paltry" and "insipid." Her existence, meanwhile, created out of fusion with this self-same Heathcliff, is torn in two, one part enmeshed in the legitimate order of family and institutions, the other in the Heathcliff that is herself. She cannot choose either to abandon Edgar or deny herself. In this self-destruction she herself has invited, her life ebbs.

Cathy's compromise affects Heathcliff with a total loss of identity, for, once alienated from her, his wholeness is destroyed. Even after his return to Wuthering Heights, his knowledge that their break is irreparable makes joy impossible. Nothing is left to him but an insatiable craving for the lost Eden that was his life with Cathy, and his dark wish to have his revenge on Earnshaw. His will to reunite with her survives her death, the line between life and death being significant only to ordinary men who are creatures of time and consciousness. He will not stay alone, and goes out to excavate her coffin; and she, ghostlike, comes to haunt him. Only by these pseudo-reunions can Heathcliff live out his long leftover life.

But throughout all this, Heathcliff's own elemental

powers are undiminished. He almost succeeds in dehuman-
izing the young Cathy and Hareton, when suddenly civilization reasserts itself in them. The young people want
to improve themselves, be decent. Smiles and flowers
return to Wuthering Heights, which is a garden now
hedged against the wildness outside.[76] Heathcliff could
still annihilate them, the offspring of his enemies, he could
still revenge Nature on humanity by pulling down the
roofs of Thrushcross Grange and Wuthering Heights: "I
could do it; and none could hinder me" (369), but his
will has finally vanished; no longer troubled by Cathy
and Hareton and their reviving loyalty to order and
civilization, Heathcliff wants only his wholeness again:

> I have a single wish, and my whole being, and faculties
> are yearning to attain it. They have yearned towards
> it so long, and so unwaveringly, that I'm convinced it
> *will* be reached—and *soon*—because it has devoured my
> existence—I am swallowed in the anticipation of its
> fulfillment. . . . O, God! It is a long fight, I wish it
> were over!
>
> (371)

Nature, in the person of Heathcliff, leaves Wuthering
Heights and takes his partial life to join his Cathy.

While the mythical events of the novel celebrate
Nature in all its fury and grandeur, the scene of domestic
happiness closing the story honors the civilized control
of energy. Yet, even as the novel laments the violence
with which the sublime force of fusion threatens order,
it mourns the meagerness of the garden whose imitation
of the grandness of Nature attains only parody. Heathcliff's and Cathy's childhood world, where the union of
"I" and otherness had not yet been broken, must be set

aside for the world of human values and institutions. The unity known to the hero and heroine of *Wuthering Heights* is inconceivable within society as we have developed it—Civilization is irreconcilable with Eros.

This basic ambivalence structures the work into an uncompromising document of modern man's ultimate reality. Without moral prescription, *Wuthering Heights* succeeds in defining and evaluating the very basis of definition and evaluation, the craftsman of this remarkable metadefinition exploiting all the techniques then available to her in the English novel. The person of Heathcliff, the ghost, the dreams,[77] the incest,[78] and the necrophilia—all are culled from conventions of the Gothic underground. But this very meticulous genius chooses her materials carefully. Like her sister, she borrows imagery and symbolism from poetry. Books are continually being mentioned, suggesting the forces of civilization,[79] the metaphors of weather, landscape, and animals standing for the opposing energy of Nature.[80] And the many doors, windows, thresholds, and gates are barriers frustrating free concourse between these two realms.[81]

The outstanding technical accomplishment of *Wuthering Heights* is, of course, the double narrative. All the mythical experiences of Heathcliff and Cathy are witnessed by Nelly Dean, the housekeeper who persists in the commonsense moral view,[82] and she tells their story to Lockwood, a bored but sentimental Londoner. This mechanism not only obviates the need of authorial comments, thereby enhancing the credibility of the story, but also allows for a very subtle manipulation of time. The chronology of events in *Wuthering Heights* is constructed quite unobtrusively by interlocking references to dates and durations of key events.[83] There is also a double temporal frame, however, consisting of straight chronological time and mythical time. Ordinary time begins with Lockwood's first visit to Wuthering Heights and ends with his last visit there, a period of less than a year, November 1801 to September 1802. Mythical time, covering the demonic events of the Heathcliff-Cathy generation, which extend over a decade, is reduced, by Nelly's narrative, to a mere evening of Lockwood time. Then, in Chapter XXXI, over a period of about a month, Lockwood time catches up with Heathcliff-Cathy time. At this point, all his stories up to date, Lockwood pays a third visit to Wuthering Heights. His fancied romance with the young Cathy implies a contrast between the transcendental Heathcliff-Cathy medium and Lockwood's foreshortened time that shrinks events to the scale of hours and weeks. Clocks and calendars measure out Lockwood's life, while the great lovers soar into the primeval timelessness of their myth. Nelly's last installment, which she tells one evening in September when Lockwood suddenly returns, covers the months since January. Heathcliff's time, too, has been forcibly "shortened" by then to days and weeks, a reasonable change since the emphasis of the story gradually shifts here from the dying Heathcliff to the romance of Hareton and young Cathy, who share with Lockwood the same order of time and civilization. With Heathcliff's death and the promise of the young couple's marriage, the two time-schemes are joined. At the end of the story, myth is swallowed up in time. Dramatically, Lockwood's comings and goings are hardly significant; from the formal point of view, however, his casual movements do add measurably to the substance of the book.

The double narrative has the effect of a hall of mirrors, reflecting and re-reflecting the characters in such a complex scheme that the novel defies summary. Cathy herself tells Nelly about her feelings for Heathcliff, and

Nelly in turn tells Lockwood, who then writes it down. This process is even more difficult than it might seem because the reliability of all these speakers must be tested from many points of view. The book is thus for the reader, too, a vigorous experience in self-definition. To listen to the voices of *Wuthering Heights* is to overhear the unspoken there in the middle of the hurricane, to catch wind of that silence of chaos.

Notes

1. "Mr. Clough's Poems," *Literary Studies* (London, 1911), II, p. 278.
2. Introduction to the *Sermons*, IV (1841), p. lxv, quoted by Basil Willey, *Nineteenth Century Studies: Coleridge to Matthew Arnold* (London, 1955), pp. 62–63. My debt to his *Nineteenth Century Studies* and *More Nineteenth Century Studies* is far greater than this paragraph might show.
3. Willey, p. 90.
4. With a slightly different emphasis, Newman's theology becomes subjectivism. In fact, French "Modernism," condemned by the Pope early in this century, seriously abused this aspect of Newman. See Charles Frederick Harrold, *John Henry Newman: An Expository and Critical Study of His Mind, Thought, and Art* (London, 1945), pp. 357–369.
5. E. E. Hale, *J. R. Lowell and His Friends*, p. 136. Quoted in Katharine Chorley, *Arthur Hugh Clough: The Uncommitted Mind* (London, 1962), p. 132.
6. Clough wrote to his sister in 1847, "The Evangelicals gabble it, as the Papists do their Ave Mary's—and yet say they know; while Newman falls down and worships *because* he does not know and knows he does not know.

    "I think others are more right, who say boldly, We don't understand it, and therefore we *won't* fall down and worship it. Though there is no occasion for adding—'there *is* nothing in it—' I should say, Until I know, I will wait. . . ." *The Correspondence of Arthur Hugh Clough*, ed. Frederick L. Mulhauser (London, 1957), I, p. 182.
7. *The Poems of Arthur Hugh Clough*, eds. H. F. Lowry, A. L. P.

Norrington, and F. L. Mulhauser (London, 1951). My references are to this edition throughout.

8. Chorley, p. 92; see also p. 175 and p. 242.

9. See Walter E. Houghton, *The Poetry of Clough: An Essay in Revaluation* (New Haven and London, 1963), p. 81.

10. Clough must have read Browning by then, for in a letter dated December 15, 1847, he referred to *Bells and Pomegranates* as the model for his poems. *Correspondence*, I, p. 190.

11. In his article, "The Satiric Poetry of Arthur Hugh Clough," *VP*, I (1963), pp. 104–114, Michael Timko treats this poem as purely dramatic and warns against identification of the king with Clough. But this point can be overemphasized. The characters in Clough's poems are hardly ever impersonal, purely dramatic personae. Rather they stand out as ironically deformed *self*-portraits. In short, the "distinguishing element" between Clough's voice and his characters' is the falsetto he adopts for himself when he speaks through his characters, and it is this style of self-mockery which suggests what Timko calls Clough's "moral realism."

12. For a good contemporary discussion of this point, see Henry Sidgwick, "The Poems and Prose Remains of Arthur Hugh Clough," *Westminster Review*, October 1869, reprinted in *Miscellaneous Essays and Addresses* (London, 1904), especially p. 76. Clough himself explains as follows: "Why is it Palinurus and Somnus, Faust and Mephistopheles even are not quite expressive to us, we want to be told that they mean contradictory elements of our own unity" (Balliol MSS, quoted by Chorley, p. 251).

13. The devil's heyday is over with the end of the Romantic period. No longer a sublime fallen angel, the devil for the Victorians is either a rogue (Thackeray's early stories in the *Paris Sketch Book*) or an out-and-out moralist (Tennyson's devil in *The Devil and the Lady*).

14. See Houghton's chapter on *Dipsychus*, pp. 156–207, especially the subsection on the Spirit, pp. 163–172.

15. Clough may have taken a hint from his Spirit. In his 1851 lecture on Wordsworth he repeated his attack on the poet—granted, in a soberer style. See *Prose Remains of Arthur Hugh Clough*, ed. his wife (London and New York, 1888), p. 315.

16. "East Coker," III, *Four Quartets* (London, 1941), p. 19.

17. Along the line suggested in another article by Michael Timko, "The 'True Creed' of Arthur Hugh Clough," *MLQ*, XXI (1960), pp. 208–222, Clyde de L. Ryals argues in his "An Interpretation of Clough's Dipsychus," *VP*, I (1963), pp. 182–188, that *Dipsychus* is Clough's *Sartor Resartus*, and its hero, his Teufelsdröckh. I

would agree with him that the "acceptance" of the here and now is certainly the final event of the poem. Yet the manner in which the hero makes his submission is hardly in the spirit of an "Everlasting Yea": Even after welcoming the world, he continues to question his decision and evade the compact. Further, it is hard to imagine why Clough would have devoted practically the whole poem to caricaturing the spiritually enfeebled man (leaving only a portion of the last scene to his positive action) if it were his *Sartor Resartus.* (After all, Herr Teufelsdröckh's conversion occurs in the middle of the book.)

18. Lytton Strachey may be a treacherous guide to the Victorians, but the notorious inaccuracies are more than compensated by his wit. See his caricature of Clough's latter days in the chapter on Florence Nightingale, *Eminent Victorians* (New York, 1918), pp. 169–170.

19. *Miscellaneous Essays and Addresses,* p. 60. Sidgwick elsewhere gives a different version of the situation. In reference to *In Memoriam,* he wrote Tennyson's son: "To begin, then: our views on religious matters were not, at any rate after a year or two of the discussion started in 1860 by *Essays and Reviews,* really in harmony with those which we found suggested by 'In Memoriam.' They were more sceptical and less Christian, in any strict sense of the word: certainly this was the case with myself: I remember feeling that Clough *represented* my individual habits of thought and sentiment more than your father. . . ." Quoted by Hallam Tennyson in *Memoir,* I, p. 301.

20. See Clough's letter to Burbidge in 1844, for instance. *Correspondence,* I, p. 131.

21. Clough's letter to J. C. Shairp, *Correspondence,* I, p. 178.

22. *The Poetical Works of Matthew Arnold,* eds. C. B. Tinker and H. F. Lowry (London, 1950). This edition is used throughout.

23. *The Letters of Matthew Arnold to Arthur Hugh Clough* (hereafter called *Letters to Clough*), p. 63.

24. The 1853 Preface, *Poetical Works,* p. xviii.

25. See his letter of July 20 [1848], *Letters to Clough,* p. 86.

26. Ironically, it is Arnold who told Clough in March of the same year to "look at Alexander Smith's poems" and let him know what he thought of them. *Letters to Clough,* p. 133.

27. *Selected Prose Works of Arthur Hugh Clough,* ed. Buckner B. Trawick (Alabama, 1964), p. 144.

28. For this reason, it is fruitless to read the Preface as a gloss on Aristotelean poetics. Arnold's departures from *Ars Poetica* are quite obvious: The Preface is prescriptive, Aristotle's poetics is inductive; Aristotle recognizes genre differences, Arnold ignores

them. For Aristotle, unlike Arnold, action is not limited to the external sort but may be of the inward psychic type. (For a discussion of this point, see S. H. Butcher's *Aristotle's Theory of Poetry and Fine Art,* 4th ed. [New York, 1951], p. 334.) As to my reading of the Preface as more a personal statement than a purely literary one, this grew out of one of several talks I had on Arnold with my friend Paul Marx, and I want to acknowledge my debt to his vigorous argument. For a good general discussion of the Preface, see Sidney M. B. Coulling's article, "Matthew Arnold's 1853 Preface: Its Origin and Aftermath," *VS,* VII (1964), pp. 233–263.

29. *Sohrab and Rustum,* almost certainly intended as the exemplar of the Preface, hardly fulfills its specifications: The action is pathetic rather than tragic, and the poem lives in its beautiful long similes, too obtrusive to be "mere accessories."

30. Dated November 26, 1853, *Letters of Matthew Arnold: 1848–1888,* ed. George W. E. Russell, I (New York, 1895), p. 36.

31. *Unpublished Letters of Matthew Arnold,* ed. Arnold Whitridge (New Haven, 1923), p. 18.

32. "Quiet Work" was the first poem in both the 1849 and the 1853 volumes. In 1869 Arnold wrote to Palgrave, "'One lesson' I have banished from its pre-eminence as an introductory piece," quoted in Kenneth Allott's recent edition of Arnold's poems (London, 1965), p. 106. The two poems were never intended to form a pair.

33. There are three book-length studies of Arnold and the Romantics: D. G. James, *Matthew Arnold and the Decline of English Romanticism* (London, 1961); William A. Jamison, *Arnold and the Romantics* (Copenhagen, 1958); and Leon Gottfried, *Matthew Arnold and the Romantics* (Lincoln, Nebr., 1963). As for Arnold and Wordsworth, there is an incisive article by U. C. Knoepflmacher, "Dover Revisited: The Wordsworthian Matrix in the Poetry of Matthew Arnold," *VP,* I (1963), pp. 17–26.

34. This view is advanced by Leon Gottfried in his *Matthew Arnold and the Romantics.* See pages 122–127.

35. A. Dwight Culler, *Imaginative Reason: The Poetry of Matthew Arnold* (New Haven and London, 1966), p. 74.

36. In his "Philomela: A Major Theme in Arnold's Poetry," *VNL,* 12 (Autumn, 1957), pp. 1–6, Robert A. Donovan points out that writing poetry was a painful experience for Arnold.

37. Despite Arnold's generally low estimate of Keats (see, for instance, *Letters to Clough,* p. 97), the concept of "negative capability," involving an assumption of otherness, should have met Arnold's approval. See Trilling's discussion of "The Strayed Reveller" in his *Matthew Arnold* (New York, 1955), pp. 91–93.

38. There is a very good treatment of "Tristram and Iseult" in W. Stacy Johnson, *The Voices of Matthew Arnold: An Essay in Criticism* (New Haven and London, 1961).

39. Douglas Bush makes this point in his *Mythology and the Romantic Tradition*, pp. 254–255, and *Science and English Poetry: A Historical Sketch, 1590–1950* (New York, 1950), p. 128.

40. J. C. Shairp wrote Clough in May 1853, "The terrible want of fresh heart soils Mat. to my taste. I can't read much of his last book without pain. That 'blank dejection of European Capitols' which you speak of weighs him down. There's not one skylark tone in them." *Clough Correspondence*, II, p. 437.

41. Arnold made a similar remark to his mother in a letter written in December 1854, "I have also lately had a stronger wish than usual not to vacillate and be hopeless, but to do my duty, whatever that may be; and out of that wish one may always hope to make something." *Letters*, I, p. 48. In another letter written to his sister in April 1856, he said, "To make a habitual war on depression and low spirits, which in one's early youth one is apt to indulge and be somewhat interested in, is one of the things one learns as one gets older. They are noxious alike to body and mind, and already partake of the nature of death." *Letters*, I, p. 60.

42. *The Alien Vision*, p. 179. See also Tinker and Lowry's explanation of this in *The Poetry of Matthew Arnold: A Commentary* (London, 1940), p. 273.

43. Arnold's self-preoccupation never leaves him, but it becomes more impersonal. In "Maurice de Guérin" (1863), he quotes a passage from Guérin that treats the dialogue of the mind with itself: " 'Do you know what it is,' M. Féli said to us on the evening of the day before yesterday, 'which makes man the most suffering of all creatures? It is that he has one foot in the finite and the other in the infinite, and that he is torn asunder, not by four horses, as in the horrible old times, but between two worlds.' " *The Complete Prose Works*, ed. R. H. Super, III, *Lectures and Essays in Criticism* (Ann Arbor, 1962), p. 23.

44. Mr. Fraser Neiman's able study, "The Zeitgeist of Matthew Arnold," *PMLA*, LXXII (1957), pp. 977–996, points out Arnold's two different attitudes toward the *Zeitgeist*. "In the letters to Clough," he writes, "the *Zeitgeist* expresses for Arnold a force to be abhorred, local, negative," while a decade later he had come to see in it a "cosmic spiritual power that wills the development of human reason and that reveals development in the sequence of historic time" (p. 982).

45. *The Letters of Elizabeth Barrett Browning*, ed. Frederick G. Kenyon (London, 1898), I, p. 429.

46. DeVane considers the meeting of the three quite possible and suggests Clough's talk "may have been the final touch which put Browning's poem in motion," *Browning Handbook*, p. 197.

47. Elizabeth Barrett repeatedly asked Browning to write a straightforward (nondramatic) religious poem. See her letters of January 15, 1845, and May 26, 1846; also, DeVane's *Handbook*, pp. 196–197.

48. See DeVane, *Browning Handbook*, p. 203.

49. The nucleus of *Christmas-Eve* is in Elizabeth Barrett's letter to Browning, dated August 15, 1846, a discovery made by F. R. G. Duckworth. See the last chapter of his *Browning: Background and Conflict* (London, 1931), pp. 187–189.

50. Browning's own words, *The Letters of Robert Browning and Elizabeth Barrett Browning*, I, p. 6. See also Duckworth's last chapter.

51. Hallam Tennyson, I, p. 304.

52. References are made to the Eversley Edition in this and in the following chapters.

53. T. S. Eliot, "In Memoriam," reprinted in Killham's selection of critical essays on Tennyson, p. 207.

54. Carlisle Moore, well-versed in Victorian conversion, makes this point in his "Faith, Doubt, and Mystical Experience in 'In Memoriam,'" *VS*, VII (1963), pp. 155–169.

55. The most comprehensive treatment of Tennyson and the motifs of dream, vision, and trance in his work is in E. D. H. Johnson's *The Alien Vision*. Incidentally, Johnson's article, "'In Memoriam': The Way of the Poet," *VS*, II (1958), pp. 139–148, argues that the poem is a record of the Tennysonian search for true poetry.

56. In his brilliant essay on *In Memoriam*, J. C. C. Mays discusses the complex relationship between Tennyson's belief and his art. See "'In Memoriam': An Aspect of Form," *UTQ*, XXXV (1965), pp. 22–46.

57. Tennyson's description of the relationship between the speaker and his friend—he speaks in terms of the divided self (LXXXV), the Brocken Spectre (XCVII), and marriage—is somewhat reminiscent of that of the poet and his Ideal Beauty in Shelley's poetry.

58. Hallam Tennyson, I, p. 396. For the poem's autobiographical references, see Ralph Wilson Rader's *Tennyson's Maud: The Biographical Genesis* (Berkeley and Los Angeles, 1963).

59. For an analysis of the flower imagery in *Maud*, see E. D. H. Johnson's article, "The Lily and the Rose: Symbolic Meaning in Tennyson's *Maud*," *PMLA*, LXIV (1949), pp. 1222–1227. Also

John Killham's essay, "Tennyson's *Maud*—the Function of the Imagery," in his *Critical Essays,* pp. 219–235.

60. *Novels of the Eighteen-Forties* (London, 1961), p. 261.

61. *The Shakespeare Head Brontë,* eds. Thomas James Wise and John Alexander Symington, *The Brontës: Their Lives, Friendships and Correspondence* (Oxford, 1932), I, p. 155.

62. *Lives, Friendships and Correspondence,* I, p. 297.

63. Fannie Elizabeth Ratchford's term. See *The Brontës' Web of Childhood* (New York, 1941), p. 106.

64. *The Shakespeare Head Brontë,* IV and V, *Jane Eyre: An Autobiography by Currer Bell* (Oxford, 1931), I, p. 2. This edition is used throughout this discussion.

65. The name "Helen Burns," as an oxymoron of Classicism and Romanticism, suggests the sort of compromise Jane must make later on. Similarly, the name of her other friend, "Miss Temple," is not arbitrarily chosen.

66. See Richard Chase, "The Brontës, or, Myth Domesticated," *Forms of Modern Fiction,* ed. William Van O'Connor (Bloomington, 1959), pp. 102–119.

67. St. John Rivers' evangelical zeal and suppressed sexuality can be thought of in terms of the priest-villain tradition of the Gothic romance. But he is perhaps more accurately seen in the light of Arnold's Hebraic acridity. Of interest here, too, is the split between his "classical" features and the (Romantic) literary ambition he had entertained before becoming a missionary.

68. Looking at Jane's pictures, Rochester comments, "There is a high gale in that sky, and on this hill-top. Where did you see Latmos? For that is Latmos" (I, p. 161).

69. *Lives, Friendships and Correspondence,* II, p. 243.

70. Walter Allen, *The English Novel,* p. 217.

71. For discussion of the Gothic elements in *Jane Eyre,* see Robert B. Heilman, "Charlotte Brontë's 'New' Gothic," reprinted in *Victorian Literature: Modern Essays in Criticism,* ed. Austin Wright (New York, 1961), pp. 71–85.

72. Mark Schorer's Introduction to *Jane Eyre* (Boston, 1959), p. xi.

73. Robert Bernard Martin points out the likeness between the man and his house in his recent book, *The Accents of Persuasion: Charlotte Brontë's Novels* (London, 1966), pp. 74–76.

74. "Recent Novels French and English," *Fraser's Magazine* (December 1847), p. 692.

75. *The Shakespeare Head Brontë,* XI, *Wuthering Heights: A Novel by Ellis Bell* (Oxford, 1931), p. 93.

76. Civilization's resurgence at Wuthering Heights begins with Lockwood's first visit. It is ironic that, after twenty years of relative

quiet in the house, this shallow fellow could call forth Cathy's ghost and start thereby a chain of events which results in the young couple's marriage.

77. Lockwood's dream-life has been subject to many analyses, the best of which is J. Hillis Miller's in the chapter on the novel in his *The Disappearance of God* (Cambridge, Mass., 1963). See also Edgar F. Shannon, Jr., "Lockwood's Dreams and the Exegesis of Wuthering Heights," *NCF,* XIV (1959), pp. 95–109.

78. Eric Solomon overstates the case by insisting that Heathcliff is Earnshaw's illegitimate child. See his "The Incest Theme in Wuthering Heights," *NCF,* XIV (1959), pp. 80–83.

79. See Robert C. McKibben, "The Image of the Book in *Wuthering Heights,*" *NCF,* XV (1960), pp. 159–169.

80. See Mark Schorer, "Fiction and the 'Analogical Matrix,'" *Kenyon Review,* XI (1949), pp. 539–560.

81. See Dorothy Van Ghent, "On *Wuthering Heights,*" *The English Novel: Form and Fiction* (New York, 1953), pp. 153–170.

82. The complexity of *Wuthering Heights* is such that one would pause before writing a good "character" for Nelly Dean. See James Hafley's "The Villain in *Wuthering Heights,*" *NCF,* XIII (1958), pp. 199–215.

83. By now a classic, Charles Percy Sanger's "The Structure of *Wuthering Heights*" (London, 1926) is the first to note the tight structure of the novel.

Look down, look down!
You see what lies at the bottom there?
Edwin Drood

5.

Broken Music:
1870

I

Whether "Art is a Crime or only an Absurdity," whether "Clergymen ought to be multiplied or exterminated by arsenic, like rats" [1]—such are the dark thoughts of John Ruskin in 1859, the same man who only a few years earlier had written that magnificent chapter on the Gothic in *The Stones of Venice*. There is also a passage in the manuscript of *The Two Paths* (1859) where he sees art as a blind irresistible urge: "It is not, observe, a feeling to be described in any exalted terms; it is a sort of hunger, an instinct more like that of the young of a wild beast for its prey, than anything else." More, it has, he says, "hardly anything to do with conscientious or religious feeling." The published version suppresses the whole passage: Preferring Gothic (Christian) style to Greek (pagan), Ruskin stubbornly argues his moral concept of art and life. But while Ruskin thus managed to control his "unreasonable, unaccountable, insatiable fury," there were others who could not or did not wish to. Moral commitment on the part of the artist was becoming more and more difficult for some and simply unattractive for others.

The year 1859 brought forth many books reflecting the impact of heretical forces which had been gathering for decades [2]: FitzGerald's *The Rubáiyát of Omar Khayyám,* George Eliot's *Adam Bede,* Meredith's *The Ordeal of Richard Feverel,* the first installment of Tennyson's *Idylls of the King,* Mill's *On Liberty,* and, of course, Darwin's *The Origin of Species.* In this year that saw the death of Macaulay, Hunt, and DeQuincey,[3] younger voices like Ruskin's grew more articulate and at times clamorous. There was still the puzzlement and confusion of the earlier Victorians, but the Empedocles of 1859 was not necessarily driven to the brink of the crater by them. With his volume of verse and jug of wine, the wilderness was transformed into paradise for him.

In another, if much more modest, work published that year there is a remarkable treatment of self-division. George Eliot's "The Lifted Veil" is in many ways a strange story. It was written about the same time as *Adam Bede,* but it has none of the provincial realism of either that work or her earlier *Scenes of Clerical Life.* In fact, quite the contrary: The tale is very Gothic in inspiration.

Latimer, the narrator of the story, recalls that he was a sensitive boy fond of poetry, but he was educated in a rigid "system" rather like the "ordeal" imposed on Richard Feverel. Sent to Switzerland at sixteen for further study, he developed there what he calls the "poet's sensibility without his voice," [4] the temper of a lonely Romantic seeking his soul in the mountains. Following an illness, he is visited by a very clear vision of Prague, a city he has never even seen. If this is to be taken as a poetic vision, it is certainly a dismal one, bearing no sign of beauty or life in it. He has several more of these deathly "previsions" and begins to see into other minds as well. This double consciousness makes contact with others intensely painful for him, revealing as it does all kinds of sordidness under their polished social surface.

When Latimer falls in love with his brother's fiancée, he has another prevision, this time of his own married life. Everyone appears to him now in a double image: the one he sees with his ordinary vision, the other with his extraordinary insight and foresight—"flowing on like two parallel streams which never mingle their waters and blend into a common hue" (307). His foresight is first verified by a visit to Prague, where he finds that the scenes of the city exactly correspond with the vision he has had. However, such verification of his foreknowledge is no deterrent to his marrying Bertha, just as predicted. As in the devil compact, desire is stronger than fear. Heretofore, Bertha has been the only one able to resist his insight, but suddenly one evening the clearest vision comes to him of the "narrow room of this woman's soul." The thought that he can read her thoughts makes him a horror to her, and with the help of a maid she plots his death. At that point, for some reason, his insight into other minds begins to weaken, and in their place he has more and more frequent visions of the future. He cuts himself off from other people, and lives for a long period solely in his "solitary future."

During a visit by his old friend, who is now a famous physician, Bertha's accomplice falls ill and dies. The doctor is able to revive her momentarily, and before she expires again she tells them of the plot to poison Latimer.

The couple separate, and he spends his remaining years wandering, aching for human companionship but always frightened off by the realities his insight discloses. When his time comes, the scene he has foreglimpsed time and again is fulfilled down to the smallest detail. He is writing the last of his story when he dies.

Latimer's double consciousness is attuned to ordinary phenomena on the one hand and very sharply to inner reality on the other. He can see how his apparently successful extroverted brother is also a dull brute, and the lovely Bertha a Borgia at heart. However, Latimer gets no advantage from this "gift" of insight and is entirely at its mercy. When his wife puts her murder scheme into operation, he inexplicably loses his power and almost falls her victim, the poet or seer being, by this reading, completely at a loss in practical life. Something more is asserted here, however, than the mere uselessness of the Romantic vision. Certainly, the notion that perception of inner reality leads to loneliness and exile is a familiar Romantic theme, but this perceived inner reality had also provided a gateway to salvation. And there is nothing transcendental about Latimer's extraordinary vision, which enables him to see only the sordid "narrow room" of the heart. His story thus concerns not primarily the duplicity of appearance and reality and man's inability to reconcile the two, although that is undoubtedly an important motif, but the monochromatic "darkness," the burden and the curse of bare reality.

If insight brings only despair, the "prevision" will likewise provide "no short cut, no patent tram-road, to wisdom" (306). George Eliot, well-confirmed in her anti-Idealism at this time, rejects Christian teleology outright, yet in denying the redemption of time through the timeless she seems to be denying as well any secular optimism about escaping the tyranny of time through greater knowledge and control of the future. "So absolute is our soul's need of something hidden and uncertain for the maintenance of that doubt and hope and effort which are the breath of its life, that if the whole future were laid bare to us beyond to-day, the interest of all mankind would be bent on the hours that lie between" (318). What she discards as theology or metaphysics must be preserved in everyday morality, which is validated in experience; or, as Latimer says, "We learn *words* by rote, but not their meaning; *that* must be paid for with our life-blood, and printed in the subtle fibres of our nerves" (326). That his life-blood and nerve fibres have been deeply informed with an evangelical severity is plain. Insight and foresight as means of transcending the personal and temporal restrictions of being are a curse. Reality unveiled is too blinding a horror. Latimer can love Bertha only when under the "delicious illusion" (317) of her goodness and beauty. With reality veiled, the meaningful moral act is possible; unveiled, there can only be suspicion and hatred and violence. If we look for George Eliot's "teaching," such is the lesson. This precept, however, is reinforced in the story neither by a redeeming heroic act nor by a sinful one. The young man is merely a victim of his "gift," his "disease." That he can see so clearly that reality is hell is a fact of no moral significance whatever. It is his problem ultimately and there is nothing that can be done about it. One of the great interests of this short story is its clear presentation of the author's fundamental ambivalence toward reality revealed in her half-hearted endorsement of "delicious illusion": it is necessary, but false; false, but necessary nonetheless.

The view of ordinary life as a veil concealing inner reality is a Shelleyan notion, as the title suggests,[5] and many incidents in the story are traceable to Mary Shelley: the friendship of scientist and poet, the revivification, the Faustian devil-compact, the Wandering Jew, the hero's isolation, and the locale itself, all are *Frankenstein* motifs. The requirements that the novel treat the ordinary and the probable are acceptable to writers just to the extent that they can reconcile in their work the real and the ideal, truth and belief. However, once that balance is threatened, they can no longer be expected to edify as well as tell the truth. The writer's intellect requires the truthful observation of even very unpleasant reality, while the practical reason wants an interpretation of that reality for purposes either of edification or of art. To represent an illusion as a fact—for any reason whatever—is intellectually unforgivable; to present reality just as it is—without any mediating order—amounts, for many Victorian writers, to artistic failure if not to moral failure. Given this dilemma, the serious writers must turn to a less restrictive mode. In the romance the writer's obligations to truth are relaxed by that genre's conventional suspension of disbelief. No longer nagged by worries about the probability of events and characters, they can move freely about in the world of imagination, a world where almost anything can happen as long as it fits the special logic of that realm. Allegory being a prominent feature of that realm, the romance allows the writers to concentrate on any imminent "problems" they might want to present. It is in this sense that George Eliot, perhaps the greatest of the nineteenth-century novelists of the so-called "orthodox tradition," was not altogether outside the romance development starting with Mary Shelley and continuing on to the Brontës and Dickens.

II

The turn toward the past in a troubled culture is only part of a larger and more pervasive return to the self. For many Victorians, upset by the compromise and lack of clarity in the contemporary scene, contemplation of a great unbroken past was soothing and restorative. The Romantics were quite different: Their "return to the past" was implied by their rallying cry "return to Nature" —the past by definition closer to Nature—but "the past" implied for them, in turn, the future, at least until disillusionment or disgust darkened their optimism. Still, the past persisted, providing the Oxford Movement with the ground of faith, Tennyson his City built to Music, FitzGerald the Persian garden, Browning the Yellow Book, and Arnold his "sweetness and light." The historicism of these men was nowhere so much an attempt at objective reconstruction of the past as a desperate use of it. Each saw in the past what he needed to see, each found a myth where he needed to find one. And as the *Zeitgeist* sent forth the myth of the future and the universal, these men tried to counter it with the historical and the particular, with "temporizing the essence," to use Burke's helpful phrase again. Thus Ruskin's Gothicism, like the Gothic romance itself, is at once an effect and a precondition of the medieval revival of the mid-nineteenth century.

The Gothic element is strong in a good deal of the writing appearing around 1870, which is a convenient *terminus ad quem* of High Victorian literature.[6] In *The Ring and the Book,* a sort of sensation novel in verse, Browning dissects the criminal mind in the person of Guido whose mask, devised by a calculus of appearances, hides a deterministic animalism. Although his fascination with the complicated compulsions of his villain nearly overturns it, Browning's belief in the efficacy of free choice finally rights itself. There is the Gothic, too, in "Balin and Balan" in *Idylls of the King,* where, with the laureate's wasteland view of his time projected on a chronicle of Arthur's disintegrating Round Table, Tennyson can explore the netherworld of the self and its duality, the heart of darkness of the Victorian protagonist.

Gothicism is a slightly different phenomenon among the younger poets. Rossetti, possessed by the notion of the double, is curiously torn between the Shelleyan desire to merge with his Ideal Beauty and the fear rampant in folklore that such encounters spell death. No attempt is made to reconcile the two emotions. For James Thomson there is no longer even a hope for union with his Shelleyan double. In a world presided over by despair, gray merging with darker gray, black continuing into black, all attempts at self-definition are meaningless.

Finally, Dickens, the greatest Gothicist of the age, brings to his last finished novel the full range of insight garnered in a lifetime preoccupied with the problem of self-identity. His career, which began in 1830 and closed in 1870, coincides with High Victorianism, and he, too, like others of that time, persists in that fairy-tale moralism with which they would brighten and soften their nightmare knowledge of a chaotic world. In *Our Mutual Friend* the dark understanding of the decomposing self becomes more and more burdensome, and in his last work, *Edwin Drood,* emerges as a full-blown Jekyll-and-Hyde theme.

While the Gothic tradition thus provides uninhibited fictional expression for personal crisis, Matthew Arnold, having already gone through his *Sturm und Drang,* must now recompose the broken music of the self in his prose discourse where he develops a program for infusing English life with the spirit of culture. Closely looked at, his cultural dualism of Hellenism and Hebraism will show itself as the same two diametrical orientations that tore him apart psychologically in his youth. With his customary irony and wit Arnold avoids formulating the crisis as a rigid either-or and advocates instead an experiential psychology aimed at an inner joy very similar to the Cyrenaicism of Pater.

III

As in Eliot's "The Lifted Veil," the dualism of appearance and reality in the self is also a theme of Tennyson's Arthuriad, *Idylls of the King*.[7] The warfare of "Sense and Soul"[8] or "the True and the False"[9] informs the whole history of King Arthur's court. The Round Table is held together solely by the knights' faith in Arthur and his divine kingship. As long as there are faith and love between Arthur and Guinevere and between the royal couple and their knights, the Order of the Round Table, the model for the world, will destroy evil and drive out the heathen. However, when the guilty love of the Queen and Lancelot begins to fester, and doubt about the king's divinity spreads, the unity of sense and soul proclaimed at Camelot breaks down. With this disintegration, the world falls apart.

The *Idylls* chronicles the whole history of the Round Table, its good times and bad, although it forewarns of the fall even at the very beginning with hints of misgivings about Arthur's origin. "The Coming of Arthur" is really as much about people's unwillingness to accept his king-

ship as it is a celebration in his honor. Furthermore, the
first book of "The Round Table," despite its happy ending, is already troubled about truth and illusion: As
Gareth worries, men "Doubt if the King be king at all, or
come / From Fairyland . . . / Or whether there be any
city at all, / Or all a vision" (242–246). But Merlin counsels faith: "For an ye heard a music, like enow / They are
building still, seeing the city is built / To music, therefore
never built at all, / And therefore built for ever" (271–
274). The two books that follow pursue the problem of
faith with even more energy. In contrast to Arthur's un-
shakable trust in Guinevere, Geraint has doubts about his
wife's fidelity and is led inevitably into a vicious circle:
The more suspicious he becomes the severer test he must
impose on her, and the more tormenting the test the
more he himself is tortured. Nothing is ever proven by
this, and the worst of it is that both are brought perilously close to destruction. Put in the context of the Higher
Criticism, the poem's concern with faith and certitude is
clear enough. Faith in the divine needs no rational justification, for belief itself will bring about a salubrious unity
in the faithful soul. In fact, attempts to establish rational
grounds for faith not only will not succeed but will
destroy the hard-won unity. This argument assuredly does
not eliminate the possibility of erroneous or false belief, but this did not concern the poet. What the *Idylls*
argues is the need—call it illogical, call it psychological—
for an absolute faith that alone will make Arthur king,
alone make belief reality, and man's multiple self whole
again. The poem envisions a world in which the loss of
such faith signals men's disintegration.

   The *Idylls of the King* is determinedly High Victorian in its "message." But its depiction of a waste-

land world, condemned in the poem yet ever-present, is acutely modern. If the *Idylls* is preeminently an account of the war of sense and soul, the destruction of Arthur's court is an analogue to that fragmentation of the self. There is in this sense a "parabolic drift" [10] in the poem that strongly suggests an equation of Arthur with "Religious Faith," Modred with the "Skeptical Understanding," Merlin with "Science," [11] and so on, although it is absurd to insist on literal application of these correspondences.

Self-division besets several of the characters. Assuredly, King Arthur expresses the authorial view, from offstage, as it were, throughout the Idylls. However, in "Guinevere," where he supposedly comes forth to act on his own, he is little more than a disembodied voice whose sermonizings are an embarrassment. Although most of the characters vary from appearance to appearance, often matching the style of the particular idyll,[12] Guinevere and Lancelot stand out as much more fully developed dramatic personae. The Lancelot of the *Idylls* is indeed a modern Everyman tormented by his duplicity and consequent guilt-feelings. This "flower of all the west" ("Lancelot and Elaine," 248) finds himself driven to the very "wastes and solitudes / For agony" (250–251). And when the innocent Elaine offers her love, he cannot accept it, for his "faith unfaithful [keeps] him falsely true" (872). In such a confused state, Lancelot begins to lose his sense of his own identity:

> For what am I? what profits me my name
> Of greatest knight? I fought for it, and have it.
> Pleasure to have it, none; to lose it, pain;
> Now grown a part of me; but what use in it?
>   (1402–1405)

His hopelessly entangled good and evil—

> . . . but in me lived a sin
> So strange, of such a kind, that all of pure,
> Noble, and knightly in me twined and clung
> Round that one sin, until the wholesome flower
> And poisonous grew together, each as each,
> Not to be pluck'd asunder. . . .
>
> ("The Holy Grail," 769–774)

—must be somehow undone. The only answer lies in the Grail, the quest for which is doomed to failure. Lancelot may finally be a negative figure in Tennyson's moral scheme, but his anxiety and despair are authentic within the poem and in the experience of many of the late Victorians.

The Red Knight, Arthur's antithesis in "The Last Tournament," calls the moral will self-deception; in the name of honesty, he ignores values and promotes existence:

> "Tell thou the King and all his liars that I
> Have founded my Round Table in the North,
> And whatsoever his own knights have sworn
> My knights have sworn the counter to it—and say
> My tower is full of harlots, like his court,
> But mine are worthier, seeing they profess
> To be none other than themselves—and say
> My knights are all adulterers like his own,
> But mine are truer, seeing they profess
> To be none other; and say his hour is come,
> The heathen are upon him, his long lance
> Broken, and his Excalibur a straw."
>
> (77–88)

Similarly, Tristram is a naturalist for whom the paradox of sense and soul is dissolved into a monism of sense experience. By blending good and evil to a range of grays, this immoralist locates the core of being in the flux of pleasurable experience. However, since such "downward" resolution ("The Last Tournament," 332) is considered far too subversive in the Tennysonian world, Tristram is identified as a "wild beast" and made a victim of another, craftier beast of prey.

A much clearer picture of the divided self is to be seen in "Balin and Balan," a surprisingly modern treatment of the doppelgänger motif. Balin, called "the Savage" (51) by Arthur, fights ceaselessly against his violent "moods" (137); as a reminder to himself, he paints a "rough beast" (192) on his shield to represent his "slain self" (174). But Balin cannot fully function without Balan, his rational self, "[his] brother and [his] better" (52), who counsels him and helps him suppress his violence. As the poem opens, their story is interwoven with that of Pellam, the woodland king who has challenged Arthur's authority with a grotesque religion of his own invention. The scheme is set: Arthur's civilization is pitted against Pellam's primitivism, with Balin and Balan, Arthur's emissaries, sent out to explore the dark world of Pellam's woods.

Balan departs first on the expedition, leaving his brother alone with no control over his "moods" other than his shield. However, Balin, by exchanging the savage on his shield for Guinevere's cognizance, provides himself with a symbol for rational control (the "crown," the head). Thus order prevails, until he chances on Guinevere's illicit tryst with Lancelot in the rose garden.[13] His ideals dashed, Balin hurries after his brother into the "heart of darkness" [14] that is the netherworld of his own being. His journey to Pellam's hall becomes a nightmare. This seat of Nature, once—for the Romantics—a paradise, is now a very hell, overgrown as it is with "lichen," "streaming grass," "a knoll of moss," "ivy-tods," and haunted with "bats" and "owls."

Balin's rational control disappears. By the time he encounters Vivien with her insinuations and outright lies, he has been practically reduced to the wood-demon he had intended to put down. Vivien succeeds in her deception, and Balin, in despair, tramples the "royal crown" (532) on his shield. Balan, hearing the unearthly roar in the forest and believing it to emanate from the wood-demon, attacks. His warning cry ("Guard thou thine head" [544]) is unheeded, and the brothers clash, inflicting mortal wounds on each other. They die "lock'd in either's arm."

In the structure of *The Ring and the Book* (1868–69) Guido's quite different appearance in two books, as "Count Guido Franceschini" and as "Guido," exhibits his essential duplicity: the wolf of Book V masked with the name and courtly manner of an ancient family, the clever eloquence, and the wolf of Book XI shorn of his sheepskin. This doubleness is of a highly sophisticated order, a careful manipulation of a meek front that has no counterpart whatever in his inner reality. Though modeled roughly on the Gothic villain,[15] Guido is definitely not one to be tormented by the awful cycle of passion and remorse. In fact, what makes his evil so powerful and persuasive is his audacious assertion of man's animality untouched by human "pallor":

Let me turn wolf, be whole, and state, for once,—
Wallow in what is now a wolfishness
Coerced too much by the humanity

That's half of me as well! Grow out of man,
Glut the wolf-nature,—what remains but grow
Into the man again, be man indeed
And all man? Do I ring the changes right?
Deformed, transformed, reformed, informed, conformed!
The honest instinct, pent and crossed through life,
Let surge by death into a visible flow
Of rapture. . . .
                              (XI.2049–2059)

Like Tristram in "The Last Tournament," Guido embodies the modern attitude toward values and existence.
Man is no longer seen as a being divided, half-beast and
half-angel, but as beast whole and undivided—a lamb occasionally, but more often a predator, a wolf. Life is
brutal force; death, "nullity"; and ethics, by this view,
the elementary mathematics of energy.

Give me my gorge of color, glut of gold
In a glory round the Virgin made for me!
Titian's the man, not Monk Angelico
Who traces you some timid chalky ghost . . .
                        (XI.2112–2115)

O thou Lucrezia, is it long to wait
Yonder where all the gloom is in a glow
With thy suspected presence?—virgin yet,
Virtuous again, in face of what's to teach—
Sin unimagined, unimaginable,—
I come to claim my bride,—thy Borgia's self
Not half the burning bridegroom I shall be!
                        (XI.2207–2213)

Against such a dazzling background, Pompilia is no more
than a bleating lamb, an "insipid harmless nullity" (XI.
1126). Her very holiness is idiocy.

The Ring and the Book denounces what Browning felt were perverted post-Darwinian attempts at simplifying and unifying human nature. To Browning man's true existence must be founded on his instinctual goodness (Pompilia) and the ability to act on this goodness (Caponsacchi). Like so many of his contemporaries worried that the overcultivation of the intellect would break the will to judge and to act, Browning, too, makes a statement on this peculiarly Victorian disease:

> Here, after ignorance, instruction speaks;
> Here, clarity of candor, history's soul,
> The critical mind. . . .
> (I.916–918)

For Tertium Quid neither side is all wrong: "There are difficulties perhaps / On any supposition, and either side" (IV.1571–72). Against this "educated" relativism, Browning sets the Pope who unequivocally rejects the compromise:

> Go!
> Never again elude the choice of tints!
> White shall not neutralize the black, nor good
> Compensate bad in man, absolve him so:
> Life's business being just the terrible choice.
> (X.1229–1233)

Despite all the devices of indirection and obliqueness employed in the poem, Browning is here totally unequivocal in his insistence on "choice." *The Ring and the Book* is not a "relativistic" [16] poem as it is often reputed to be: With its Pope speaking for the poet, it reaffirms the power of will that determines and integrates man's self.

IV

When Arnold gave up writing poems, his demons seem to have migrated to his prose. Whereas argument dominates in his poetry, the subjects of his critical essays become metaphors. It makes no difference what the topic—whether education, literature, society, religion or history—the tenor of all these metaphors shows an amazing consistency: "life," or—to use terms less Arnoldian—the modern illness of being as he saw it and his ever-renewable prescription for the cure. The recommendations he *must* make (sage, as he is, not analyst) in each area, therefore, exactly correspond to the exhortations to which he earlier aspired, but failed to execute, in his poetry.

Most of the critical essays bear this out. *On Translating Homer* (1861) is a discussion of various Homeric translation styles, covering Chapman, Pope, Cowper, down to Francis W. Newman. Arnold sets the criteria for these efforts which he believes adequately describe Homer's "grand style"[17]—"rapid," "plain," "direct," and "noble" (102)—and he measures the Elizabethan, eighteenth-century and nineteenth-century versions against these key terms, thereby of course proving all wanting. With a closer look, however, it appears that his four terms refer primarily to psychological properties. A particular translation style represents, for Arnold, a dominant psychological trait, or *Zeitgeist,* of the time of the rendering. Thus, the Elizabethan is "fanciful" and "eccentric"; the eighteenth-century, "artificial"; and the contemporary, "quaint, garrulous, prosaic, low" (119). In fact, the whole modern literary development is fatally lacking in the critical spirit (140), and rapidity, plainness, directness, and the noble are all antithetical to the modern temper brooding on the self. The subject, translation style, is merely a trope for the problem that concerns him at the moment.

In essays such as "The Function of Criticism at the Present Time" and "The Literary Influence of Academies," the approach is the same: "Peace," "cheerfulness," "disinterestedness," "glow," a "free play of the mind," and "curiosity" are desirable, and "impatient irritation," the "feeling of depression," "ennui," the "overstrained," the "gloom-weighted," and the "morbid" undesirable. This use of psychological description to indicate the whole range of cultural activities says a great deal about Arnold. He always tried to see life whole, all its aspects related. Further his observations and evaluations on everything in life, from literature to religion, are all tied to his personal experience. As his critical horizon expanded over the years, experience became more and more the source of his thought, rapidly approaching the status it enjoys in the pragmatic philosophy of Dewey and James.

Arnold's trips to the Continent and to the English countryside provided him many opportunities to study different ways of life, and once again his way of characterizing a culture or a social class is metaphorical. In his Introduction to *The Popular Education of France* (1861) he describes French and English classes in terms of individual attitudes and life styles. But despite his insight, he is no anthropologist,[18] for his argument is mainly evaluative and prescriptive. The middle classes may have achieved "liberty" but lack "high reason and a fine culture"; the aristocracy, once "in the grand style"—the same "literary" phrases here apply to his description of social classes—but now in decline, conspicuously lacks the power of "ideas." [19] All three classes are partial, incom-

plete, and the totality he proposes at the end is the notion of the "state"—like the self, unfragmented by conflicting impulses.

Culture and Anarchy (1869), his major essay on the
possibility of the total development of man, follows directly on "Culture and Its Enemies," which was itself a
development of a series of brilliant journalistic lampoons.
The controversial nub of the work lies in his discussion
of all those elements—culture, nationality, class, religion,
liberalism—that go to make up the whole social fabric of
England at that time. Toward his definition of "culture,"
Arnold provides a great array of terms, few of which
lend themselves to analysis. To Frederic Harrison this
"culture" is "fiddlestick or sauerkraut," [20] which he attributes to the vagueness of his formulation. However,
as Arnold himself declares—no doubt with tongue in cheek
—his catch-phrases are meant to "elude" [21] his readers.
The more closely one might try to pin down a single
term, the more baffling will he find the whole range of
synonyms and antonyms for that term. Arnold's aim in
the book is not primarily to discourse on culture in a
systematic way, but to start his readers questioning conventional values. This challenge itself is essential to his
program for culture.

Given the problems of definition, Arnold's paired
phrases—"Hellenism" and "Hebraism," "culture" and
"religion," "sweetness and light" and "fire and strength,"
"spontaneity of consciousness" and "strictness of conscience"—obviously do not always lend themselves to
schematization. They should rather be taken as rhetorical restatements—from several subtly differing points of
view—of two fundamentally different life styles, that of
intellectual detachment and that of moral commitment.
And just as the loose periphrasis of the book is a red flag,

the ideas of the essay urge the modern Englishman to liven his awareness, to detach himself from that "one thing needful," in short to "Hellenize." After all his verbal side-stepping, Arnold finally comes to say plainly that "culture goes beyond religion" (94).

Culture, or Hellenism, is nowhere clearly or completely defined by Arnold. But he does come toward it from interesting directions:

> Now the force which we have so much neglected, Hellenism, may be liable to fail in moral strength and earnestness, but by the law of its nature,—the very same law which makes it sometimes deficient in intensity when intensity is required,—it opposes itself to the notion of cutting our being in two, of attributing to one part the dignity of dealing with the one thing needful, and leaving the other part to take its chance, which is the bane of Hebraism. Essential in Hellenism is the impulse to the development of the whole man, to connecting and harmonizing all parts of him, perfecting all, leaving none to take their chance.
>
> (184)

There is a great deal more in *Culture and Anarchy*, certainly, than what might be seen as an impersonalized version of Arnold's own fight against the warring selves within. At the same time his Hellenism, by which he would attempt to develop the "whole man," is not a concept that can be left out with impunity from a consideration of his earlier poems, whose dominant preoccupation was exactly that predicament in which the wholeness of man was threatened.

Arnold's holism does not focus only on the self but on the wider socio-political questions summed up by the political usage "the conditions of England." To Arnold, concerned not so much with class divisions as with promulgating a neo-Burkean philosophy, the state is rooted in each one's "best self," which is nurtured by culture, or "the study of perfection" (134). This "best self," identical in the Arnoldian multi-equation to "right reason," will gladly accept the center of authority. As a person is to his best self, so is society to the state, the totality of which coincides with the aims of culture.

In *Culture and Anarchy* Arnold's secularization of man's inner life is rather broadly set forth. But once he has put "culture" even a thin cut above "religion," he must in some manner redefine this religion so that the two will coextend over the province of life. In his three books on Christianity, *St. Paul and Protestantism* (1870), *Literature and Dogma* (1873), and *God and the Bible* (1875), the redefinition is carried several steps further. *St. Paul and Protestantism* identifies the two terms he had once held opposed: "Hebraism at its best is beauty and charm; Hellenism at its best is also beauty and charm" and will only differ "in their lower forms." [22] What both are "at their best" are qualities properly belonging to the realm of Hellenism, "beauty and charm." The patness of the equation tends to obscure the root newness of its concept of religion, that both religion and culture are means toward the same end—culture! His secularization of religion—into a species of aesthetics one moment and psychology the next—is nearly complete. St. Paul, according to Arnold, had "come by" his religion "psychologically and from experience" (48). His notion of sin, in the Arnoldian "theology," provokes this comment:

Paul did not go to the Book of Genesis to get the real testimony about sin. He went to experience for it. "*I see,*" he says, "a law in my members fighting against the law of my mind, and bringing me into captivity." This is the essential testimony respecting the rise of sin to Paul,—this rise of it in his own heart and in the heart of all the men who hear him.

(88)

The sense of self-division becomes, for Arnold, the foundation of the Christian concept of sin!

Literature and Dogma is the culmination of his program for psychologizing Christianity. Early in the book, Arnold makes his famous apportionment of life—three quarters for conduct (religion) against one quarter for intellect (culture).[23] (Later, he will subdivide the intellectual fourth between art and science [210].) But all this arithmetic is really just a good show. By the time he was writing this book, if not earlier, religion and culture had become thoroughly interchangeable notions: There is, for evidence, his description of "Jesus' new way," His "sweet reasonableness" (87)[24]—two words, one recalls, that, at least in *Culture and Anarchy*, were properties of Hellenism, not Hebraism. *Literature and Dogma,* the climax of Arnold's radical program for redefining religion as psychology, rejects as *"Aberglaube"* ("extra-belief") almost the whole dogma of Christianity, from the divinity of Jesus to miracles. Stripped of their theological overlay, the commandments are offered as a "truth of psychophysiology" (208–211), a very effective psycho-therapy whose sole justification rests on its experiential efficacy. Asked for verification, Arnold would explain, "How? why, as you verify that fire burns,—*by experience!*" (325), anticipating, of course, Pater's hard gemlike flame.

With the help of "experience" Arnold could finally manage to re-tailor the torn self of modern times, an objective never far from his mind from the early days of his friendship with Clough when he first talked over the problems of poetry, country, and Christianity. His thinking toward the end of his life came very close to the pragmatism of William James, which sees religious experience from a psychological point of view. To focus too sharply on Arnold as the perplexed poet of the High Victorians is to distort or miss entirely the great range and depth of his modernity.

V

His father, learned in neo-Platonism and the Renaissance, no doubt influenced him a great deal, but Dante Gabriel Rossetti was also an enthusiast of the Gothic and Romantic writers quite on his own.[25] In "How They Met Themselves," a painting which he started on his honeymoon, a knight and his lady almost faint with fear as they confront their doubles who are bathed in a ghastly halo. Dividing the canvas is the knight's sword, drawn as though to drive away these wraiths. The picture perfectly describes Rossetti's imaginative mode, taking its stock of symbols from the Gothic to give form to his Victorian anxiety. The notion of encounter with the double, foreboding the breakdown of self in constant concourse with the self, will soon become an "obsession" [26] with him. In the very discovery of the notion there was a kind of "imaginative fulfillment" [27] for Rossetti.

One of Rossetti's early tales on the theme is "Hand and Soul" (1849).[28] Chiaro, the young art student, idles his time away and only goes back to his work when he becomes jealous of another painter.[29] Soon his own fame spreads, but he is bothered by religious doubts, and worries about his sincerity. He begins to feel that religion has been a mere cover-up for his worship of beauty. He changes his painting style, choosing subjects that are morally edifying. As a result, he loses his popularity and his career declines.

It happens that a fierce fight erupts between the two great Pisan families which have been feuding for generations, and blood spills all over one of Chiaro's frescoes, a "moral allegory of Peace." In his anger and frustration, Chiaro becomes feverish and lapses into delirium. A woman appears before him; "I am an image, Chiaro, of thine own soul within thee." [30] She advises Chiaro that he was wrong in believing that faith and love of beauty are incompatible and tells him to paint her portrait in order that "thy soul stand before thee always, and perplex thee no more" (I,395). In the last scene, he finishes the painting and the beautiful woman, his epipsyche, lulls him to sleep with her quiet voice.

Rossetti's early prose poem has elements both of High Victorianism and the aesthetes. There is Chiaro's conversion, after which he dedicates his art to God and morality, but there is also disillusionment with the efficacy of this art: His peace fresco is destroyed by the blood of war. Then there is the growing emphasis on his efforts to join beauty with faith—the truly beautiful is bound to please God—but it is the Romantic imperative, "Paint thine own soul," which closes the story. Rossetti here revives the impulse—inhibited in Tennyson, Browning, Clough, and Arnold—to invite his soul without guilt-feelings. At the same time, he is not the pure Romantic either. Chiaro's soul, after all, comes to him in the form of a death-dealing wraith. Also, although the tale is nowhere explicit on this point, the reference at the end to "the many dead" does suggest that, after finishing the portrait, the artist never wakes to see his soul again. Her

counsel on reconciling faith and beauty, moral aestheticism and "pure" aestheticism would then amount to mere
wishful thinking on his part, which would never be actu-
alized. Between his two selves, as between the two warring
houses of Pisa, Chiaro the painter perishes.

Another early tale on the theme of the double is
"Saint Agnes of Intercession" (once called "An Autopsy-
chology" by the author), an incomplete story published
in 1850. The narrator relates how, from early childhood, one of his favorite art works was an old-fashioned
engraving of St. Agnes by a fifteenth-century Italian
painter. Later, as an art student, he enters in exhibition
a portrait he has painted of his fiancée Mary Arden. On
opening day, breathless with expectation of seeing his
picture again—"his naked soul, himself" (I,403)—he
rushes off to the gallery only to be buttonholed by a
pompous art critic. It seems that Mary's portrait reminds
the critic of something he has seen by an Italian painter
Angiolieri, especially his portrait of St. Agnes. It is then
that the young painter suddenly recognizes the extraordinary similarity between Mary's features and those of
St. Agnes. He leaves immediately for Italy to find Angiolieri's works, and after a long search finally locates them.
He learns there that St. Agnes had been modeled on the
painter's love who died very young, and more amazing,
that Angiolieri's self-portrait shows features identical with
his own. The night of this discovery he has a dream. The
scene is the London exhibition hall, but this time his
painting is the St. Agnes of Perugia. Mary is there with
a man in a masquerade costume and as he tries to speak
to him, this man "turned round suddenly, and showed
me my own face with the hair and beard quaintly cut"
(I,419–420). Sensing an impending calamity, he returns
to London immediately, only to become seriously ill with

a raging fever for several weeks. Just as soon as he gains a little strength he goes to visit Mary, with deep forebodings that the funeral bells he heard that morning were for her. The story breaks off at this point.

"Saint Agnes" is more eventful than "Hand and Soul," and less ornate in style. On the whole, it is a readable work. Aside from the "autopsychological" elements, which are more prominent in this second story, Rossetti seems to have a clearer awareness of the catastrophic outcome of the self's encounter with the self. In his use of the portrait-double motif he stands between Maturin and Poe earlier and Wilde later on. However, despite the artist's more certain knowledge of this doom, there is the notion in the story that art as an embodiment of the artist's soul has an immortality independent of the artist. Finally, apropos of Rossetti's own artistic development, the story says something about its author's future. The sense of identity the young painter feels with Angiolieri parallels Rossetti's enthusiasm with the Pre-Raphaelites. To invoke a Dantean unity of flesh and spirit in the face of Victorian rationalism is a project on the order of reviving Angiolieri's fifteenth-century soul in the nineteenth-century artist. In all his work from here on, Rossetti will be found hovering over a nebulous region between spirit and flesh, two realms whose alliance even Rossetti no longer really believes possible. The result is a body of fatally incoherent poetry. "Saint Agnes of Intercession" foretells the failure of his poetry to arrange a meeting of his nineteenth-century self with his fifteenth-century self.

When Rossetti's wife died—rather mysteriously, as it happened—he placed a manuscript in her coffin. Some seven years later (October 1869) the grave was opened to retrieve these poems, and both body and manuscript were supposedly found perfectly preserved. As though

to improve on this macabre realization of Gothic fancy,
a legend grew that the girl's luxuriant blond hair continued growing after her death and that at the time the
coffin was exhumed it was found filled with golden strands.
With the publication of the 1870 volume of *Poems*, Rossetti claimed that "Most of these poems were written
between 1847 and 1853. . . . The 'Sonnets and Songs' are
chiefly more recent work," [31] suggesting, of course, that
many had been addressed to his dead wife—and possibly
were those supposedly recovered from the grave. In fact,
"most" of the love sonnets in *The House of Life* were
written after 1868 for Janey Morris and other women.[32]

Regardless of who she was, she is everywhere in *The
House of Life* the object of Dantean passion, of the love,
in particular, of the *Vita Nuova,* which identifies the lady
with divine wisdom. As "Heart's Hope" (V), one of the
earlier sonnets in the sequence, states boldly: "Thy soul
I know not from thy body, nor / Thee from myself,
neither our love from God." His terms such as "soul,"
"body," "love," and "God" are vague, and we can know
from them only Rossetti's uppermost desire for total unity
wherever he can find it, whatever it is.

The poet's inability to see and convey the precise
nature of this unity is readily apparent in the more fully
developed poems such as "The Kiss" (VI):

What smouldering senses in death's sick delay
Or seizure of malign vicissitude
Can rob this body of honor, or denude
This soul of wedding-raiment worn to-day?
For lo! even now my lady's lips did play
With these my lips such consonant interlude
As laurelled Orpheus longed for when he wooed
The half-drawn hungering face with that last lay.

I was a child beneath her touch,—a man
When breast to breast we clung, even I and she,—
A spirit when her spirit looked through me,—
A god when all our life-breath met to fan
Our life-blood, till love's emulous ardors ran,
Fire within fire, desire in deity.

While the third line attributes a spiritual quality, "honor," to the "body," the "soul" is spoken of in physical terms: "denude" and "wedding-raiment." The interest here is not so much Rossetti's criss-crossing of the spiritual and the physical as with his vagueness as to which of the two orders is reality. Is he saying that the "body" in its "wedding-raiment" is the symbol for the "soul" with its "honor," or the converse? If the physical order is the symbol for the spiritual, the notion of "soul" here is not substantial enough to carry its weight in a metaphor. But if the spiritual order thus symbolizes the physical, in what sense can a nonobject be said to stand for a material one? In the second quatrain the mythical implications of the Orphic "interlude" are ignored, leaving the figure at the level of mere rhetorical ornamentation. The pun on "lay," like those on "play" and "denude," therefore, comes through as a *faux pas*.

The sestet is on the whole a little more coherent. The speaker's transformation from "child" to "man" is realistically convincing. But between lines 10 and 11 he is suddenly a "spirit" for no other reason than that her "spirit" ("eyes"?) has "looked through" him. The last three lines elevate him to a deity, a change even more mysterious. Why must he be a "god" simply because the lovers' "life-breath" seems to be churning their "life-blood"? In the Rossettian mana of words, the act of love is an instant sacrament, without benefit of any of the richer metaphysical sanctions utilized, for example, in Donne's sonnets.

"Nuptial Sleep" (VIa), originally a continuation of "The Kiss," was so naughty as to provoke Buchanan's furious attack on the whole "Fleshly School of Poetry." Its treatment of the subject is one of the boldest in Victorian poetry. Its poetic technique, unfortunately, is another matter:

> At length their long kiss severed, with sweet smart;
> And as the last slow sudden drops are shed
> From sparkling eaves when all the storm has fled,
> So singly flagged the pulses of each heart.
> Their bosoms sundered, with the opening start
> Of married flowers to either side outspread
> From the knit stem; yet still their mouths, burnt red,
> Fawned on each other where they lay apart.
>
> Sleep sank them lower than the tide of dreams,
> And their dreams watched them sink, and slid away.
> Slowly their souls swam up again, through gleams
> Of watered light and dull drowned waifs of day;
> Till from some wonder of new woods and streams
> He woke, and wondered more: for there she lay.

In the octave, his allusions to the storm and to flowers is deliberately ambiguous, referring to the sexual act happening in the foreground as well as to the natural scene of the poem. However, the relationship between the two sets of reference is too feeble to convey any other impression than that of a factual description of the sexual act, which is then flourished by inoffensive objects strewn about like the flowers in Victorian upholstery patterns. In the sestet, "souls," meaning simply consciousness, is similarly unwarranted. In fact, its antithesis "bodies" would fit the rest of the poem far better. Again, in line 13, the "new woods and streams" are linguistically a lie, being only a euphemism for sexual phenomena. Such random metaphoric ornamentation, which barely covers the subject matter, is conspicuously the kind of arbitrary joining by which Rossetti tried all along—from "The Blessed Damozel" to *The House of Life* [33]—to simulate a Dantean fusion of spirit and flesh, heaven and earth.

As for the unity of the man and the woman in love, it appears almost Shelleyan in these poems except that Rossetti does not aspire to the oneness; he is certain of having achieved it. In "The Portrait" (X), for instance, returning to the motif of "Hand and Soul" and "Saint Agnes," he has his speaker believing that the portrait of his lady represents "the perfect whole [of her inner self]" (though it must of course be sensual, too—"Above the long lithe throat / The mouth's mould testifies of voice and kiss"). At the same time the portrait represents the whole "I," or self, of his soul fused with hers: "Let all men note . . . They that would look on her must come to me." This "oneness" is elaborated in a longer poem also entitled "The Portrait":

> This is her picture as she was:
> It seems a thing to wonder on,
> As though mine image in the glass
> Should tarry when myself am gone.

Here the notion is emphasized by the use of the "double" motif. Except for the circumstance that here the lady is the "I's" double, this poem might indeed be considered a text for his painting "How They Met Themselves":

In painting her I shrined her face
'Mid mystic trees, where light falls in
Hardly at all; a covert place
Where you might think to find a din
Of doubtful talk, and a live flame
Wandering, and many a shape whose name
Not itself knoweth, and old dew,
And your own footsteps meeting you,
And all things going as they came.

But such a compound of man and woman, flesh
and spirit, is unstable: He will not stay convinced that
the spiritual love he idealizes and the carnal desire that
drives him are really the same. *The House of Life* includes a number of sonnets expressing his distress on this
account. The psyche-epipsyche union dissolves in "Severed
Selves" (XL), echoing the Arnoldian lament: "Two separate divided silences, / Which, brought together, would
find loving voice / . . . . / Two souls, the shores wave-
mocked of sundering seas:— / Such as we now." And
in "Lost Days" (LXXXVI), the speaker's possible selves
confront each other in hell, only to realize the war on the
self as the only continuing reality:

                    but after death
God knows I know the faces I shall see,
Each one a murdered self, with low last breath.
'I am thyself,—what hast thou done to me?'
'And I—and I—thyself,' (lo! each one saith,)
'And thou thyself to all eternity!'

In "A Superscription" (XCVII), the speaker is a lost self
who calls himself alternately "Might-have-been" and "No-
more, Too-late, Farewell." Obviously, between the speaker

and the "thou" (his present self) there is no hope for reconciliation.

"Lost on Both Sides" (XCI) is perhaps one of the better sonnets in the volume. The octave builds a metaphor on the story of two men who, having once fought bitterly over a woman, become reconciled only at her death. The sestet compares "their feud forlorn" with each man's inner struggle. Like the woman, one's inner peace, too, must perish between opposed hopes:

> So through that soul, in restless brotherhood,
> They rode together now, and wind among
> Its bye-streets, knocking at the dusty inns.

Even here the ambiguous relationship of symbol and referent is such that one of Rossetti's more literal-minded readers once insisted that the poem is autobiographical.[34] But the bleak feeling of ruination is maintained, and the octave's dramatic situation is well suited to the allegorical statement of the sestet.

Finally, in "He and I" (XCVIII), the speaker is so hounded by his other self that he no longer knows which of the two is living his life:

> Whence came his feet into my field, and why?
> How is it that he sees it all so drear?
> How do I see his seeing, and how hear
> The name his bitter silence knows it by?
> This was the little fold of separate sky
> Whose pasturing clouds in the soul's atmosphere
> Drew living light from one continual year:
> How should he find it lifeless? He, or I?

The realization that his identity has been usurped by the "he," with no longer even an outside chance of reclaiming it, brings with it the sense of the utter loss of existence. Desolation and torment alone are in prospect.

VI

For James Thomson, too, the desolation of the decomposing self permeates the dreadful night of his vision. Even Nature in "The City of Dreadful Night" (written between 1870 and 1873) is devoured by despair and terror. The country migrant to the gloomy and often bizarre monolith of the city must pass first through a desert where he is assaulted by "Sharp claws, swift talons, fleshless fingers cold" [35] and where stars, sun, and sea are deformed into nightmares. There is in the poem then none of the dramatic polarization of countryside and city that is found in Romantic poetry. The city *is* the whole world, its mankind and its nature painted darkly against the monochrome of desolation. In this respect, Thomson's city is different from the Unreal City of *The Waste Land*. Eliot's version juxtaposes the sterility of modern life with man's remembrance of the past and hope for regeneration, thus mitigating his fearful loss of belief in the present. Thomson's wasteland admits no such hope. There is only the present futility, the present extended dying. The poem's essential feature is in fact this consistent oneness, the total lack of contrast, tension, or conflict within either its image structure or its argument.[36]

The plan of the poem allows for both description and narrative by alternating odd-numbered, seven-line sections for the first and even-numbered, six-line sections for the second, a structure which, had there been any tension between the what of description and the what of narration, might have made all the difference to the poem. As it is, the structure seems arbitrary and me-

chanical, mainly because in Thomson's world his single
element, hopelessness, thickens to coagulation, stopping
all motion. The narrative sections are increasingly indistinguishable from the descriptive ones, toward the end
the sole difference being the presence of one or more
characters in the narrative episodes. But even that difference does not help much, for the characters are not themselves identifiable one from another: All are residents of
the city, and all alike are aimless wanderers in the timeless
night. And since the main narrator has throughout the
poem essentially the same personality as these wanderers
he comes across, the poem has the effect, all told, of one
unbroken groan.

Thomson's idiosyncrasies are noticeable immediately. In Section I, for instance, a description of the city
is followed by another slightly more specific description
in Section III, and the sections are so alike as to be
practically interchangeable:

> The street-lamps burn amidst the baleful glooms,
> Amidst the soundless solitudes immense
> Of rangèd mansions dark and still as tombs.
>
> (I)

> Although lamps burn along the silent streets;
> Even when moonlight silvers empty squares
> The dark holds countless lanes and close retreats;
>
> (III)

The full effect of the redundancy accumulates over the
length of the poem. Then there are the members of the
congregation in Section XII who have come to the city
from all walks of life—political and social reform, the
opium den, the theater. With all this variety, all have

gathered there for the sole purpose of waking from their "daydreams" to "this real night." All the diversity of man with all its possibility for interest and drama is thus canceled by the sameness of destination reiterated in the refrain. Similarly, in Sections VI and VIII, where the speaker overhears voices floating up from the dark river walk, the speeches are not in themselves uninteresting, but because no specific events are related, only opinions that are all much the same, the voices merge with each other and with countless others rising out of the night.

The lack of dramatic events and character conflict is not in itself a defect. As is the case in so many Victorian conversion poems, where the discovery of faith alone energizes the monologue, a good dialectic of argument would to some extent compensate for the dramatic deficiency. But in Thomson's poem, as in Hardy's work, there is no such dialectic. The very thesis obviates its possibility: "There is no God; no Fiend with names divine / Made us and tortures us; if we must pine, / It is to satiate no Being's gall" (XIV). An impersonal and amoral "Necessity Supreme" operates this world, allowing man no freedom except to choose his time, place, and manner for suicide. The poetic potential in the sermon here, delivered by an atheist minister in a "church" devoid of all churchlike features, is left undeveloped. Similarly, the last section which is an emblematic treatment of Dürer's "Melencolia," presents the colossal woman of the picture "Undaunted in the hopeless conflagration. . . . Sustained by her indomitable will." "Will" and "fate," the fundamental paradox of life, are excellent potential for drama in this passage. But Thomson will not let them play their parts.

With total despair the only response to life, man is reduced at last to silence. "The City of Dreadful Night" radically approaches this condition. In Section XVI the "infinite Past is blank and dumb," the "infinite To-come" also "blank." Time thus obliterated, man's life is a mere "mockery, a delusion." With no amelioration in sight, acquiescence is the only attitude: "Speak not at all: can words make foul things fair? / Our life's a cheat, our death a black abyss: / Hush and be mute envisaging despair." This counsel for silence is so cogent as to cast the very existence of "The City of Dreadful Night" in doubt. For what is the point of a poem whose only *raison d'être* is "To see what shifts are yet in the dull play" (XIX)? "The City of Dreadful Night" is a poetic dead end, an antipoem to deny the principle of poetry itself.

Paradoxically, however, it is this utter monotony and immobility of the poem, sustained by refrain, repetition,[37] and emphasis, that makes it memorable. To this end the structure is reinforced by a number of static images. The futility of life is compared, for instance, to a blank-faced watch:

> Take a watch, erase
> The signs and figures of the circling hours,
> Detach the hands, remove the dial-face;
> The works proceed until run down; although
> Bereft of purpose, void of use, still go.
>
> (II)

Such passages, emblematic rather than dramatic, arrest the flow of the poem in several impressive stills. One of the best of these images, for which Thomson is indebted to the Pre-Raphaelites and the emblem poets, is that of the great conflict between an angel statue and a sphinx (XX) in which the sphinx by silent instantaneous thumps of its huge paw shatters the angel, leaving at the end a pile of stones in the brilliant moonlight with the cold majesty of the sphinx above staring into the void. The episode, anticipating Yeats's "Second Coming," builds a remarkable scene solely with still-photos, as it were, of antagonists frozen in combative postures.

Against this immobility, the consciousness of self-division takes on new meaning. The guilt and remorse and anxiety are there, but there is no evidence of struggle. Since whatever route man may choose leads only to desolation and despair, choice between contrasting or conflicting courses is meaningless in this city. Unlike the paralysis of the earlier Victorians, the city's ubiquitous hopelessness nullifies action. The standstill is the natural mode for this death-in-life. Thus, whether one's half-self (Section X) should stay alive and keep the watch by the bier of his dead love or die himself and join her makes no difference whatever. Similarly, the doppelgänger journey (Section II) through the whole cycle of life is expressed by an equation of "perpetual recurrence,"

$$\frac{\text{LXX}}{333} = .2\dot{1}\dot{0}.[38]$$

But since the doubles see things exactly alike all along the way, there can be no tension or conflict between them. The double no longer signifies the self at war with the self, only an ever-present self-consciousness.

The final murder of the warring half-self is committed in Section IV. The self, here a sort of Childe Roland, another wasteland voyager of this time, survives one nightmare after another on his journey through hell because he is not in the least afraid: "No hope could have no fear." But when he meets the graceful woman with a red lamp, he feels for the first time hope and as a

result fear and conflict. His self is cut in two by opposed
emotions of hope and no hope, love and hatred.

> As I came through the desert thus it was,
> As I came through the desert: I was twain,
> Two selves distinct that cannot join again;
> One stood apart and knew but could not stir,
> And watched the other stark in swoon and her;
> And she came on, and never turned aside,
> Between such sun and moon and roaring tide:
> And as she came more near
> My soul grew mad with fear.

His one self stands by as the shrouded woman with the
bleeding heart bends over his other self, making love to
him until the tide rises and swallows them both. The
death of his loving, believing self leaves him deformed
and without hope in the barren desert. The union of the
two, so much the expressed craving of Rossetti's poems,
is now unthinkable.

The *Nachschein* of Christianity that still illuminated
the world of Arnold and George Eliot is snuffed out for
Thomson, replaced by the night light of a self-consciousness anathema to the older writers. But however dark,
"The City of Dreadful Night" is not without its own
strange majesty. The coagulating despair of the poem
might even be regarded as therapeutic, a glue for the
fragmented self, if it were not for the fact that such
argument is mere word play and reduces to absurdity.
Where there is no hope or freedom to act, the self, as
ordinarily defined, has no referent; the self does not exist
until hope or freedom is exercised. In the nullity of the
word and the nullity of the self, Thomson glimpsed the
nothingness that lies at the bottom of contemporary life.

VII

The city is also the scene for the last complete novel by Dickens. The publication of *Our Mutual Friend* (1865) was met with several bad reviews,[39] and the next hundred years, until very recently, brought many more.[40] Gissing, Chesterton, and Orwell all loved Dickens, but felt this book was not up to his usual standards. Still another interpretive commonplace is to regard the work as first and foremost a tract in social criticism. It is to this tradition that much of the general failure to appreciate *Our Mutual Friend* is traceable.

Certainly, the dust piles are prominent in this pessimistic book, their filthiness as impudent as the luxury of their owners' great estates is ostentatious. However, in their constant presence, they point to other notions than class struggle and the myth of money: nothing less than the whole problem of identity in a world where things —and men—are not always what they appear to be. Of course, dust must be self-identical with dust—a substance is what it is—but the property of dust by which it produces wealth for its owners makes it identifiable, finally, with that wealth. As for the men who manipulate filth and filthy lucre, they, too, struggle for self-definition. When a man finds what he is looking for in the junk-filled dust piles, the dust is as good as gold to him; indeed, to ignore what is commonly held to be desirable in life (the golden aspect of dust) completely is to cut oneself off from society, become an outcast like Betty Higden. But at the other extreme, where the essential identity of dust as mere dust is ignored and the golden aspect of dust becomes everything in life, people like the Podsnaps and the Veneerings cut themselves off from their own essential humanity. Only Mr. Boffin seems able to comprehend the ambivalent dust. Just as capable of pricing "the Mounds to a fraction" [41] as of renouncing all claim to the Harmon fortune, the Golden Dustman emerges as the champion of Dickensian humanism. He can live in this world and keep his essential humanity.

The Thames, too, is important in this structure filled almost to overflow with people and events. In fact, Swinburne called the river "the real protagonist" [42] of the novel. Like the dust piles the Thames has a double identity, but in its roles as killer and as regenerator its action is beyond human interference and its power almost supernatural. In the course of the story, the Thames drowns four men and nearly succeeds in carrying off two others, but it offers a new life to two and at least the possibility of renewal to a third. Lizzie and Betty, both alien to the prevailing dust-as-gold values, are both drawn to the river: Lizzie "can't get away from it" (II,i); and Betty, as she lies dying, hears the river whisper to her, "Come to me, come to me! . . . I am the Relieving Officer appointed by eternal ordinance to do my work" (III,viii). Almost as though they are sealing their common kinship with the river (their common name, Elizabeth, suggests they are closer even than kin), Betty dies in Lizzie's arms, and becomes thereby the younger woman's guardian angel. Lizzie says later on, "What she did, I can do" (IV,vi).

Robert Morse has seen in this "principle of *doubleness*" a "unifying sub-theme" [43] for the novel's panoramic plot. The pairing of the characters, the examples of duplicity, disguise, false claims, hourglass reversals, and dual natures are all aspects of the principle. However, this "doubleness," more than an integrating device, bears the substantial weight of the novel: the crisis of identity by which every character exhibits some degree of duality, from duplicity and hypocrisy to a fully developed dual personality.

Dickens' obsession with the problem of identity is already in evidence in his earliest work. And unlike Thomson's monism, Dickens' imagination constructs reality—and the identity problem—in vibrant, and often violent, polarities, affecting formal as well as thematic aspects of his work. For one, there is that peculiar uncertainty of relationship between Dickens the author and Dickens the man. What start out as well-projected dramatic characters abruptly become strangely immediate voices confessing the writer's emotions. The interpolated tales in *Pickwick Papers*, for example, confront certain dark experiences which complement only to contradict the Pickwick story proper, a picaresque tale which is for the most part quite innocent of evil. Fagin and Sikes of *Oliver Twist* are pasteboard villains straight out of the romances until suddenly toward the end they begin to project a very uncharacteristic fear and anxiety with an emotion so intense and personal as to sharply reduce the narrator's distance from the criminals. Without doubt, Dickens was aware of this. There is that little-noticed pun in *David Copperfield,* which is in any case his most autobiographical novel: Mr. Dick has trouble writing a memorial because the chopped head of "King Charles" keeps getting into it—Charles Dickens' way of letting the reader in on the fun.[44]

There are large structural features, too, that reflect the Dickensian dualism. The double plot is especially strong, clearly emerging from the web of subplots in practically every novel—with the exception, of course, of *Great Expectations.* In *Dombey and Son* the Dombey household and the Midshipman family are both sources of plot development which join only at the very end. Similarly, in *Hard Times* the Gradgrind set and the Rachael-Blackpool set come into contact infrequently, although the novel evolves from the contrasting values of the two. The double plot, then, more than a merely structural maneuver, reveals Dickens' Manichean inclination to see the world in terms of irreconcilables, and it also explains his dependence on the happy ending for their resolution. Related to this is the double-narrator framework of *Bleak House* with its omniscient voice intoning the ever-expanding chaos of the world and Esther Summerson providing the conventional cause-and-effect moral view in her retrospective account.[45] The typically Dickensian shift between close observation and all-out sentiment should be mentioned in this connection. That the writer who could record the details of human wretchedness and urban filth of his time with unerring precision could also be so helplessly sentimental, so downright weepy on occasion, is not to be explained entirely by a sociology of his culture. This imbalance is singularly Dickens', and the modal shifts in his writing—always baffling and very often annoying—must finally be located in his temperamental constitution.

Dickens' grotesque imagery is traceable directly to his double vision, which detects in human beings the attributes of things. As Dorothy Van Ghent puts it very well, his imagination performs "surgical division" on a personality, cutting it into a "me-half" and an "it-half."[46] Conversely, he animates objects as though for a fairy tale. Such transformations are no indication of belief in a universal oneness of existence but of the contrary: an all too painful knowledge of its sinister disorder. Krook's metamorphosis into two chemical elements causes a "spontaneous combustion" that returns him to vapor and cinder, the fog and the mud of the *Bleak House* world.

Surrogation (or doubling) in characterization is a more direct way of handling the problem of troubled identity. That Dickens' characters are not dramatic was for long a standard complaint, but psychology, symbolism, and the advent of writers like Edmund Wilson make critical sense of them and reconstituted the old Dickens. By this view, the Dickensian character is not supposed to be an imitation of a complete personality but a symbolic abstraction of some one trait. As the plot joins two or more of these symbolic characters in conflict, they begin to correspond to what is usually meant by the dramatic character. Dickens likes lots of people in his books, and there is a demographic advantage to his method. Instead of compounding aspects of several individuals into one "round" character, he deforms an individual into two or more parallel or contrasting characters. Thus Pickwick's increasingly serious heroic vision of the world is set off by Sam Weller's increasingly serious ironic vision. Character doubling is endemic in *Dombey and Son*. Aside from the central pairing, in which Carker epitomizes an evil Dombey might have been capable of had his pride developed along different lines,[47] there are many others— Dombey and Edith, Dombey and Sol the Midshipman, Dombey and Mr. Toodle, Dombey and Florence, and Dombey and his son.

The characterization of Pip is the most outstanding example of surrogation. Pip's sense of guilt is far too pervasive and profound to have been caused by his snobbery alone, much less by his unwitting involvement with criminals. If Pip is taken as a character in his own right, the treatment of guilt in *Great Expectations* would not get beyond *The Book of Snobs*. But there is that special relationship binding Pip and Orlick.[48] For one thing, Orlick's melodramatic and violent hatred is aimed at Pip but also at people like Mrs. Joe, Magwitch, and Pumblechook who are authority figures for Pip. Orlick is constantly at Pip's heels, always lurking about in the shadows like Frankenstein's monster. With Orlick's accusation of Pip for the assault on Mrs. Joe and Pip's acquiescence to the monstrous charge, the picture is complete: Pip and Orlick are the symbolic representation of a personality divided in the classical Freudian sense. In fact, Pip's sexual passivity can only be adequately explained by Orlick's lecherous interest in Biddy and by his successor's (Drummle's) brutal beatings of Estella. In this use of doubling there is at least the tacit assumption that the psychological reality can no longer be contained within a single character but requires two or more for any adequate expression. Dickens does utilize other novelistic possibilities of imitation, too. In his later years, he became increasingly interested in creating characters crossed by opposing impulses. The Gothic-Byronic archetype was near at hand, and he made frequent use of it. Both Steerforth in *David Copperfield* and Harthouse in *Hard Times* are Gothic villains, though more accomplished in the science of deportment than a Manfred or an Ambrosio.

It is *Our Mutual Friend* that makes full thematic use of the split-personality type in its attempt to show the inner life of its characters within the usual novelistic definition of that term. This is true even of the lesser characters in the book. Alfred Lammle and Sophronia Akershem marry for money, unaware that each is being deceived by the other. With their discovery of the brilliant double deception after the wedding, they savagely turn on each other, yet decide, after all, to stick it out and put up a front not only of wealth but of bliss, as well. They succeed in this plan to the extent that their talk of their grand palace, never beyond the blueprint stage, arouses jealousy in their group. But Sophronia, nasty as she is, feels compunction—if only for a moment—when she encounters an instance of real generosity. "Why, confound the woman," her astonished husband exclaims, "she *is* sentimental!" (IV,ii). Then there is Charley Hexam, that "curious mixture . . . of uncompleted savagery, and uncompleted civilisation" (I,iii). He also struggles to get ahead, and to some extent he succeeds. To do so, he has to abandon his old self, and in the process of establishing his new identity he destroys himself. (Hexam's case is much like that of Pip, though more harshly drawn.) Charley's teacher, Bradley Headstone, seems Wrayburn's double, but he also lives two distinct lives of his own, just like the Gothic villains: "Tied up all day with his disciplined show upon him, subdued to the performance of his routine of educational tricks, encircled by a gabbing crowd, he broke loose at night like an ill-tamed wild animal" (III,xi). He has still another double, his violent self, in the character of Rogue Riderhood. Jenny Wren, the dolls' dressmaker, constantly escapes into a private world of fairy birds and fairy flowers. This mere child, however, whose back is bad and whose legs are queer, treats her abject father as though he were her small, spoilt son, as she empties his pockets to take his earnings away and scolds him, shaking her fist like a sadistic shrew. Jenny has still another side: she commutes regularly between life and death. It is this Jenny who, as an "interpreter between this sentient world and the insensible man" (IV,x), guides the half-dead Eugene Wrayburn back to life. The only titled character in the novel, Lady Tippins, belongs to the aristocracy only because her late husband had been "knighted in mistake for somebody else" (I,x). Fascination Fledgeby, the idle gentleman, is in fact a brutal and greedy money-lender, and the venerable and generous Jew, Mr. Riah, compelled as he is to play the role of moneylender to cover for his master Fledgeby, comes to hate himself and at the end must resolve the conflict by quitting his job. Again, as Silas Wegg plots darkly under his guise of humble "literary man," his partner Mr. Venus loyally helps Mr. Boffin, while pretending to Wegg that he is his accomplice. Mr. Boffin's playing the miser is as central to this reading of the novel as John Harmon's masquer-ading as John Rokesmith. Finally, foggy London itself, the hero of *Bleak House,* is here "divided in purpose be-tween being visible and invisible, and so being wholly neither" (III,i)!

Of the major characters, there are two important pairs: John Rokesmith (John Harmon in disguise) and Bella Wilfer; and Lizzie Hexam and Eugene Wrayburn. Up to the very end, when both couples marry, their rela-tionships remain uncertain. This is not because of any external obstructions to their union—as is the case in so many romances of the time—but because the lovers them-selves fail to resolve their own inner conflicts. Three of them (the exception is Lizzie) know their own minds no better than they know their lovers', and their first task is to discover some path out of their confusion.

John Harmon, for one, taking advantage of the er-roneous identification of the drowned man Radfoot who had tried to kill him, assumes a new identity, first that of Julius Handford, then that of John Rokesmith. In the single most important chapter, "A Solo and a Duet" [49] (placed at the middle of the novel), Rokesmith re-traces his past in a long dialogue of the mind with itself.

When he returned to England, he was, as he puts it, "divided in my mind, afraid of myself and everybody here, knowing of nothing but wretchedness that my father's wealth had ever brought about" (II,xiii). The "division" is resolved by the choice of a new identity. The old dust-as-gold values, inherited from his father, are left behind in the river with Radfoot, who is, of course, an altogether adequate double, looking exactly like Harmon and embodying his old money values. The whole experience by the river amounts to a kind of baptism for Harmon, who is then born again to a new life.

As Rokesmith, Harmon is immediately presented with a dilemma. He genuinely falls in love with Bella, but because Bella wants to marry money, there is no chance of her accepting a poor secretary like Rokesmith. To the contrary, he is afraid that if he tells her he really is Harmon, she will marry him immediately, and he detests the idea of "buying" a wife in this way. Although he decides against telling her, the temptation is never completely put to rout. At this point in the story, Dickens again uses the device of the sacrificial double: the orphan, whom the Boffins had adopted and named "John Harmon" in memory of Harmon, is seriously ill, but just before passing away, he gives all the presents he has received to a sick boy in the next bed. With this young Johnny's death, the old Harmon values die a second time, and when Rokesmith at last proposes to Bella and she takes it as some preposterous insult, he is only toughened in his resolve to bury forever his dust-as-gold Harmon identity:

[He] heaped mounds upon mounds of earth over John Harmon's grave. His walking did not bring him home until the dawn of day. And so busy had he been all night, piling and piling weights of earth above John

Harmon's grave, that by that time John Harmon lay buried under a whole Alpine range; and still the Sexton Rokesmith accumulated mountains over him, lightening his labour with the dirge, "Cover him, crush him, keep him down!"

Bella meanwhile undergoes her long struggle to define her real self. The daughter of a clerk of modest means, she regrets acutely having missed out on marrying into the Harmon fortune. After her adoption by the Boffins, her resolution to marry money only intensifies, though she is never free of guilt feelings about it. Time and again she tells her "cherubic" father, "I am the most mercenary little wretch that ever lived in the world." She is also a habitual mirror-gazer. Turning to her mirror immediately after rejecting Rokesmith's proposal, she despises the images she sees there, and when Mr. Boffin, with the idea of reforming Bella, begins to act out her mercenary theory by pretending himself to be a fanatic miser, hateful and suspicious,[50] Bella interprets the change in him as due to his acquisition of a fortune, and her high respect for wealth gradually declines. She acknowledges his brutal treatment of Rokesmith, but still wonders to herself in the mirror why she should blame Boffin. "The looking-glass preserving a discreet ministerial silence when thus called upon for explanation, Bella went to bed with a weariness upon her spirit which was more than the weariness of want of sleep" (III,v). Mr. Boffin's moral education itself works as a mirror for Bella, and soon she is quite fairly divided between her dust-as-gold self and her gold-as-dust self: "Why," she asks herself, "am I always at war with myself?" At this point Mr. Boffin arranges to have her meet Lizzie, who inspires Bella by the genuine love she has for Eugene. Finally when a

pretended outburst of fury at Rokesmith on the part of
Mr. Boffin repels Bella completely, she decides to leave
his house. Her mercenary self now banished (" 'Now I
am complete,' said Bella," III,xv), it is a new Bella who
loves Rokesmith, the poor clerk, and the two, true to
themselves and to each other, marry. We are given to
understand that it is this new self-aware integrity of
both Bella and Rokesmith that assures not only that they
will inherit the Harmon fortune, but that they will, like
the Golden Dustman and his wife, put it to wise and
generous use.

In the other important couple of the novel, Eugene
and Lizzie, it is Lizzie, the poor river girl, who is the
constant lodestar. As her brother described her, "What
she is, she is, and shows herself to be" (II,i). Eugene,
before he falls in love with her, is an indolent Wildean
dandy: "In susceptibility to boredom," he tells Morti-
mer, "I assure you I am the most consistent of mankind"
(I,xii). He is a man for whom "everything is ridiculous."
As Eugene comes to love Lizzie, however, there is a change
in him: "earnestness" begins to concern him. The conflict
between his developing love for Lizzie and the dictates
of a society that he detests but that runs his life grows,
and by the time he visits Lizzie in her place of exile, he
is hopelessly torn apart. A Byronic figure of pose and
passion, Eugene the real lover (the gold-as-dust Eugene)
is engaged in total war with Eugene the seducer (the
dust-as-gold Eugene). Precisely at this moment of "crisis," his dark self and insane rival Headstone assaults
him, and he is dragged into the river. But the "Relieving Officer" that kills also resurrects; Lizzie comes
to the rescue and Jenny takes care of him. Deep in a coma
he keeps "wandering away I don't know where" and worries that he might "lose myself again" (IV,x). His strug-

gle with death is a struggle between his warring selves, which are only restored to integrity by his deathbed marriage to Lizzie. "When you see me wandering away from this refuge that I have so ill deserved," he tells her, "speak to me by my name, and I think I shall come back" (IV,xi). His name has come to represent his restored identity, no longer bored, no longer embattled.

The two marriages are the inevitable outcome of the characters' final reconciliation of their own warring selves. Rokesmith, Bella, and Eugene all find themselves through free experimentation with different identities. Bella and Rokesmith, it is true, find their way back at the end to the course charted originally by the old Harmon, but they are different people for having chosen it for themselves. By the free renunciation of the mere given, they have established a totally new relationship to the old life patterns. "If Mr. John Harmon had lived," Bella's father once speculated to Rokesmith, "he mightn't have suited Bella, or Bella mightn't have suited him, or fifty things, whereas now I hope she can choose for herself" (II,xiv). That the course they in fact come to follow turns out to be the one laid out for them should not confuse the issue. What Bella herself is, what she has chosen to make of herself, makes the difference between life and death in the dismal swamp.

Dickens' last novel, *The Mystery of Edwin Drood* (1870), has inspired a great amount of speculation as to what the fragment might have become had he lived to finish it. As it stands, no one can tell for sure whether Drood will die or not or who Datchery really is, and however ingenious the theory [51] and however carefully worked out, it is, for obvious reasons, bound to be conjectural. (Even Forster's testimony as to his friend's plans for this book leaves questions unanswered.) Such theories, brilliant as they often are, often brilliantly miss the point—*Edwin Drood* as it has come to us, *Edwin Drood* as it is.

There is overpoweringly about this novel an air of death. Almost as though reflecting Dickens' own exhaustion, the cathedral town of Cloisterham sinks into gloom:

> Not only is the day waning, but the year. The low sun is fiery and yet cold behind the monastery ruin, and the Virginia creeper on the Cathedral wall has showered half its deep-red leaves down on the pavement. There has been rain this afternoon, and a wintry shudder goes among the little pools on the cracked uneven flagstones, and through the giant elm trees as they shed a gust of tears. Their fallen leaves lie strewn thickly about. Some of these leaves, in a timid rush, seek sanctuary within the low-arched Cathedral door. . . .
>
> (ii)

The cheerful sunlit scene of the *Pickwick Papers* is gone, its place overgrown with ruin and decay. And the Gothic imagination is much more total here than in *Our Mutual Friend*,[52] moving Dickens that much closer to symbolism. John Jasper may or may not be a Thug bent on ritual murder, but the cutthroat atmosphere strongly suggests it. The Drood world is a fantasy world of the opium dream.

And it is an anxious world, a frightening world, its sense of the psychic underground focused on the sinister character of Jasper. A figure directly in the tradition of the priest-villain, this man lives two distinct lives—a pious choirmaster by day and a dope fiend by night. Dickens, fascinated with the evil of this man, dwells on his passion for Rosa and on all the sick contents of his subconscious. At one point, Jasper, deep in the delirium of his fix, shouts out his dreadful vision of life: "It was a journey, a difficult and dangerous journey. . . . A hazardous and perilous journey, over abysses where a slip would be destruction. Look down, look down! You see what lies at the bottom there?" (xxiii). Dickens writes rather casually here about the "two states of consciousness that never clash, but each of which pursues its separate course as though it were continuous instead of broken (thus, if I hide my watch when I am drunk, I must be drunk again before I can remember where)" (iii). With Edwin Drood, Dickens foreshadows the dual personality novel of the nineties.

VIII

Within a few years, Pater's gentle and weary intoning of division as the condition of modern life would betray no quiver of regret. Man's identity, like his body, consists of atoms. Nothing stays constant for Pater, all is in Heraclitean flux. Arnold's "disinterested" criticism is transformed into the effort to "know one's own impression as it really is." [53] But even this "impression," no more the universal vision of the Romantics, is merely that of "the individual in his isolation, each mind keeping as a solitary prisoner its own dream of a world." [54] Although Pater's idea is to make each separate impression perfect, relinquishing all efforts to unite them into the continuity that is a man, it would be a mistake to equate his notorious hard, gemlike flame with a *carpe diem* hedonism. Even as hedonist, he is "a moralist." [55] Yet, while the record of Marius' pilgrimage told what kind of "hardness" and what sort of "gem" was this flame of ecstasy, his philosophy is sharply distinguishable from that of the earlier Victorians by his indifference to the self-limits supposedly necessary for man to root himself substantially in time and society. Pater's reflections fold back doubly and trebly on the mind itself. In the series of impressions which is a man's life, he may indeed burn, "catch at any exquisite passion," but he cannot act, cannot mingle, cannot read his time right or guide it.

The disillusionment that descended on European literature in the nineteenth century was of an extraordinary sort. Chesterton felt that Christianity was much more dead in the eighteenth century than in the nineteenth, but political idealism was much more alive.[56] With the collapse of High Victorianism, both were dead. And man without God, without his fellow man, lacking history and self-conviction, felt himself strapped to a lifelong treadmill.

Late in the 1870's a long house party was given—in *The New Republic* (1877)—by William Hurrell Mallock, a nephew of Hurrell and James Anthony Froude. The guest list included some of the most distinguished Englishmen of the age: Arnold, Ruskin, Huxley, Pater, and Jowett. Their conversation ranged over religion, aesthetics, industry, fashion, culture, and the self. Unlike the Veneerings and their dreadful friends, these people were refined and learned. At the same time—also unlike the Veneerings—they were absolutely tired out and pessimistic. Through Mr. Herbert, Mallock has Ruskin say:

> Aristotle says that what is truly a man's Self is the thinking part of him. This sooner or later all the other parts obey—sooner or later, willingly or unwillingly; and if this Self be base, the whole man will be base; if the Self be noble, the whole man will be

noble. And as it is with the individual man, so it is with the ages and the generations. They obey their several Selves, whatever these Selves may be. The world once had a Self whose chief spokesman was a Jewish peasant called Jesus; and sooner or later the world followed him. Later on, it had a Self whose chief spokesmen were Dominics or Luthers or Loyolas; and in like manner the world followed them. Later still, it had got another Self, and the chief spokesmen of this were Voltaires and Rousseaus. And in each case the world was convinced at heart, consciously or unconsciously, that the vital truths of life were to be sought for only where these Selves sought for them. With Jesus and with Luther it sought them in duty and in a turning to the true God; with Voltaire and Rousseau, in justice, and in a turning from the false God. And now, where do you seek them? Where does the Self of your age seek them— your Self, that thinking part of you before which you all either quail or worship? Does it seek them either in justice, or loving-kindness, or in the vision of the most high God! No—but in the rotting bodies of dead men, or in the writhing bodies of live cats. And in your perplexity, and your amazed despair, ever and again you cry to it, what shall we do to be saved? Show us the Father! Show us the high and holy One that inhabiteth Eternity! And what does your Self answer you? It answers you with a laugh, "There is no high and holy One at all. How say ye then to me, Show us the Father? For the Earth saith, He is not with me; and the depth saith, He is not with me; and our filthy phials of decaying animal matter say, He is not with us. Argal, ye poor foolish seekers, He is nowhere." You may try to escape from your own Self, but you cannot; you may try to forget its answer, but you cannot. Loudly you may affirm with your lips; but the importunate denial is ever at your heart. *Patriae quis exsul se quoque fugit?* [57]

The writers of the nineties were to devise some new escape acts, as we shall see, but their success is moot at best.

Notes

1. *Letters of John Ruskin to Charles Eliot Norton* (Boston and New York, 1905), I, p. 85. Both this quotation and the next (*Works*, XVI, 290) appear in William A. Madden's "The Burden of the Artist," *1859: Entering an Age of Crisis*, ed. Philip Appleman, William A. Madden, and Michael Wolff (Bloomington, 1959), pp. 249 and 263.
2. Most historians take this date as *the* turning point in the Victorian period; see, for instance, the editorial assumption of *1859: Entering an Age of Crisis*. However, the year is, in my view, more a culmination of crisis than its beginning.
3. G. M. Young, *Victorian England: Portrait of an Age* (New York, 1953), p. 154. Young calls Macaulay the "last of the Augustans." Hunt and DeQuincey would then be "the last of the Romantics."
4. *Silas Marner, The Lifted Veil, Brother Jacob, The Works of George Eliot,* Cabinet Edition (Edinburgh and London [1878]), p. 284. This is the edition used for the discussion of "The Lifted Veil."
5. See Shelley's sonnet, "Lift Not the Painted Veil." The view of actuality as a veil concealing the higher reality is axiomatic throughout nineteenth-century poetry (for example, Stanza LVI of *In Memoriam*).
6. See footnote 7 to the Preface.
7. Tennyson added four idylls in 1869: "The Holy Grail," "The Coming of Arthur," "Pelleas and Ettarre," and "The Passing of Arthur" (which incorporates "Mort D'Arthur"). The poem as a whole was not complete until 1888.
8. Hallam Lord Tennyson, *Memoir*, II, p. 130. The phrase appears in the poem "To the Queen" attached to the *Idylls*.
9. Tennyson's name, later abandoned, for the first four idylls.
10. *Memoir*, II, p. 127.
11. *Memoir*, II, p. 123.

12. The *Idylls,* by its deliberately varied approaches to the characters, is quite experimental. A case could be made for the idea that Tennyson is challenging the reader to examine poetic reality by exposing him to different styles of characterization—the novelistic, the allegorical, the heroic, the homiletic, and so on.

13. The war between the purity of the lily and the sensuality of the rose is prefigured in *Maud.* E. D. H. Johnson's "The Lily and the Rose" provides a good analysis of this imagery. See footnote 59 to Chapter 4.

14. I am indebted to Nancy M. Engbretsen's unpublished dissertation (New York University, 1963) which reveals the essential imaginative kinship between "Balin and Balan" and Conrad.

15. DeVane mentions *Cenci* in this connection. Wylie Sypher sees Browning's villains as a cross between the melodramatic-Byronic figures and Dostoevsky's underground man. See his Introduction to the Norton Edition of *The Ring and the Book* (New York, 1961), pp. v–xxi.

16. After many qualifications, Robert Langbaum, in his *The Poetry of Experience,* calls *The Ring and the Book* "relativist."

17. *On the Classical Tradition, The Complete Prose Works of Matthew Arnold,* ed. R. H. Super, I (Ann Arbor, 1960), p. 128. References in this section are made to Super's edition which has to date published Arnold's prose works up to *Culture and Anarchy.*

18. Frederic E. Faverty, *Matthew Arnold, the Ethnologist* (Evanston, 1951). He argues that Arnold is a very good social scientist indeed.

19. *Complete Prose Works,* II, pp. 5–12.

20. "Culture: A Dialogue," *The Choice of Books and Other Literary Pieces* (London, 1886), p. 103.

21. *Complete Prose Works,* V, p. 124.

22. *The Works of Matthew Arnold* (London, 1903–1904), IX, p. xxxvi.

23. *The Works of Matthew Arnold,* VII, p. 15.

24. This "culturization" of Jesus, or Hellenizing of Hebraism, is already apparent in *St. Paul and Protestantism* (see pp. xx and xxxvi), but it is more fully developed in *Literature and Dogma.*

25. His brother tells us that his youthful reading includes Byron, Shelley, Keats, Tennyson, Poe, Maturin, Eugène Sue, Hoffman, Alfred de Musset, and Dumas. William Michael Rossetti, *Dante Gabriel Rossetti: His Family-Letters with a Memoir* (London, 1895), I, pp. 100–103.

26. F. L. Lucas, *The Decline and Fall of the Romantic Ideal* (Cambridge, 1948), p. 104.

27. R. L. Mégroz' subtitle for the chapter dealing with the motif of the double in his *Dante Gabriel Rossetti: Painter Poet of Heaven in Earth* (London, 1928).

28. Reminding one of earlier claims to inspired writing of Gothic stories, Rossetti says he finished the tale in "one night," *Family-Letters*, I, p. 415.

29. Graham Hough sees the Chiaro-Giunta-Bonaventura relationship as an autobiographical reference to the Rossetti-Hunt-Millais relationship. *The Last Romantics* (New York, 1961), p. 51.

30. *The Collected Works of Dante Gabriel Rossetti*, ed. William M. Rossetti (London, 1888), I, p. 392. Unless otherwise stated references are made to this edition.

31. All references in this discussion of the sonnet sequence are made to Paull Franklin Baum's edition of *The House of Life* (Cambridge, Mass., 1928), p. 230.

32. For dates of individual sonnets, see Baum, *passim*, and Oswald Doughty's *A Victorian Romantic: Dante Gabriel Rossetti*, 2nd ed. (London, 1960), pp. 381–382, 685–687.

33. There are few good treatments of Rossetti's poetry. Two exceptions are Hough's chapter in *The Last Romantics* and Harold Weatherby's "Problems of Form and Content in the Poetry of Dante Gabriel Rossetti," *VP*, II (1964), pp. 11–19, both of which discuss the unstable fusion of flesh and spirit in Rossetti's poetry.

34. Lafcadio Hearn, in *Pre-Raphaelite and Other Poets*, p. 102, quoted by Baum, pp. 205–206.

35. *The Poetical Works of James Thomson (B.V.)*, ed. Bertram Dobell (London, 1895), I, p. iv. References are all to this edition.

36. William David Schaefer's "The Two Cities of Dreadful Night," *PMLA*, LXXVII (1962), pp. 609–615, explains that Thomson began the poem with two different concepts of the city. His *James Thomson (B.V.): Beyond "The City"* (Berkeley and Los Angeles, 1965) is also helpful.

37. Repetition of course conveys the sameness, the feeling of ennui, of the existential hell. As a technique, however, it perilously resembles the mimetic fallacy, turning the reading of the poem itself into a hellish experience!

38. The 70 years of a normal lifetime, divided by the three mystic terms, faith, love, and hope, is nothing but 2, 1, 0, 2, 1, 0 . . .—misery (the number 2 is close to the mystic figure 3, and yet it can never reach it; it is also a very small number near 0, or nothingness), a greater misery (1), nothingness (0), and once again, misery. . . . The equation is an interesting indication of the mechanical quality of Thomson's imagination, his need to find security in abstraction.

39. The young Henry James, among others, felt that the author's imagination was "lifeless, forced, mechanical." "Our Mutual Friend," *The Future of the Novel*, ed. Leon Edel (New York, 1956), p. 76. The review originally appeared in *The Nation*, December 21, 1865.

40. See for example the attacks on this novel in Monroe Engel, *The Maturity of Dickens* (Cambridge, Mass., 1959), p. 132; K. J. Fielding (*Charles Dickens* [London, 1958]); and Robert Barnard ("The Choral Symphony: 'Our Mutual Friend,'" *A Review of English Literature*, II [July, 1961], pp. 89–99).

41. Book I, Chapter xv. For this discussion I used the Nonesuch Edition, eds. Arthur Waugh, Hugh Walpole, Walter Dexter, and Thomas Hatton (London, 1937–38).

42. "Charles Dickens," *Quarterly Review*, CXCVI (July, 1902), p. 34.

43. "Our Mutual Friend," *Partisan Review*, XVI (1949), reprinted in *The Dickens Critics*, ed. George H. Ford and Lauriat Lane, Jr. (Ithaca, 1961), p. 207.

44. The fun begins soon after David meets Mr. Dick (Chapter XIV) and continues throughout the novel. The year 1649 "when King Charles the First had his head cut off" is also made much of. Dr. Strong's dictionary is said to require 1649 more years for completion (Chapter XVI). *David Copperfield's* serialization started in 1849.

45. Here I am indebted to J. Hillis Miller's excellent chapter on *Bleak House* in his *Charles Dickens: The World of His Novels* (Cambridge, Mass., 1959).

46. "The Dickens World: A View from Todgers's," first published in *Sewanee Review*, LVIII (1950), and later reprinted in *The Dickens Critics*, p. 215.

47. Steven Marcus finds that the initials of the two characters correspond to Charles Dickens'. See *Dickens: From Pickwick to Dombey* (New York, 1965), p. 346.

48. The best discussion of the Pip-Orlick relationship is Dorothy Van Ghent's in her *The English Novel*. See also Julian Moynahan's "The Hero's Guilt: The Case of *Great Expectations*," *Essays in Criticism*, X (1960), pp. 60–79.

49. The chapter title has a double significance, referring, of course, to Rokesmith's monologue and subsequent dialogue with Bella, but also to the selection in which they each talk to themselves, in a kind of *dialogue* of the mind with itself. The importance of the chapter is emphasized in another way: Rokesmith's identity is disclosed here for the first time.

50. Some readers, unconvinced that Mr. Boffin is just playing a part for Bella's sake, feel that Dickens may have changed his plan for

the novel while writing it. However, they are ignoring the fact that the Golden Dustman's miserliness only begins (in III,iv) *with* his discovery of Rokesmith's true identity. His pretending to be a miser, therefore, cannot be interpreted as anything but a conscious move in a well-thought-out strategy for reforming Bella.

51. See especially discussions by J. Cuming Walters, W. Robertson Nicoll, Andrew Lang, and Richard M. Baker.

52. The immediate reasons for Dickens' Gothicism in this novel seem to be his determination to outdo Collins' *The Moonstone* (published in *All the Year Round* in 1868) and his meeting in Paris with Eugène Sue, one of several important French Gothic writers. However, Dickens' Gothicism goes deeper than that. As Walter C. Phillips argues, in his *Dickens, Reade, and Collins: Sensation Novelists*, Dickens stands in the middle of the romance tradition deriving from the Gothic romance and Byronism.

53. Preface, *The Renaissance: Studies in Art and Poetry*, 3rd ed. (London and New York, 1888), p. x. For his further transformation of Arnoldian disinterestedness to uninterestedness, see *Plato and Platonism* (New York, 1901), "[The young scholar's] duty is rather to follow intelligently, but with strict indifference, the mental process there, as he might witness a game of skill . . . ," p. 6.

54. The Conclusion to the *Renaissance*, p. 248.

55. T. S. Eliot's word. See his "Arnold and Pater," *Selected Essays*, new ed. (New York, 1950), p. 389.

56. *The Victorian Age in Literature*, pp. 110–111.

57. *The New Republic: Or, Culture, Faith, and Philosophy in an English Country House*, ed. J. Max Patrick (Gainesville, Florida, 1950), pp. 219–220.

Part III
The Art of the Self

Life imitates Art far more than Art imitates Life.
"The Decay of Lying"

We make out of the quarrel with others, rhetoric, but of the quarrel with ourselves, poetry.
"Per Amica Silentia Lunae"

6.

Masks in the Mirror:
The Eighteen-Nineties

André Gide met Oscar Wilde several times during the early nineties, and on one occasion that he recalls, Wilde inquired of him what he had been up to since their last meeting. Gide, a serious young man already taking sincerity seriously, recounted a few trifling incidents, which prompted Wilde to ask, Did he really do that? Was he *really* telling the truth? "Absolutely," said Gide, apparently gulled. "Then why repeat it?" countered Wilde. "You must see that it is not of the slightest importance." And he continued lecturing, "You must understand that there are two worlds—the one exists and is never talked about; it is called the real world because there is no need to talk about it in order to see it. The other is the world of Art; one must talk about that, because otherwise it would not exist." [1]

This Wildean anecdote, like the Wildean epigram, comprises the time, Wilde himself being, of course, its most perfect exemplar. If life seemed on the whole dull and inconsequential, art at least was something to talk about, and perhaps of occasional consequence. The argument is inescapable: One must live one's life as though it were art. But to consciously imitate art is finally to switch roles with it. Dorian Gray trades lives with his art-double, the idealized portrait, and makes for a time a beautiful life for himself—one is tempted to say, a life pretty as a picture. Of all the writers of the nineties it is surely in Wilde that the art of the self is at its most deliberate, its most artificial. Ultimately Wilde's art is the art of the lie, staged spectacularly as in a Cecil Beaton production. Next to the glories of that negotiated life, ordinary existence—even Dorian's monstrous reality as disclosed at last in the portrait—diminishes and dies.

To Stevenson, the real world was not so boring really as it was simply unmanageable. More precisely, it was the self that was unmanageable, problematic in relation to the rest of life, for the biggest problem was what to do about the hypocrisy of one's own life and the lives around one. In a sense, his essay into the double life, *Dr. Jekyll and Mr. Hyde,* is a more conventional statement than *Dorian Gray,* for all their thematic similarity. In Stevenson, hypocrisy, the lie at the very core of life, is still moralistically conceived. While Jekyll and his ilk continue to live the lie of respectability, the "idealized" double who is Jekyll's joyboy must carry the burden of disguise. Jekyll fears disclosure of the Hyde who is his "true" identity in the same way that the Puritan fears disclosure of his secret sexuality, not for reason primarily of shame but for fear of losing forever the exquisite pleasure of that second life. The paradox of Stevenson is that his joy can never free itself, whether in art or in the art of life, from the brand of gutter guilt that was **his heritage.**

Hardy saw the lie at the core of life more darkly than either of these men. By some strange sport of time, dread was discovered too soon, and in *Tess* as in *Jude* the self was not allowed its self-deception, nor art its little play on life. It was as though Hardy's illusionist, recognizing his idealized double, his epipsyche, as indeed his true mirror-image, and horrified at this too pure vision of his own identity, backed away from it as from a wraith. The illusionist was himself an illusion.

The double, whether as epipsyche, self-portrait, or monster, is for these writers the vehicle of self-creation. Indeed, consciousness of self implies doubleness, the consciousness aware of itself. Whether it is the "metaphysical" double of Hardy's novels or the "aesthetic" double of Wilde, the writers of the nineties take the insufficiency of the mere *ur*-self, the born identity, as axiomatic. Life experience, the development of self-consciousness, is for them mere matter for the life of art. At the point where art is found to be illusion, a lie at last, the life which is its source, and which in turn models its further life on art, is unavoidably a lie—and this, whether the lie is looked upon as salvation (Wilde) or damnation (Hardy). Either way the autonomy of art relative to life is beyond compromise. Wilde is clear on this in "The Decay of Lying": "As long as a thing is useful or necessary to us, or affects us in any way . . . it is outside the proper sphere of art." [2]

This distinction was present, too, in the theory of the novel at that time. It was abruptly in the eighties, fully a hundred years after Walpole's Preface, that the novel-romance controversy flared again among English writers. This time the romance genre was contrasted with the naturalistic novel of Zola. One of Stevenson's early theoretical statements, "A Gossip on Romance"

(1882), argues that a romance should "embody character, thought, or emotion in some act or attitude that shall be remarkably striking to the mind's eye."[3] Although an author will certainly draw his material from ordinary life, mere representation is not his purpose. "Fiction," Stevenson believes, "is to the grown man what play is to the child" (201). The following year, he attacked the overuse of detail in modern literature, arguing that the contemporary interest in realism has little to do with the "fundamental truth" of a work of art, being simply concerned with its "technical method" ("A Note on Realism"). The romance, just as the novel, must of its nature tell the truth. The distinction between the two forms rests rather on their differing degrees of inclusiveness: The realist tends in his "insane pursuit of completion," to "immolate his readers under facts"; the romancer, in contrast, is likely to become "merely null and lose all grip of fact, particularity, or passion."[4]

In "A Humble Remonstrance" (1884), Stevenson agrees with Henry James's "Art of Fiction" but goes further (James had denied any difference either between the novel and the romance or between the novel of character and the novel of incidence), asserting that there is no distinction between fiction in prose and fiction in verse, or even between fiction and "nonfiction" such as history or biography. Common to all genres is the art of narrative, which is not representative of real life. Stevenson, borrowing a phrase from James, insists that no art can be expected to "compete with life." Where life is "monstrous, infinite, illogical, abrupt, and poignant," art is "neat, finite, self-contained, rational, flowing, and emasculate."[5] Like a proposition in geometry, an art object expresses existence, but it cannot reproduce it. It is not a "transcript of life" but a "simplification

of some side or point of life, to stand or fall by its significant simplicity" (p. 100). To Stevenson art cannot
be life, though it can *have* a life of its own.

After more than a century of theory, which strictly
segregated the two streams of English fiction—the novel
and the romance—the men of the nineties, already redefining their lives, redefined their books. However "realistic" a literary work may be, it cannot be a point-by-
point reproduction of "reality," because "reality" is un-
ascertained. Rather, the artist makes reality by shaping
the inchoate material often called "reality." Understanding this, these artists were led to another notion, which
Wilde would so nicely formulate, that art is to a far
greater degree independent of mere life than the realist
or the naturalist would accept. Art leads a life of its own,
with the consequence that the artist can employ in his
art whatever he finds suitable, however irrational or
inexplicable it may be. In fact, the artist begins about
this time to surrender the common sense and commonplace entirely to the life-styles of the "ordinary" middle
classes, while appropriating the extraordinary and the
improbable as his proper domain. And, just as the poet
forges his language of symbolism—unintelligible to all
but the initiate—to express his vision of reality, so the
novelist discovers new forms and techniques—point of
view, altered time sequence, and stream of consciousness [6]
—that alone express his.

Intricately involved in this asserted alienation of the
artist is the marked resurgence of Gothicism. That this
mode had been all along highly attractive to many
writers is clear from the strong current of the Gothic
imagination throughout Victorian literature. However,
the earlier restraints on it (Charlotte Brontë's dominion
over the "nether world," for instance) are no longer

very effective. The sudden plethora of dual-personality stories in the nineties,[7] partly the result, no doubt, of the huge circulation figures run up by both *Dr. Jekyll and Mr. Hyde* and *Dorian Gray,* is surely better explained in terms of the great impetus the form provided writers to explore the dark side of human nature.

I

Dr. Jekyll and Mr. Hyde (1886) was by no means the first product of Stevenson's fascination with the dual personality. From childhood he had been familiar with the legend of Deacon Brodie, daylight cabinetmaker and moonlight burglar, and a full twenty years before *Dr. Jekyll and Mr. Hyde* he was already working on a play based on Brodie's life.[8] In 1883 he wrote a wretched and revolting story ("The Travelling Companion"), which was turned down by his publisher and which he himself soon decided to destroy. He called it a "carrion tale," and later explained why he had written it: "I had long been trying to write a story on this subject, to find a body, a vehicle, for that strong sense of man's double being which must at times come in upon and overwhelm the mind of every thinking creature." [9]

Then there is "Markheim" (1884), which somewhat resembles *Crime and Punishment.*[10] The hero, intent on robbery, enters a pawnshop on Christmas eve on the pretext of looking for a present. There, like Dorian Gray prematurely encountering his portrait, the sight of himself in an antique hand-mirror unhinges him: "Why, look here—look in it—look at yourself!" he cries to the pawnbroker, "Do you like to see it? No! nor I—nor any man." [11] There is too awful a self-recognition in the mirror, a "damned reminder of years, and sins and follies [in] this hand conscience" (132). At the height of his self-aversion Markheim murders the man, only to be confronted at every turn in the stifling little room by some presence, some "shadow of himself." In one glass after another "he saw his face repeated and repeated, as it were an army of spies; his own eyes met and detected him" (135).

Out of his anguish, there appears another man Markheim at once recognizes as a "likeness to himself" (146). The double is that other self, his conscience. Markheim at first tries to justify himself to this double. What he seems to be, he argues, is not his true nature but merely a disguise, a mask: "I have lived to belie my nature. All men do; all men are better than this disguise that grows about and stifles them" (147). Arguing in the Godwinian vein, he is, he insists, merely what the "giants of circumstance" have made of him, his true self having no responsibility for anything the "lie" happens to do. Underneath his false face anyone can see the "clear writing of conscience" (148). The double admonishes him for all this self-defensiveness, and when the shopkeeper's servant girl suddenly returns he advises killing her and running. However, Markheim, realizing that he is still free and, like the hero in Sartor Resartus, can still prefer good to evil, confronts her and tells his crime. During this confession, the features of his double brighten and soften, and he gradually disappears. Markheim has reconciled the double agents of action: his true free self and circumstance. The "other self" has no reason any longer to live.

"Markheim's" resolution of free will and circumstance is glib, and the reversal at the end—the thief-murderer's sudden conversion—is tacky. Despite the good description of the dealer's apartment and the uncanny way in which this room almost converges with Markheim's interior, the story is slight and remains only a preface to *The Strange Case of Dr. Jekyll and Mr. Hyde.*

It is best to envision the world of the story—the men and the landscape—before turning to the Jekyll-Hyde relationship itself. To begin with Mr. Utterson, a highly respected citizen and counselor: In his professional life, he is always correct and trustworthy, yet there is something furtive and suppressed about him. He is "austere with himself." He never smiles. He is "cold, scanty, and embarrassed in discourse" (Chapter 1).[12] He claims to like the theater, though he has not been to a play in twenty years. He makes no new friends and socializes only with men he has known well for a very long time. As for his renowned tolerance of other people's misconduct, this looks suspiciously to be the result not of sophistication or even good will but of indifference, though there is the subtlest suggestion of vicarious pleasure. Utterson, too, it turns out, has a past not quite innocent. When it occurs to him that blackmail may be at the root of Hyde's connection with Jekyll, he considers the possibility of a similar threat to himself: "And the lawyer, scared by the thought, brooded a while on his own past, groping in all the corners of memory, lest by chance some Jack-in-the-Box of an old iniquity should leap to light there" (Chapter 2). When his friend and client Sir Danvers Carew is murdered, the event stirs no deeper feeling in him than worry "lest the good name of another should be sucked down in the eddy of the scandal" (Chapter 5). And when his relative Mr. Enfield correctly observes the unspoken rule of never asking questions—"the more it looks like Queer Street, the less I ask" (Chapter 1)—Utterson concurs. Only the sight of Mr.

Hyde's unpleasant face cracks the smooth varnish of his existence, making him feel "(what was rare with him) a nausea and distaste of life" (Chapter 2).

Dr. Hastie Lanyon is, by contrast, an outwardly healthy and genial man, yet he too is shielded from life by an imposing respectability. Estranged from Dr. Jekyll for ten years, Dr. Lanyon is a scientist of "practical usefulness" (Chapter 9), who sees Jekyll as a man gone wrong with his "scientific heresies" (Chapter 3). As it happens, when the great Dr. Lanyon confronts a phenomenon which his matter-of-fact science cannot explain, his life is "shaken to its roots" (Chapter 9). He says to Utterson, "I sometimes think if we knew all, we should be more glad to get away" (Chapter 6). Too late he has learned something of the ghastly aspect of life, and, with undiminishing horror at it all, he shrivels and dies.[13]

The important men of the book, then, are all unmarried, intellectually barren, emotionally stifled, joyless. Nor are things much different in the city as a whole. The more prosperous business people fix up their homes and shops, but in a fashion without chic. Houses give an appearance of "coquetry," and store fronts invite one like "rows of smiling saleswomen" (Chapter 1). The rather handsome town houses in the back streets of Dr. Jekyll's neighborhood are rented out to all sorts—"map-engravers, architects, shady lawyers, and the agents of obscure enterprises" (Chapter 2). Everywhere the fog of the dismal city is inescapable, even creeping under the doors and through the window jambs (Chapter 5). The setting hides a wasteland behind that secure and relatively comfortable respectability of its inhabitants.

In such a milieu Dr. Jekyll stands out as "the very pink of the proprieties" (Chapter 1). Although his studies tend toward "the mystic and the transcendental"

(Chapter 10), like those of Faust and Frankenstein before him, he still manages to maintain a considerable scientific reputation. Despite Jekyll's social and professional caste—in fact, because of it—it is he, rather than Utterson or Lanyon, who brings forth Mr. Hyde.

It will be remembered that, for a period long before the emergence of Mr. Hyde, Dr. Jekyll had experienced a "profound duplicity of life"; alongside his "imperious desire" for dignity and reputation, there was that "impatient gaiety of disposition" (Chapter 10). But for those in the Victorian wasteland, gaiety and respectability are not easily reconciled. Dr. Jekyll, in particular, sees the two as mutually exclusive: A respectable pleasure would be a contradiction in terms. The exacting nature of his moral ambition was such that the most innocent delight resulted in shame. Meanwhile, his Faustian studies, which had already made him conscious of the "perennial war among [his] members" (Chapter 10), suggested a practical means of settling the whole question. However, where Faust was Promethean, irrepressible, by definition, Jekyll, the latter-day Faust, must at all costs button himself down, hold his place as a reputable man and even rise in the establishment if he can. And so, though pleasure had been suppressed for a long time by the dreary decency that was his life, Dr. Jekyll will enjoy it, after all, in the person of a totally new identity, Edward Hyde.

Hyde, once unleashed, arouses disgust in everyone. Dr. Jekyll's servant, for one, feels "kind of cold and thin" in his marrow after meeting Hyde for the first time (Chapter 8), and even the "Sawbones" has the urge to do away with him. To catch sight of Hyde is to be reminded of the hidden *"je"* in each of us, the "troglodytic" (Chapter 2) animal that lies in wait for the moment of release. In most societies men are not required to suppress the *"je"* totally, and they agree to curb it. But in Jekyll's world, the *"je"* must be ruthlessly suppressed—most unequivocally so by the man known as "the very pink of the proprieties," Dr. Henry Jekyll, the most thoroughgoing *"je*-killer" of them all.

Hyde, at once Jekyll's Mephistopheles and his (Frankenstein) monster, looks like the very incarnation of evil, but at the beginning he is in fact merely Jekyll's unrepressed spontaneous existence. Going about in the guise of Mr. Hyde, Dr. Jekyll discovers a new freshness and joy in his life. He feels "younger, lighter, happier in body" and is conscious of a "heady recklessness," of a "current of disordered sensual images running like a mill-race in my fancy, a solution of the bonds of obligation, an unknown but not an innocent freedom of the soul" (Chapter 10). Not respectable certainly, and therefore utterly despicable by the standards of the Utterson-Enfield-Lanyon world.

However, Hyde gradually shows himself dissatisfied with his role as mere "impatient gaiety" and becomes scornful of the rights of others. His "every act and thought [are] centred on self" (Chapter 10). In fact, his pleasure comes to depend on his torturing others. At this point, the self and society are enemies to the death.

Soon after the episode in which Hyde tramples the child, the Jekyll-Hyde metamorphosis becomes involuntary. The doctor goes to bed Henry Jekyll and awakes as Edward Hyde. The hidden *"je"* released by the social "I" threatens now to overpower it. Yet he believes it is still within his strength to control Hyde. Resolving to forego the "leaping impulses and secret pleasures," he determines to live once again the life of an "elderly and discontented doctor" (Chapter 10). Of course, having once allowed his *"je"* the taste of freedom, he finds he cannot long suppress it. Soon Edward Hyde leaps out "roaring" (Chapter 10) from the cave of Henry Jekyll. When the brutal murder of Sir Danvers Carew is disclosed, Jekyll's remorse is intense, if short-lived, recalling the amnesiac reaction of countless Gothic villains after indulging their sadism. Hyde is now a known criminal, hunted down not only by Utterson (who calls himself "Mr. Seek" [Chapter 2]) but also by the police, and the doctor can no longer risk taking advantage of the Hyde persona for his sojourns in the netherworld. The next time he goes out it is in the guise of Dr. Henry Jekyll. No wonder, then, that the metamorphosis should have become completely involuntary and the magic drug virtually ineffectual. There are no longer any marks to distinguish the two. The hideous face is forever joined to the social mask. The joining, however, is in no sense a reconcilement of the Jekyll-Hyde duality. Rather, it signals a return to the starting point of Jekyll's whole experience. Only the annihilation of one of the two selves "reconciles" them: at the end of the story the doctor finally suppresses the *"je"* by murdering Hyde, thereby, of course, becoming a "self-destroyer" (Chapter 8), a suicide.

Chesterton is the first to have pointed out the autobiographical elements in *Dr. Jekyll and Mr. Hyde*. He argues that Edinburgh, not London, is the scene of the story, on the basis that the black and white distinction of good and evil, the horror of tainting respectability with the disclosure of human failings, is Puritan, especially Caledonian. Chesterton sees Jekyll's fastidiousness as the trait of one who "knew the worst too young; not necessarily in his own act or by his own fault, but by the nature of a system which saw no difference between the worst and the moderately bad." [14] Stevenson himself, being the only child of a very pious couple, suffered from

their Puritanical suppressions from his earliest days. Although he did rebel in adolescence, leaving home for a
bohemian love-life in the Edinburgh slums, he was
soon being suppressed again, this time by his wife, the
respectable Fanny Osborne Stevenson. Since he did require her secretarial services, it gradually developed that
both his work and his personal correspondence were regi-
mented and censored by her.[15] No one has yet, of course,
disclosed a Hyde lurking in the shadows of Stevenson's
life, and the biographical interest must remain ancillary
to the book itself. On its own, quite apart from its
author's problems, *Dr. Jekyll and Mr. Hyde* is fascinating
for its depiction of the two levels of man's being. It
also provides a very convenient epithet ("Jekyll-and-
Hyde") for the psychopath. For these reasons we can
say that Stevenson was perhaps too successful in both
story idea and execution. For the mastery of the book is
the vision it conjures of the late Victorian wasteland,
truly a de-Hyde-rated land unfit to sustain a human being
simultaneously in an honorable public life and a joyful
private one.

II

Hardy's main sources and influences are the two familiar tributaries—the Elizabethan villain and old folklore and balladry—that formed the long and deep flow
of Gothicism in nineteenth-century English writing. His
Elizabethan villain once regularly haunted the ruined
Castle of Catatonia, whose star boarders then went on
to thrill the Romantics and the mid-Victorians. And his
use of folklore and balladry, always a full reservoir of
old legend, superstition, and witchcraft, is clearly con-

substantial with the Gothic imagination.[16] Yet Hardy tells how he decided not to read the superbly Gothic *Wuthering Heights* after hearing it was a depressing novel—an amazing admission from the author of *Tess* and *Jude,* It is not known whether he ever read *Jane Eyre,* but between Charlotte's book and *Tess of the d'Urbervilles* (1891) there are striking resemblances. Both are stories of a poor girl's seduction. Thornfield Hall echoes with the ghostly laughter of its tenant vampire, and Tess hears the ominous sound of the d'Urberville Coach. The thunder striking on the eve of Jane's wedding and the cocks crowing on Tess's nuptial afternoon both signal disaster to come. At Thornfield the gabled roof hides the vampire, and the old d'Urberville vault, where Tess decides to give herself once more to Alec, is stocked with coffins. It is true the heroines are rather different people: Jane is plain and something of a prig, whereas Tess is one of the most attractive and fully sexed women of all Victorian literature. But there is in both novels the same love triangle, and in both, the two men attracted to the heroine are diametrically opposing characters—making a pattern well understood if looked at in terms of Arnold's dichotomy of Hellenism and Hebraism. In *Jane Eyre* this dualism is strongly suggested, but in *Tess* it is fully implemented. Each of the four men, however, shows traits of the Gothic tribe: Alec d'Urberville, like Rochester, is the pure type of Gothic villain, passion overruling reason at crucial points, and Angel Clare's priestly villainy is also true of St. John Rivers. "Angel" is of course an idealist, his harp tuned to pagan morality, but his humanism shows its cruel side immediately after his discovery of Tess's past indiscretion. Alec, in contrast, despite his brief conversion, is fundamentally and thoroughly a pitchforked devil. He mockingly calls Tess

"coz," recalling the circumstance that Jane and St. John
Rivers are cousins by birth.

Such thematic affinities broadly establish Hardy's kinship with Charlotte Brontë, which is not of course to
attribute to them the same temper, sensibility, and reading of life. Indeed, what is sometimes called Hardy's
"cosmic sensitivity" is much more noticeable in Emily
Brontë, and later in D. H. Lawrence, than in Charlotte.
Finally, it is in their different treatment of self-division
that their differing outlook on life is most clearly exposed.

In Alec the fraudulent identity is obvious. First, his
claim to the old family name is unrightful, being based
on the sheer theft of it by his father, a nouveau riche
who needed a good name to go with his money. Second,
this bored sensualist is supposedly completely transformed
into a hell-fire preacher: As expressed in the succinct
oxymoron of Chapter 45, in Alec "Animalism had become fanaticism; Paganism Paulinism." [17] But when
he meets Tess again, he must protect himself against, as
it were, the old Alec in him. In a compact sealed at
the grave of a thug who "sold his soul to the devil"
(Chapter 45), he makes her swear not to seduce him.
After all that, his religious drive slows ("duty and desire
ran hand-in-hand" [Chapter 46]) and before long peters
out altogether. Meanwhile his sensual craving for Tess
grows and becomes his sole preoccupation: "I thought I
worshipped on the mountains, but I find I still serve in
the groves!" (Chapter 46). Alluding to Milton, he identifies himself with Satan: "You are Eve, and I am the old
Other One come to tempt you in the disguise of an inferior animal" (Chapter 50). Alec switches back to
sensuality as abruptly and thoroughly as he originally
converted to evangelicalism.

Angel Clare's dualism, like that of St. John's, is

more subtle than either Alec's or Rochester's. If Jane's husband cuts rather a Byronic figure, Tess's man is "less Byronic than Shelleyan." Being "imaginative and ethereal," his love for her is capable of jealously protecting the loved one "against his very self" (Chapter 31). Clare may be said to have been created on the model of the *Alastor* poet.[18] The ideal beauty he sees in Tess is his own creation, having nothing to do with the person Tess understands herself to be. She is tormented by the discrepancy, by her lover's inability to meet her: "O my love, my love, why do I love you so! . . . for she you love is not my real self, but one in my image; the one I might have been!" (Chapter 33). Unable to recognize his delusion (like Sue Bridehead's in Hardy's next novel it has a large component of sexual fear), Clare is oblivious to her suffering: "What I am in worldly estate, she is. What I become, she must become. What I cannot be, she cannot be" (Chapter 34). The great irony of the novel is that Tess is the truest "epipsyche" he could have, a fact she realizes only when he confesses his past transgressions and asks her forgiveness: "How strange it [is]! He seem[s] to be her double" (Chapter 34). He, however, can never accept it. Confronting his double in her, he shrinks as if from a Rossettian wraith. She horrifies him with her true likeness to himself. His double, then, is not what he sought; he wanted rather some idealized impossibility: " 'I repeat, the woman I have been loving is not you.' 'But who?' 'Another woman in your shape' " (Chapter 35). His "hard logical deposit" then rejects everything about her with a ruthless consistency. The "gentle" Clare conceals in his depths this "will to subdue the grosser to the subtler emotion, the substance to the conception, the flesh to the spirit" (Chapter 36), and with much more brutality than even Alec is capable of rejects all possibility of union with otherness.

The self-recognition scene done, Tess begins in fact to waste away into the Rossettian wraith. However, by now she herself had "spiritually ceased to recognize the body before him as hers." She had allowed it to "drift, like a corpse upon the current, in a direction disassociated from its living will" (Chapter 55). Nonetheless, by disowning this body which has failed them both, she becomes for the first time an active agent. Tess asserts her whole being in the murder of Alec, a being undistorted either by Clare's earlier false idealization of her or by her own self-destructive guilt. There is a diabolical double irony here: Only when the self dissociates from the body is it free to act and fulfill itself—in an act of murder. Yet Tess says on the altar at Stonehenge, "It is as it should be" (Chapter 58). In *Jane Eyre* the descent from Latmos exacts its toll, though both Jane and Rochester are presumed to live a long, happy life afterward. In *Tess of the d'Urbervilles*, a mere few days of happiness are bought at the price of her life.

Read as a "realistic" novel, *Jude the Obscure* (1895) is unquestionably Hardy's most preposterous. Several of the characters—not just the notorious "Little Father Time" —are little more than programed puppets. The story strings together fantastic events and coincidences in utter disregard of the laws of reality, not to say the novelistic law of verisimilitude. Furthermore, its plan, as Hardy himself admits, is too "geometrically constructed." [19] With marriages made, unmade, and made again in the book, the effect is often sentimental and melodramatic, quite different indeed from the work, say, of Hardy's two great contemporaries, James and Conrad.

But *Jude* may also be taken as a historical document, depicting quite justly the late nineteenth-century English intellectual milieu, particularly around Oxford where Tractarianism, Arnold's Hebraism and Hellenism, even Ruskin's "two paths" have all long since become sets of obsolete alternatives. Gothic cathedral and "Corinthian" are alike in ruins. And the two roads that branch off only to meet again no longer go anywhere:

> The great western highway from London passes through it, near a point where the road branches into two, merely to unite again some twenty miles farther westward. Out of this bifurcation and reunion there used to arise among wheeled travellers, before railway days, endless questions of choice between the respective ways. But the question is now as dead as the scot-and-lot freeholder, the road wagoner, and the mail coachman who disputed it; and probably not a single inhabitant of Stoke-Barehills is now even aware that the two roads which part in his town ever meet again, for nobody now drives up and down the great western highway daily.
>
> (V,v)

So many Victorian sages, having joined the ancient dead in the gallery of framed portraits at Christminster, leave the scene of this book to the forces of secularism, skepticism, neopaganism, and feminism—all very much in the minds of Hardy's contemporaries. As a " 'purpose' novel," [20] too, *Jude* made a powerful impression on contemporary readers. Its outspokenness on sexual matters, a shock and scandal at the time, rid the English novel of excessive prudishness and helped prepare the way for the uninhibited novels of the twentieth century. Its attack on the denial of higher education to the working class served as an impetus for the establishment of Ruskin College at Oxford and for other measures signaling democratic progress.

In the broad terms of its understanding of human behavior, *Jude the Obscure* stands somewhere between nineteenth-century moral psychology and twentieth-century clinical psychology. Sue Bridehead is Hardy's masterly characterization of the *belle dame sans merci*, the frigid woman, or the "pure thing" [21] as Lawrence calls her, whereas Arabella, raised by a "pig-breeder," is Sue's antithesis—all sex and no intellect. Arabella and Sue exemplify what Schopenhauer, anticipating Freud's eros and thanatos, called the Will-to-live and the Will-not-to-live. Jude is torn between the two—between Sue's highly developed intellect and Arabella's sexuality. Of course in neither can he find both satisfactions, and he dies frustrated and alone.

In addition to this familiar Hardyan dualism, however, *Jude the Obscure* furthers the Shelleyan theme already apparent in *Tess*. Sue is Jude's intellectual beauty, epipsyche, and double. Phillotson is struck with "the extraordinary sympathy, or similarity, between the pair." They seem to him "one person split in two," and he sees their paramount desire "to be together" as "Shelleyan" (IV, iv). Jude addresses Sue as "you spirit, you disembodied creature . . . hardly flesh at all," and Sue too thinks of herself as Jude's epipsyche, quoting Shelley. Throughout the novel she is referred to as "a phantasmal, bodiless creature" (V,i), "flexible and light as a bird" (V,v). As long as Jude's idealizing self dominates, he and Sue are in perfect union, or as she calls it, in perfect "two-in-oneness" (VI,ii).[22] In utter disregard of social convention and traditional wisdom, the couple attempt to guide their life together solely by ideal rationality. Estranged from their own class while not yet integrated with any other, they wander homeless in the "sordid" human world.

However, as the Poet in *Alastor* had discovered, the rarefied air gradually strangles. Even the pure union of Jude and Sue requires consummation in the mixed and ordinary. But as the beast in Jude begins to stir, society starts to persecute them. A wide rift appears to them between "the ideal life a man wish[es] to lead, and the squalid life he [is] fated to lead." [23] Jude's self-division cannot help but affect their idealized union, and with Arabella's reappearance on the scene, Sue for the first time gives herself to Jude. In physical surrender she recognizes the incompleteness of their former relationship, and its false basis: "Our life has been a vain attempt at self-delight," she tells him, "But self-abnegation is the higher road." The "creed-drunk" Sue has only replaced her Shelleyanism with a different doctrine—the Judeo-Christian religion and the social conventions of her time and place. "We should mortify the flesh—the terrible flesh —the curse of Adam!" (VI,iii). Despite her continuing aversion to sex, she yields to Phillotson, to whom, as she now acknowledges, she is tied "sacramentally."

Jude's was not the only failure; the Shelleyan epipsyche took to the air as well. But in *Alastor* there is a glory, if not of triumph, at least of a sublime sort of defeat. In *Jude,* the ceremony of glory is drowned. Abandoned by his epipsyche, Jude almost indifferently turns to Arabella. Here again there can be no real union, for his spirit is unengaged. Forsaken by Arabella, too, he dies alone, incomplete, in full cognizance of all his futility. Similarly for Sue, there is scarcely a glimmer of hope. What she has embraced is hardly the full "here and now" of English life, but merely the "function-fulfilling organ" [24] of a Phillotson. As Arabella says of Sue, "She's never found peace since she left his arms, and never will again till she's as he is now!" But how different this wandering soul from the soul of a Heathcliff or Cathy! [25]

III

Hardy was not a man to be easily consoled, whether by art or by life. For the author of *Tess* and *Jude* art, like the ideal in life, is an illusion which comes to nothing. To the decadent of the time, however, art stands in for life, answering very well for its myriad inadequacies. What the famous principle of art for art's sake really amounts to is an assertion of art's dissociation from the material of life. Life, in fact, is too busy imitating art to obey the Arnoldian version whereby it—life—should be the observed category, imitated by art to produce a kind of "art life" drawn from life. But the tautology involved in the Wildean notion of life as art—life becomes art which is art—is not disturbing to the decadent, probably because if art is antiseptically cloistered from life, life then in this special sense is finally quite irrelevant to life. And art—whether mirrored in the masks of the nineties, the shrines of the Yeatsian icon, or the living theaters of the cool and the absurd—art is the thing which comes to us bearing the only liveliness, the only reality there is.

As Wilde advised, one must continue to talk about art, talk it up, to assure its viability and its vibrancy. But can talk about art equal the practice of art? Possibly, if the art one is talking about is the art of talking itself, which to Wilde was the medium of life. Predictably, Wilde's natural medium was the stage. Arthur Symons was to recall that the Wildean intelligence was intrinsically "dramatic," and the man himself "not so much a personality as an attitude." Not really a sage, he maintained the attitude of a sage; not quite a poet, he maintained the attitude of a poet; not fully an artist, he maintained the attitude of an artist. "And it was precisely in his attitudes he was most sincere." [26] Playing the artist was a serious art with Wilde. Arnold prophesied it and Wilde fulfilled it—the proposition that because art makes for coherence and magic in a life devoid of both, being an artist is the only way to live. Further, because modern life fatally imitates art, the life of the Wildean artist must itself be art. A delicate balance is maintained between art as life and life as art, but the tendency with Wilde is toward the latter at the expense of the former. "I have put my genius into my life," said Wilde, "and only my talent into my works." [27]

The life performances of Beckford and Byron were discussed earlier, and brief references have been made to the attitudinizing of poets such as Poe and Whitman. There were longer discussions of both Browning, who, it should be noted, aspired to the stage, and of Dickens, who of course was famed for his readings. Wilde was a very special test of this lively tradition. With his warmth and self-indulgent personality—like a spoilt child—his existence demanded an audience, and an affectionate and responsive one at that. But the touted autonomy of art is irreconcilable with this notion of life as art: To believe that art is for the sake of art, one should be an alienated, lonely figure. And, insofar as such an artist basks in his own limelight, he is like the performer who declaims to his audience that he needs no audience, while fully expecting it to applaud him for the style of his declamation. Wilde managed to juggle this bundle of paradoxes until society caught up with him in 1895 in the malice of the mad Marquess of Queensberry.

To the actor Wilde the importance of his theatrical tools, the mask and the mirror, is so great as to be almost an obsession. The motif of the mask appears constantly in the plays. Lord Darlington says to Lady Windermere, "You would have to be to him the mask of his real life, the cloak to hide his secret" (*Lady Windermere's Fan*, II), and Mrs. Erlynne to Lady Windermere, in a vocabulary powerfully suggesting Dr. Jekyll's confession, "You don't know what it is . . . to have to creep in by hideous byways, afraid every moment lest the mask should be stripped from one's face" (III). Mrs. Arbuthnot says of herself: "She is a woman who wears a mask, like a thing that is a leper" (*A Woman of No Importance*, III), and Lady Chiltern accuses her husband, "Oh what a mask you have been wearing all these years! A horrible painted mask!" (*An Ideal Husband*, II). The mask hides a no-man's face, and although everyone fears exposure of his nothingness, to others one's mask *is* one's face.[28] The mirror, on the other hand, reflects not only the mask but, hopefully, the hidden truth of the face. The mirror, a recurrent image in Victorian literature—Tennyson's "The Lady of Shalott," Arnold's "Empedocles," George Eliot's *Adam Bede* and *Middlemarch,* Dickens' *Our Mutual Friend*—takes on a distinctly new cast in Wilde. For most of the earlier Victorian writers this self-consciousness is to be suppressed, whereas for the writers of the nineties—as for the Romantics—introspection, mirror-gazing, is a sanctioned activity. For the world, wear your mask; for a true glimpse of yourself, consult your mirror. The mask is for others' inspection, the mirror for one's private introspection.[29] In *The Picture of Dorian Gray* (1890), the portrait is the "most magical of mirrors" (Chapter 8), duplicating the corruption of Dorian's soul, while his ageless hand-some face is a mask hiding the soul's progress in evil. Of all Wilde's works, *Dorian Gray* has been called his "Wild-est and Oscarest," [30] and in this sense the book can be said to mirror its author, whose own witty masquerade may have fooled his audience but hardly himself.

The materials for the making of *Dorian Gray*, its literary sources and influences, have been quite thor-oughly searched and researched. As to its Gothicism, Wilde got the notion of the doppelgänger portrait from *Melmoth the Wanderer* by his great-uncle Charles Ma-turin. Dorian's house, with its hidden closet and isolated "schoolroom," is a type of haunted castle, and there is the opium den toward the end of the book like the one Casper visited in *Edwin Drood*. The book's Satanism is a borrowing from the Byronic and villain-hero tradition. Lord Henry is the classic devil figure, Dorian's prayer ("I would give my soul for that!") a rudimentary devil-compact,[31] and throughout the story his greed for life is unmistakably Faustian. Campbell's disposal of the corpse recalls the experiments of *Frankenstein* and *Dr. Jekyll and Mr. Hyde*. Poor Sibyl's suicide derives from the "persecuted maiden" of Victorian and pre-Victorian mel-odrama. There is just a hint of incest between Sibyl and her brother. And the ending is, of course, straight out of Poe's "William Wilson." What we have got from all this study is an understanding of the practical nature of this actor-author by which each of his "sources" is in turn "taken up, used, and dropped," in his persistent efforts at demonstrating his "truth of masks." [32] The book, or Wilde himself for that matter, is thus no more "derived" from these sources than a Shakespearean actor could be said to be derivative of Hamlet or King Lear. Le Gallienne calls Wilde an "astonishing, impudent microcosm," [33] a mirror, he implies, of the macrocosm of England at that time. So if we want to read larger sociohistorical "forces" at work in *Dorian Gray,* they are precisely those, including decadence and dandyism, that formed the age of the nineties.

Apropos of this relation of Wilde and his age, there is a certain work noted for its absolute statement of the decadent philosophy which is referred to several times in *Dorian Gray* itself, although without identifying it as *À Rebours* by Huysmans.[34] Chapter 11 in particular seems a deliberate imitation of both theme and style of the Huysmans work. Wilde's hero pursues a cultivation, or "spiritualization," of the senses, and in what amounts to a potpourri of Rossetti, Pater, and Whistler, with a strong indication of Huysmans, Dorian Gray moves with his "new Hedonism" from ordinary sensuality to a vaguely Gothic sort of ritualism to the connoisseurship of perfumes, jewels, and the exquisite embroideries of old church vestments. In the double-mirrors passage, very closely resembling a scene in *À Rebours,* Dorian like Des Esseintes is in the grip of ennui. Both are young men estranged from their contemporaries and engaged instead in scouting the farthest limits of selfhood. Yet certain differences between these two very similar works stand out. The kind of sensual intensity that is so brilliant in the Huysmans work is nowhere approached in the Wilde. *Dorian Gray* tends to read in its entirety as a succession of purple patches and epigrams. Sparkling and crackling though they are at times, they are randomly placed in the melodrama. In the Huysmans, the hero's search for the sensual absolute is very convincing; in the Wilde, there is only the pose of the explorer. The ornamental style of the English book arouses suspicion that a discrepancy may exist between Wilde's intended hedonism and diabolism and his actual literary product, which is finally quite Philistine in its performance.

The book provides a good deal of evidence for this disparity of matter and manner. Lord Henry is often put forth as Wilde's spokesman, and in fact he does parrot the Wildean aesthetic. For instance, Wotton pontificates at one point how the aim of life is "self-development," and that realizing our nature perfectly is "what each of us is here for." He continues, "People are afraid of themselves, nowadays. They have forgotten the highest of all duties, the duty that one owes to one's self" (Chapter 2). Well, Wilde himself is on record as having said essentially the same thing some four years *later* (an order of events reinforcing the picture of Wilde imitating art in his life) in the letter to Alfred Douglas known as *De Profundis:* "To reject one's own experiences is to arrest one's own development. To deny one's own experiences is to put a lie into the lips of one's own life." [35] Wotton's epigrams are so much Wilde's own that they would blend completely in any Wildean essay or letter. His expression of the new hedonism and aestheticism of the *Fin-de-siècle* is clearly Wilde's. In the dramatic context of the novel Lord Henry, of course, is the tempter offering eternal youth and beauty in return for Dorian's soul. According to Lord Henry, this exchange marks the emergence of "the real Dorian Gray." Later, however, Dorian is seized with remorse for having made such a pact and renounces Lord Henry as the devil. The relationship of the two thus appears at one point to be that of prophet and disciple, at another, that of devil and victim, and the question is, Which does the novel intend?

In the other temptation episode, "Prince Charming's" seduction of Sibyl Vane, there is a similar ambiguity. The situation, straight out of sentimental melodrama, is handled rather nicely. "Before I knew you," Sibyl tells Dorian, "acting was the one reality of my life. It was only in the theatre that I lived. . . . I was Rosalind one night, and Portia the other" (Chapter 7). With Dorian she comes to know, she believes, "what reality really is," comes to see through "the hollowness, the sham, the silliness" of her stage life (Chapter 7). Being in love, really and truly, she can no longer play at being in love. For Dorian, of course, by now an accomplished student of Lord Henry, the play is the thing. "You used to stir my imagination," he admonishes, "Now you don't even stir my curiosity. . . . Without your art you are nothing." Quite unmoved by her grief and more than a trifle annoyed, he drops her. "There is always something ridiculous about the emotions of people whom one has ceased to love." Dorian's reaction is understandable: Sibyl's suffering is a bore, although our bad temper is directed less toward this helpless creature than toward her creator. The hero's lapse in gallantry is perfectly consistent with his principles. By this time he had advanced remarkably in his course of Satanic aesthetics, and yet he carries off no laurels from the author. In fact—and amazingly—Dorian begins to feel somewhat ashamed: "My own personality has become a burden to me" (Chapter 18). He tries to atone for the guilt he feels by denying himself the pleasure of seducing a village girl, and his death at the end is surely some sort of poetic justice. Which sort is not at all clear, for it is not at all clear what his guilt consists of. Is he to be accused of denying Sibyl's self-demeaning and sentimental love for him? Or damned for his apostasy to the new hedonism? If the novel is to any extent sympathetic toward Sibyl, and Sibyline love, what then becomes to the new hedonism? But if, otherwise, it supports Dorian's Satanism, why is he punished? Wilde's

Caliban sees his face in *Dorian Gray*. But which face? Dorian's handsome one, his corrupt one, or Sibyl's teary one? The novel carries this indecisiveness at a very fundamental level.

One writer on Wilde sees the uncertainty as a problem of two distinct Wildes: the showpiece ("the dandy, the wit, the sophisticate, the cynic, the paradoxer, the brazen sinner"—in short, "the Devil's Advocate") and the anti-Wilde, a mystery to all but a few of his most intimate friends (the "ordinary human being, *l'homme moyen sensuel*, the sentimentalist, the tortured sinner, the penitent").[36] According to this view, it is the Devil's Advocate who secures the privacy and rather modest existence for the anti-Wilde, the "realer," moral Wilde. But is this scheme itself real? Wilde is the performer, the public man even in his most private life, and in the typical attitude he strikes, dandy and sentimentalist are indistinguishable. It is simply not the case that the anti-Wilde is the truer Wilde. Even the supposedly clinching evidence, the letter in which Wilde defines himself in relation to the personae of his book ("Basil Hallward is what I think I am; Lord Henry what the world thinks me; Dorian Gray what I would like to be—in other ages, perhaps.")[37] becomes, when read carefully, counterevidence for the anti-Wilde thesis. Take the "Basil Hallward" Wilde of 1890 and 1891, the triumphant hero of aestheticism constantly in the limelight and always the lion of high society. Could this Wilde possibly see himself as clumsy and unattractive, the dull, lonely, alienated artist? Further, the "Dorian" Wilde presents still another enigma. It is understandable that Wilde may have longed for the same beauty, grace, and eternal youthfulness that Dorian possessed. But Dorian's character? In short, Basil Hallward and Dorian Gray are poor correlatives, if indeed they were ever intended as such, of Oscar Wilde's "reality" and "ideal." As for the "Lord Henry" Wilde, he is epigrammatic, Satanic, the ultimate dandy. Lord Henry certainly approximates the picture the world and Oscar painted of Oscar. However the job here is to discover Wilde as he was, not Wilde as he looked to the world.

All this is not to say that Wilde himself did not try to justify the work as moral. To those papers and periodicals which had attacked the serialized version of *Dorian Gray,* he pointed out the "moral" of the book:

> All excess, as well as all renunciation, brings its own punishment. The painter, Basil Hallward, worshipping physical beauty far too much, as most painters do, dies by the hand of one in whose soul he has created a monstrous and absurd vanity. Dorian Gray, having led a life of mere sensation and pleasure, tries to kill conscience, and at that moment kills himself. Lord Henry Wotton seeks to be merely the spectator of life. He finds that those who reject the battle are more deeply wounded than those who take part in it. Yes; there is a terrible moral in *Dorian Gray*—a moral which the prurient will not be able to find in it, but which will be revealed to all whose minds are healthy.[38]

To Arthur Conan Doyle he wrote, very much in the style of Coleridge on the "Ancient Mariner," that the "moral" of the book is "too obvious." [39] Was this to say then the work of art should have a moral, but concealed? If so, how would this rather sedate position square with his aesthetic doctrines? Or with the Preface of the book for that matter?

There is no such thing as a moral or an immoral book. Books are well written, or badly written. That is all.

No artist has ethical sympathies. An ethical sympathy in an artist is an unpardonable mannerism of style.

Furthermore, *Dorian Gray's* overly "obvious moral" amounts to little more than a tablet of thou-shalt-nots: "Don't kill your conscience," "Don't be excessive," "Don't worship physical beauty," and "Don't be vain"! Is this such a "terrible moral"?

Walter Pater reduced the book to a very simple moral: Vice and crime make people "coarse and ugly." [40] After all the rodomontade, Wilde's Satanism never gets much beyond middle-class squeamishness.[41] In *De Profundis,* surely one of the most pathetic documents of modern times, this attitude comes through even clearer—and shabbier. Abandoning his once outrageously anti-bourgeois pose, he blames Douglas for having made him foul his family name ("a name they had made noble and honored not merely in Literature, Art, Archeology and Science, but in the public history of my own country").[42] Is this then finally the real Wilde? This bourgeois sentimentalist worrying over his disgraced line, forgetful, when under pressure, of the merry buffoon of former days masquerading with a lily one day and a sunflower the next?

Wilde is more than a "playboy of the Nineties." [43] There is something about him that reflects quite faithfully the predicament of the last decade. Through Dorian, Wilde talks about man in a way that challenges the definition of the self held by earlier Victorians: "He used to wonder at the shallow psychology of those who conceive the Ego in man as a thing simple, permanent, reliable, and of one essence" (Chapter 11). Just before this he wonders if insincerity is such "a terrible thing" and cannot believe it is. He sees it rather in a very positive light as "a method by which we can multiply our personalities." The figure of Faust as self-multiplier is a constant, as we have seen, throughout nineteenth-century English letters, but what is new in this Wildean Faust is his unselectiveness. The archetypal Faust generates a powerful urge to identify the self with the whole of life as the creator of life, but here the self, in this integral creative sense, is nowhere to be found. If the Wildean insincerity implies multiplicity, sincerity must imply self-integrity. To experience all possible experiences, spiritual and sensual, religious and secular, moral and amoral, man must be a "complex multiple creature." However, to "experience" at all, one must *be,* first of all. And this is what he is unable, or unwilling, to do, since for that he would have to *choose* what he wants to see, what he wants to do, and what he would like to be. And he cannot choose. He is uncomfortable with morality, Philistine morality being vulgar; he is ill at ease in sin, immorality, after all, being unpleasant and tiring; he is suspicious about religion, God being the only one who knows for certain He exists. Then, too, he is unsure of himself about atheism, being aware he is not really self-sufficient; ill at ease with others, being destined to be alone and lonely; unfamiliar with real solitude because he is so lonesome. Probably the best way is the way out, equivocating on each dilemma as it presents itself. But if that cannot be arranged, and one must stand and fight, a paradox is a well-sharpened sword, and the deliberate presentation of different masks the best shield.

When Dorian makes the point that acting is the only reality, what he means is that acting is *really* unreal, whereas life is a little real and a little unreal, necessitating a very precise discrimination at each point. Thus, the "realness" of the actor's life—the unreal world of art itself—is the only congenial life. The two worlds Wilde distinguished for Gide are finally one—the one we all live in, artist and Philistine alike. That world which Wilde promised would exist if only one talked about it is not at all a possible one for him. The moment he abandons choice and offers himself to a random selection of masks, his possible world of art vanishes. What remains is just talk—ready, clever, incessant, and tiring after a while.

Nevertheless, *The Picture of Dorian Gray* is hardly the "bore" [44] W. H. Auden has said it is. For all its disordered art, the book is still the best mirror of the nineties' sham resolution of the Victorian paradox. The problems of the novel qua novel remind us that the Wildean indeterminacy precludes choice and thus precludes rejection of any mask. He wears each one with the sure sense that there exists an actual face behind it; the mirror, on the other hand, never shows this face, only the mask. Just as the mask fails to hide the face from others, so does the mirror fail to reflect the face to itself. For a true art of mask and mirror, English letters must await the maturing of Yeats, Conrad, and Joyce, in whose hands these performer's tools are precision instruments in service of their science of the self. And yet, inescapably, these men were different for having witnessed the mistakes and achievements of Oscar Wilde.

IV

Role-playing was a matter of dead seriousness with the men of the nineties. For some, such as Dowson,

Johnson, and Symons, the pattern of their lives grew out of a very clear perception of their own unclarity and indeterminateness. Am I really there? Look in the mirror to see. And like Wilde many of the so-called "decadents" sought the sort of ego-protection that the mask might provide. If forced to take account of the face beneath and the lies their lives often reduced to, they typically sought refuge in Bohemianism and the fog of intoxication. For these men, the division of the self was more a problem of life than of art. Ironically their troglodytes within were lily-livered, much too tame for Gothic outrage, and their discontented hearts, all too aware of their relative failure even in the "tragic reproduction of all tragic poetry" [45] which was their life, flickered briefly and were extinguished. Like the Romantics at the beginning of the century, Beardsley, Dowson, Johnson, as well as Wilde, all died young, but the Romantic analogy ends there. For what Wilde said of Symons could be applied to all his contemporaries: All were "sad example[s] of an Egoist who had no Ego." This is the basis of our interest in them: The way both their lives and their art are transported into a shadowy no-man's-land where neither life nor art can achieve substantial existence.

In many ways more intellectual than Wilde, Lionel Johnson nonetheless shared his fatal incapacity for self-definition. As a restless young man he took up successively Buddha, Shelley, Emerson, Whitman, Newman, Browning, and Pater as guides to both life and art. Yet he could never be free of an unnameable unease. "I live in the age of the 'Welt-Schmertz,' " he wrote in one of the *Winchester Letters*, ". . . my sorrows never come from consciousness of wrong; but from the vague shadow of unrest thrown over life by passing things; 'a death, a chorus ending.' " [47] He remained to his own dying day haughtily contemptuous of the "noise and glare" [48] of life, yet tucked away safe in his library Johnson still found no peace. At eighteen he had already refused to choose sides on many things: "I do not love sensuality: I do not hate it; I do not love purity: I do not hate it; I regard both as artistic aspects of life." And even in aestheticism, the young Johnson equivocated: "I cannot violate my own nature. Asceticism is wrong as a rule of life, sensuality is wrong as a disorder of life: but asceticism is right when the moment cries out with Faust, 'Entbehren sollst du'; and sensuality when it whispers, 'eat and drink, for tomorrow we die.' " [49] The ethical confusion of this statement is somewhat obscured by his precise syntactic parallels but is very clearly expressed in the arrangement of his Oxford room: on a center table a bottle of Glengarry, along with open volumes of *Les Fleurs du Mal* and *Leaves of Grass;* and on the wall, the imposing portraits of Cardinal Newman and Cardinal Wiseman.

Several of the poems reveal the same insoluble ambivalence. "The Destroyer of a Soul" is addressed to Wilde, but in the poem this good friend is only Johnson's metaphor for the enemy within. In "In Honorem Doriani Creatorisque Eius" and "Satanas," the contrast of tarnished soul and radiant vice is set forth in a cold, intense Latin. His best known poem, "The Dark Angel," shows the self watching the demon-self devouring him:

> When music sounds, then changest thou
> Its silvery to a sultry fire:
> Nor will thine envious heart allow
> Delight untortured by desire.
>
> Through thee, the gracious Muses turn
> To Furies, O mine Enemy!

> And all the things of beauty burn
> With flames of evil ecstasy.

The battle lines are drawn even more explicitly in "To Passions":

> My hatred of myself is pain
> Beyond my tolerable share.
>
> .   .   .   .   .   .
>
> Darker than death, fiercer than fire,
> Hatefuller than the heart of Hell:
> I know thee, O mine own desire!
> I know not mine own self so well.

Johnson was never able to quench these rival fires of the self and retreated more and more to the narrow room of his solitude. His devotion to beauty was awesome to his friends, even to such an impassioned poet as Yeats. More and more he withdrew behind a facade of brilliant lies about himself,[50] and drenched himself in alcohol. Santayana, recalling his friendship with Johnson, well understood that unhappy life: "The same emotional absolutism, the same hatred of everything not plastic to the fancy, which drove him from Victorian England into Celtic poetry and Catholic supernaturalism, kept him from accepting definition and limitation even there; he could not deny himself other dreams." [51]

Ernest Dowson was in the eyes of some a poet less gifted than Johnson, but he was the more typical decadent of his time. Utterly heedless of the sorts of practical measures people take to hold themselves together in life, he wandered about, drinking and reveling. It was as though he could only put up with life while drunk. During the limited intervals he was sober, he was, from most accounts, a gentle, sensitive person. And his writings, surprisingly, give hardly a glimpse of that incessant rage for disorder within him. The one romance of his life, that curious affair with a London waitress, risks being Dowson's invention, but it conveniently epitomizes his inordinate pursuit of love. Never convinced that he would or could reach fulfillment, he seemed to want to demolish its very possibilities beforehand and grieve eternally afterwards. All of his stories in *Dilemmas* (1895) and elsewhere tell the same tale of frustrated love, of a weak man's failure and melancholy retreat. The most famous of his works, "Non sum qualis eram bonae sub regno Cynarae," says about all there is to say on this theme. Cynara's lover cries out, with his "bought red mouth," for "madder music" and "stronger wine," [52] aching all the while in the shadow of his lost love. The stagy phrases only reveal Dowson's innocence, which the histrio in him did its best to cover for. Had he been born a couple of hundred years before, he might have passed for Robert Herrick celebrating the joy of passing beautiful things, but being in and very much of his time in the late nineteenth century, he simply could not resist violating these lovely things before they came to flower.

Dowson collaborated on two novels with a friend. One of them, *A Comedy of Masks* (1893), takes up the notion of the discrepancy of appearance and reality—the mask and the face. But just as his poetry falls short of the desired elegance of Horace and music of Verlaine, his novels, too, fail to realize the Jamesian kind of irony he so much admired. Inescapably enmeshed in his life, he could not pull himself away to his art. Nowadays, what we have of his work only serves to remind us that the duality of personality was by then no longer only a literary theme, but a condition of life. As his friend put it, Dowson was a twilight wanderer holding a "whispered *colloque sentimental* with the ghost of an old love." It was fated that he succumb to these "destructive forces" which, imprisoned within him, "pulled down the house of life upon his own head." [53]

In "A Prelude to Life," Arthur Symons tells of the frustration he felt as a child with the Puritan, provincial life. In a reaction very much like Stevenson's, he looked for excitement for a while in the Bohemian life of sensation. Later Symons assumed the role of public spokesman for the "symbolist movement," proclaiming its doctrines and purportedly practicing them in several stories and innumerable essays and poems. With the exception of *The Symbolist Movement in Literature* (1899), however, his writings are practically forgotten now. His poems, many of which describe the inevitable London night scenes of the time, are sentimental and diffuse. His titles in the volumes published in the nineties record his "spiritual adventures" rather explicitly: "A Café-Singer," "In Bohemia," "The Absinthe-Drinker," "Perfume," "Nocturne," "Pierrot in Half-mourning," "Hallucination," "To One in Alienation," and "The Destroying Angel," among others.

One of his earliest, "A Crisis" (1886), is as rhapsodic as *Pauline* in its self-hatred. "O cursed Self, / He muttered; for his selfhood hemmed him round, / A flame of fire about a narrow ring, / And fleeing he vainly circled, vainly beat / The fatal limits." [54] His verses secrete the guilt of the confessional: " 'Lost, lost!' / And his whole soul cowered in upon itself." In another, the "Prologue" (1893) to *London Nights,* the self as performer takes over, dominating the audience self which is alternately angry and complaisant:

> My life is like a music-hall,
> Where, in the impotence of rage,
> Chained by enchantment to my stall,
> I see myself upon the stage
> Dance to amuse a music-hall.
>
> 'Tis I that smoke this cigarette,
> Lounge here, and laugh for vacancy,
> And watch the dancers turn; and yet
> It is my very self I see
> Across the cloudy cigarette.

The struggle, recalling the antinomies of Dipsychus, is useless. In his "very self" he sees both the emptiness of the dance and his own "vacancy."

There is something very personal in Symons' theory of symbolism, with its formula for alienation, that purports to explain this double sense of the self. In his essay on Gérard de Nerval in the *Symbolist Movement,* he almost seems to anticipate his own later illness:

> Who has not often meditated, above all what artist, on the slightness, after all, of the link which holds our faculties together in that sober health of the brain which we call reason? Are there not moments when that link seems to be worn down to so fine a tenuity that the wing of a passing dream might suffice to snap it? The consciousness seems, as it were, to expand and contract at once, into something too wide for the universe, and too narrow for the thought of self to find room within it. Is it that the sense of identity is about

to evaporate, annihilating all, or is it that a more profound identity, the identity of the whole sentient universe, has been at last realized? Leaving the concrete
world on these brief voyages, the fear is that we may
not have strength to return, or that we may lose the
way back. Every artist lives a double life, in which he
is for the most part conscious of the illusions of the
imagination.[55]

Here he seems to grasp the tenuous balance of the artist's
"double life," yet he never really gets to the root of the
predicament. In the concluding passage of *Studies in
Prose and Verse,* he talks about the artist's need to make
a "choice":

He [Barbey d'Aurévilly] has realized that the great
choice, the choice between the world and something
which is not visible in the world, but out of which
the visible world has been made, does not lie in the
mere contrast of the subtler and grosser senses. He
has come to realize what the choice really is, and he
has chosen. Yet perhaps the choice is not quite so
narrow as Barbey d'Aurévilly thought; perhaps it is a
choice between actualizing this dream or actualizing
that dream. . . . Art begins when a man wishes to
immortalize the most vivid moment he has ever lived.
Life has already, to one not an artist, become art in
that moment. And the making of one's life into art is
after all the first duty and privilege of every man. It
is to escape from material reality into whatever form
of ecstasy is our own form of spiritual existence. There
is the choice; and our happiness, our "success in life,"
will depend on our choosing rightly, each for himself,
among the forms in which that choice will come to us.

(pp. 290–291)

The argument, peculiarly, recollects Rossetti as well as Pater and Wilde, but there is also an element opposed to the aestheticism of these writers: the Victorian compulsion for commitment. Still more curious, the choice he is urging is only between one dream and another, thus obviating the meaning of choice itself. There is this urgent sense of the necessity for definition, but not the slightest idea what sort of definition, and all the while the deep doubt of ever formulating one. In this uncertainty there may be the key to the diffuseness of his work.

In "A Prelude to Life" he tells how as a child he "did not know quite what [he] wanted." [56] The same vagueness and indecisiveness persisted throughout his life. Intellectual enough to have formulated the most comprehensive theory of symbolism at the time, morally aware enough to have recognized "a world of holy terror" [57] in Conrad's work, Symons nonetheless lacked a naturally strong central self and either the character or the art to synthesize one. The attack of manic-depression in 1908 which dramatically ended his writing career was inevitable. So complete was this eclipse that even the *Confessions: A Study in Pathology* (1930), a reminiscence of his experience of mental unbalance, is a disappointment.

V

Role-playing is a conspicuous feature in the lives of many writers outside Wilde's circle. Edmund Gosse, for whom the discovery of an "other self" marked the start of his adolescence,[58] managed as he grew up to abandon the old fundamentalist in him and nurture the literary connoisseur. But there were others for whom the experience of self-division was so acute that their only way of living with it was to avoid it by assuming either a different name or a different personality that would blur the clear definition of an identity they did not feel and could not face. Wilde's "C. 3. 3." and "Sebastian Melmoth" were practically forced on him by the circumstances of his disgrace, but what about W. K. Magee hiding himself behind an English name "John Eglinton," and the flight of George Russell to the ether as "AE," a name he derived from "Aeon," revealed to him in a vision? Strangest of all was the case of William Sharp, designer and producer of *The Pagan Review* of 1892, all written by him alone under a number of pen names, recalling the plans the young Browning once had for a brilliant pseudonymous career. Actually, Sharp's disguises went very deep. A devoted husband, he created a fictitious mistress and signed her name, "Fiona Macleod," to his best works. When drunk, he excused his intoxication as the result of the deep remorse he felt for his infidelity to this woman. "He never told one anything that was true," Yeats said of Sharp, "the facts of life disturbed him and were forgotten." [59] Yeats, along with everyone else who knew Sharp, had been completely taken in by the feminine handwriting of the Fiona Macleod correspondence and never suspected the hand of their friend behind it.

Sharp's impersonations seem extraordinary, but at that time there were very few who escaped these powerful forces seemingly bent on destroying the self. Gissing, Wells, Henley, Davidson, Kipling, Crackanthorpe, Barrie, Thompson, Meynell, all experienced a wide break in the self-continuum. This is not to put a sunflower in the hand of every English writer and a green carnation in his lapel. Nor is it to assume, on the other side, that these men knew only gloom and despair.[60] In fact, many of them, Max Beerbohm for instance, took the bull by the horns in their writing, and enjoyed themselves hugely. Beerbohm's parodistic dual-personality story, *The Happy Hypocrite* (1897), good-humoredly pushes the Wildean philosophy of the mask to its absurd conclusion. Lord George Hell is a cynical young buck who falls in love with a pretty actress, Jenny Mere, paralleling the romance of Dorian and Sibyl. Lord George is no aesthete, however, and he becomes genuinely entranced with the sprite. Unfortunately, neither his wealth nor rank persuades her, for her dream man must have an absolutely "saintly" face. His visit to Mr. Aeneas the mask-maker solves that problem, and Jenny responds to her new boyfriend ardently. The two walk into the woods and are wed, and Lord George, from here on George Heaven, feels tremendously renewed by pastoral bliss. Suddenly, at the "mensiversary" of their wedding his old mistress appears and threatens to reveal his former identity. The vicious woman rips off the mask expecting to show George Hell to the world, but the exposed face appears exactly the same as the assumed saintly face.

The mask becomes the face; life imitates art. This simple story "for tired men" was no doubt meant as a cool satire on Wilde in the style of his comedies and fairy-tales.[61] However, it makes even more sense if taken as a demonstration of the axiom that the role played in earnest preempts, in time, one's original earnestness. The play's the thing. In his untroubled enjoyment of the role, Beerbohm is a bellwether for the more relaxed attitude toward the art of the lie typical of the twentieth century.

For George Bernard Shaw, a showman in the Wilde-Beerbohm tradition, the divided self is a great chance for a comedy. *Arms and the Man* (produced in 1894; pub-

lished in 1898) especially demonstrates the absurdity of
the mask and all attempts to hide the presumed true self
from the world. In this play the Romantic protagonist
and his fiancée work hard at their heroic dream only to
have illusion punctured by the blunt "realist." The hero
can no longer feel sure of a single self now, counting as
many as six: "Which of the six is the real man? That's
the question that torments me. One of them is a hero,
another a buffoon, another a humbug, another perhaps a
bit of a blackguard. And one, at least, is a coward." [62] The
multiple-selves theme is not a new invention with Shaw—
or at least no fresher than his sentimental young lady in
love with the debonair officer. This satire on self-illusion
expertly combines farce and realism, but Shaw's important contribution in this play, as in others, is his socialist
interpretation of alienated identity.[63]

Samuel Butler's *The Way of All Flesh* (1903) [64] takes
the sacrosanct notions of family and respectability and
demolishes them with sure satire. Out of that shattered
Victorian world comes the record of Ernest Pontifex's
struggle to restore his sense of himself and the new world
he belongs to. What is remarkable in the novel is the way
Butler divides up his authorial personality between the
ironic narrator and the earnest protagonist.[65] He is very
much like Wilde in the way he evades out-and-out con-
frontation with the problem within, always equivocating in amusing epigrams. The dilemma of money (which
he finally champions) and respectability (which he savagely ridicules) is never resolved. He wants us to have
a laugh at Theobald Pontifex and all his absurdity, but
on the other hand it is hard to accept wholeheartedly the
"vitalist" doctrine endorsed by Ernest-*cum*-Overton, the
surrogate Samuel Butler. The discrepancy between the
purported seriousness of his intent and the casualness

with which the difficulty is glossed over is disturbing in this book.

Laughter—as produced by a Shaw or a Butler—is an appropriate way to deal with the mask, although only insofar as the mask is taken as social pretension, a false face to poke fun at. But the assumption of a mask sometimes results too from a personal necessity having little to do, originally, with the pleasures of role-playing. For, when the experience of inner division threatens the very survival of the self, the mask no longer functions as a lie outright but as a desperate test of another possibility. Wilde only imperfectly understood this, but even if he had grasped the full range of the phenomenon, he did not show the sort of patience needed to work it out thoroughly in his art.

In *The Trembling of the Veil* (1922) Yeats repeatedly returns to his great theme of the "Unity of Being," [66] and throughout the book, although particularly in the chapter called "The Tragic Generation," there are accounts of his early struggles with self-division. One passage, in particular, describes his experience of the doppelgänger: "A man walked, as it were, casting a shadow, and yet one could never say which was man and which was shadow, or how many the shadows that he cast." [67] Contrastingly, in his early poems this "disunity of being" is concealed by their dominant mood of flight and longing,[68] but Yeats was even at this time actively involved in forging his language of myth and vision. The doctrine of the Mask, the concepts of the self and antiself, and the cosmology of solar gyres and phases of the moon were intended to explain all of history, religion, ethics, and psychology, and all grew out of the same intense preoccupation with the unity of being. Yeats continued to explore this realm of self in which man and mask are the poles for the tension which life is. The germ of this fascination was everywhere, after all, and he caught it in the same hothouse atmosphere of the nineties that made the Romantic theme of the double so attractive to so many different writers.

In Yeats's story, "John Sherman" (1891), written under the pseudonym of Ganconagh, the young protagonist leaves his boyhood sweetheart and goes to London where he soon falls in love again. Sherman and this beautiful young woman plan to be married, but he gradually begins to lose confidence in himself and becomes generally troubled and indecisive. His "sense of personal identity is shaken" as he feels as though his "past and present [are] about to dissolve partnership." [69] In an attempt to brace himself and resolve his dilemma (the love triangle recalls *Jane Eyre, Tess,* and *Jude,* among many others), he invites his best friend for a visit. In character, temperament, and appearance, Sherman and his friend are antithetical, and before long friend and fiancée fall in love. Sherman breaks his engagement and returns to Ireland to propose to his old sweetheart. He has at last made up his mind. They marry, and dream together of a long and happy future in the country. For all the artlessness of the narrative, the story is noteworthy for the young Yeats's way of handling the divided self. For one thing, there is Sherman's inability to come to a decision on an important matter; then there is the polarizing of Sherman and Howard, whose characters are the two possibilities open to Yeats himself as a young man.[70]

This young Yeats was to become one of the greatest poets of the language, and it is interesting that of all his contemporaries in the nineties, he alone managed to put the artist's broken self together in his art. Following him, later poets, those potters of the well-wrought urn, understood that poor life could not help itself. The shards of the broken self could be repaired only in the new cast of their work. Even then, while their art promised wholeness, such integrity remote to life only divided again into art versus life, play-actor against person. As Ionesco would demonstrate in his play on the nonidentity of modern man, the search for the self as the center of existence is no longer a main concern in our literature:

> Bart I [*to* Ionesco]: Be careful now . . . to play the scene according to the theory of alienation.
>
>   .   .   .   .
>
> Ionesco: [*in the same tone as before*] How do I do it? . . .
> Bart II: Without any self-identification. You've always made the mistake of being yourself.
> Ionesco: Who else could I possibly be?
> Bart II: Alienate yourself.
> Ionesco: [*almost blubbing*] But how do I do it?
> Bart III: It's perfectly simple. . . .
> Bart I: Watch yourself acting. . . . Be Ionesco not being Ionesco!

Bartholomeus, the three stage managers in Ionesco's play on a play, is a latter-day alchemist producing instant alienation. After congratulating his triple-self on his progress in separating the play from any trace of the old author Ionesco, he proceeds methodically to his next operation:

> Bart I [*to* Ionesco]: Now move to the door. . . .
> [Ionesco *says no more. He moves to the door like a sleepwalker.*]
> Bart III [*to* Bart I]: Not like that!

Bart I [*to* Ionesco]: Move forward one step! . . .
Bart II [*to* Ionesco]: While you move two back! . . .

. . . .

Bart II: That's it. . . . He's alienated himself! He's
done it! [71]

Being nothing in particular, the self can be made to be
anything by this contemporary Faust—one step forward,
two back, dance, sing, write, alienate, write harder. . . .

The fire in the forge of the artist's self has petered
out, the Yeatsian smithy cooled and now abandoned.
The self divided is, as the Victorians had long ago antici-
pated, a condition of modern life, and it is only in this
disintegrity or self-dissolution that we are free, paradoxically, to be a presence in the world, a meaning.

Notes

1. André Gide, *Oscar Wilde: A Study*, trans. Stuart Mason (Oxford,
   1905), pp. 27–28.
2. "The Decay of Lying," *The Complete Works of Oscar Wilde*
   (Garden City, 1923), V, p. 24.
3. *The Works of Robert Louis Stevenson*, Vailima Edition (London,
   1922), XII, p. 193. Unless otherwise stated, references are to this
   edition throughout the discussion on Stevenson.
4. *Works*, IV, pp. 417 and 422.
5. *Henry James and Robert Louis Stevenson*, ed. Janet Adam Smith
   (London, 1948), pp. 90 and 92.
6. The phrase was of course first used by William James in *The
   Principles of Psychology* (1890). There is a chapter in the book,
   incidentally, "The Consciousness of Self," which discusses the
   problem of the divided self, and he again pursues the question in
   The Varieties of Religious Experience (given as lectures in 1901
   and 1902) in a chapter called "The Divided Self, and the Process
   of Its Unification."

7. Gothicism responded quickly to the temper and taste of the mass reader with such books as Arthur Machen's *The Three Imposters*, George Manville Fenn's *The Man with a Shadow*, Sir Walter Besant's *The Ivory Gate*, Ella D'arcy's *The Death Mask*, Robert Smyth Hichens' *Flames: A London Fantasy*, and Lyman Frank Baum's *Tod and Tot*—all but forgotten nowadays.

8. "Deacon Brodie; or, the Double Life" was coauthored by W. E. Henley, published in 1880, and produced in 1883. Later Stevenson revised it and published the new version in 1892.

9. *The Letters of Robert Louis Stevenson*, ed. Sidney Colvin (New York, 1911), II, p. 282, and "A Chapter on Dreams," *Works*, XII, p. 247.

10. Stevenson mentioned Dostoevsky in a letter to J. A. Symonds written in the spring of 1886. However it is quite possible, as Laura L. Hinkley suggests, that he had read the Russian novelist before writing "Markheim." See *The Stevensons: Louis and Fanny* (New York, 1950), p. 231. She also charts Stevenson's gradual development of the dual-personality theme which culminated in *Dr. Jekyll and Mr. Hyde*. See p. 238.

11. *Works*, XI, p. 131.

12. *Works*, VII, Chapter 1. The chapters are not numbered in this edition, but I have done so here for ease of reference.

13. Dr. Lanyon's fate bears a strong resemblance to Captain Brierly's in *Lord Jim*.

14. *Robert Louis Stevenson* (New York, 1928), p. 53.

15. This is the view of Malcolm Elwin in his *The Strange Case of Robert Louis Stevenson* (London, 1950). Unfortunately, Elwin's scanty documentation makes it hard to judge the correctness of his view of the author's personal life. Mr. Bradford Booth has informed me that his forthcoming edition of Stevenson's letters will correct Mr. Elwin's interpretation on many matters.

16. For discussions of Hardy's sources, see Morton Dauwen Zabel, "Hardy in Defense of His Art: The Aesthetic of Incongruity," *Southern Review*, VI (1940); Samuel C. Chew, *Thomas Hardy: Poet and Novelist* (New York, 1928); Carl J. Weber, *Hardy of Wessex: His Life and Literary Career* (Hamden, 1962); Ruth Firor, *Folkways in Thomas Hardy* (Philadelphia, 1931); Douglas Brown, *Thomas Hardy* (London, 1954); David Cecil, *Hardy the Novelist: An Essay in Criticism*, 2nd ed. (London, 1954); and Albert J. Guerard, *Thomas Hardy* (Norfolk, 1964).

17. References are made to the Wessex Edition of Hardy throughout this discussion.

18. Hardy's excitement with Shelley's poetry is indisputable. A two-volume edition of his poems, which he always carried about with

him, has his penciled notes in a fine script. See Weber, pp. 138–139, 244; Chew, p. 10; and Phyllis Bartlett's "Seraph of Heaven: A Shelleyan Dream in Hardy's Fiction," *PMLA*, LXX (1955), pp. 624–635.

19. Hardy's phrase from a letter quoted in *The Life of Thomas Hardy: 1840–1928* (London, 1962), p. 271.

20. Hardy denied that *Jude* is a manifesto on "the marriage question." See *Life*, p. 271.

21. "Sue Bridehead," originally printed in *Phoenix*, later reprinted in *Hardy: A Collection of Critical Essays*, ed. Albert J. Guerard (Englewood Cliffs, 1963), p. 71.

22. A. Alvarez argues that Sue expresses one side of Jude's character. He compares Sue's wearing his clothing after her escape from school to the similar situation in Conrad's *The Secret Sharer*, Guerard's *Collection of Critical Essays*, pp. 115–116.

23. Hardy's explanation, given in a letter reproduced in the *Life*, p. 272.

24. Lawrence, "Sue Bridehead," p. 75.

25. In a letter quoted in the *Life*, Hardy explains the novel as "all contrasts": Sue and her heathen gods and Jude and his reading of the Greek testament; the university community of Christminster and its slums; Jude the saint and Jude the sinner; Sue the pagan and Sue the saint; marriage and single blessedness, and so on. See pp. 272–273. Albert J. Guerard sees Hardy's conflict of impulses as one between realism and antirealism. See the chapter called "Conflicting Impulses" in his *Thomas Hardy*.

26. *A Study of Oscar Wilde* (London, 1930), p. 47.

27. Gide, p. 49.

28. In his "Romantic Pantomime in Oscar Wilde," Richard Ellmann points out that the motif of exposure is almost always the focal point in Wilde's plays. In his view, Wilde's own compulsion to confess was so strong that he might be said to have invited the scandal that exposed him. *Partisan Review*, XXX (1963), pp. 342–355.

29. Gide recounts a story Wilde told when they dined with Mallarmé. When Narcissus died, the field flowers asked the river for drops of water so that they could shed tears for him. The river refused and explained: " 'If I loved him, it is because when he hung over my waters I saw the reflection of my waters in his eyes,' " p. 26.

30. One of many happy inventions by *Punch*. Quoted by Frances Winwar, *Oscar Wilde and the Yellow Nineties* (New York, 1940), p. 167.

31. The devil-compact motif is clearly meant, as Wilde explains in

a letter dated June 30, 1890. *The Letters of Oscar Wilde*, ed. Rupert Hart-Davis (New York, 1962), p. 263.

32. Symons, p. 51.

33. *The Romantic 90's* (London, 1951), p. 157.

34. See his letters to E. W. Pratt and to Ralph Payne, *Letters*, pp. 313 and 352. Also his testimony at the 1895 trial, recreated in William Gaunt's *The Aesthetic Adventure* (New York, 1945), p. 184. As for Wilde's other French sources, Balzac's *La Peau de Chagrin*, standing somewhere between Maturin and Wilde, should be mentioned. The importance of Whistler as the one who introduced the concept of art for art's sake to England should not be overlooked. Another enthusiast of French literature, George Moore, worried over his own crisis of the self, especially in the long dialogue between the "I" and his conscience in *The Confessions of a Young Man* (1888).

35. *Letters*, p. 469.

36. Arthur H. Nethercot, "Oscar Wilde and the Devil's Advocate," *PMLA*, LIX (1944), p. 843. In the last chapter of his book, *The Paradox of Oscar Wilde* (London and New York, 1949), George Woodcock also attempts to "resolve" the Wildean "contradictions," this time on the ground of Wilde's "largeness" and "individuality," but this, too, remains an unsatisfactory explanation. Barbara Charlesworth structures her Wilde chapter by the Lord Henry-Dorian-Basil Hallward triad in *Dark Passages: The Decadent Consciousness in Victorian Literature* (Madison and Milwaukee, 1965).

37. First printed by Nethercot in "Oscar Wilde on His Subdividing Himself," *PMLA*, LX (1945), pp. 616–617. Reprinted in the *Letters*, p. 352.

38. A letter to the Editor of the *St. James's Gazette* dated June 26 [1890]. *Letters*, p. 259.

39. *Letters*, p. 292.

40. The larger part of Pater's review is reproduced in Thomas Wright's *The Life of Walter Pater* (London, 1907), II, p. 160.

41. In "A Philistine Source for *Dorian Gray?*" Oscar Maurer, Jr. suggests George Augustus Sala, Matthew Arnold's "rowdy Philistine," as a source. Though I am not persuaded by his findings, the idea of Wilde's stealing from a Philistine model is an interesting one. *PQ*, XXVI (1947), pp. 84–86.

42. *Letters*, p. 458.

43. Holbrook Jackson, *The Eighteen Nineties* (Middlesex, 1939), p. 86.

44. "An Improbable Life," *The New Yorker*, March 9, 1963, p. 175.

45. Wilde's phrase, *Letters*, p. 816.

46. Frank Harris, *Oscar Wilde: His Life and Confessions,* quoted by Roger Lhombreaud in his *Arthur Symons: A Critical Biography* (London, 1963), p. 112.

47. *Some Winchester Letters of Lionel Johnson* (London and New York, 1919), p. 122.

48. "Plato in London," *The Complete Poems of Lionel Johnson,* ed. Iain Fletcher (London, 1953). References are made to this edition throughout the discussion on Johnson.

49. A letter to B, dated April 26, 1884, *Winchester Letters,* pp. 76 and 78.

50. Johnson used to invent stories of his meeting with great men— Newman, Gladstone, and others—and he told them so convincingly that Yeats and his other friends were completely taken in. See "The Tragic Generation," *The Trembling of the Veil* (1922) collected in *The Autobiography of William Butler Yeats* (New York, 1958), pp. 185–234.

51. *The Middle Span* (New York, 1945), p. 61.

52. *The Poems of Ernest Dowson,* ed. Mark Longaker (Philadelphia, 1962), p. 58.

53. *Studies in Prose and Verse* (London [1904]), p. 271.

54. *The Collected Works of Arthur Symons* (London, 1924), I, *Poems I,* pp. 50–51. References are to this edition.

55. *The Symbolist Movement in Literature,* ed. Richard Ellmann (New York, 1958), pp. 13–14.

56. *Collected Works,* V, *Spiritual Adventures,* p. 18.

57. *Dramatis Personae* (London, 1925), p. 3, quoted by Lhombreaud, p. 232.

58. See Chapter II, *Father and Son,* ed. William Irvine (Boston, 1965), pp. 28–32, 142–143.

59. *Autobiography,* p. 228.

60. Helmut E. Gerber, for one, complains about the fallacy of equating the "eccentricities of a small group with the 'period-mind' " in his article, "The Nineties," in *Edwardians and Late Victorians: English Institute Essays, 1959,* ed. Richard Ellmann (New York, 1960), p. 54.

61. The most complete discussion of the tale is in J. G. Riewald's *Sir Max Beerbohm: Man and Writer* (The Hague, 1953), pp. 132–137. His analysis of the parallels between *The Happy Hypocrite* and *Dorian Gray* is good but overlong, whereas his contention that the tale parodies the *"person* of Oscar Wilde" is not at all convincing. For Wilde's response to the story, see *Letters,* p. 576.

62. *Complete Plays with Prefaces* (New York, 1962), III, Act II.

63. In the Preface Shaw attacks the whole histrionic tendency in

modern life, and he refers, elsewhere, to this play as an "attempt at Hamlet in the comic spirit." Archibald Henderson, *George Bernard Shaw: Man of the Century* (New York, 1956), p. 539.

64. The period of composition is of course much earlier, and Butler had finished it by 1884.

65. For a thorough discussion of this question, see U. C. Knoepflmacher's "'Ishmael' or Anti-Hero? The Division of Self in *The Way of All Flesh*," *English Fiction in Transition*, IV (1961), pp. 28–35, later incorporated into his *Religious Humanism and the Victorian Novel* (Princeton, 1965).

66. See, for example, pp. 166, 176, 183, 193, and 235.

67. *Autobiography*, p. 176.

68. Thomas Parkinson shows how in his early poetry Yeats's lifelong view of the world in antithetical terms is not brought into dramatic focus. See *W. B. Yeats: Self-Critic: A Study of His Early Verse* (Berkeley and Los Angeles, 1951), pp. 52–54.

69. *John Sherman and Dhoya* (London, 1891), p. 98.

70. For an incisive discussion of *John Sherman* as Yeats's experiment on his own personality, see Richard Ellmann *Yeats: The Man and the Masks* (New York, 1948), pp. 78–79.

71. "Improvisation," in *The Killer and Other Plays*, trans. Donald Watson (New York, 1960), pp. 143–144.

Index

Alexander, Boyd, 41n
Allen, Walter, 225n
Altick, Richard D., 44n
Alvarez, A., 337n
Arabian Nights, The, 14, 21
Aristotle, 38n, 182, 221n, 222n, 279
Arnold, Matthew, xi, xvi, 62, 66, 68, 107, 111, 131, 143, 156n, 159, 160, 172, 174–199, 202, 208, 213, 219n, 221n, 222n, 223n, 234, 243–249, 250, 264, 278, 279, 282n, 285n, 302, 306, 310, 338n; "The Buried Life," 193–194; *Culture and Anarchy,* xi, 147, 184, 245–247, 248, 282n, 382n; "Culture and Its Enemies," 245; "Dover Beach," ix, 193, 194; *Empedocles on Etna,* 191; "Empedocles on Etna," 160, 181–182, 185, 191, 195–198, 311; "The Forsaken Merman," 190–191; "The Function of Criticism at the Present Time," 244; *God and the Bible,* 247; "Heine's Grave," 199; "Human Life," 192; "In Harmony With Nature," 185–186; "The Literary Influence of Academies," 244; *Literature and Dogma,* 87n, 247, 248, 282n; "Maurice de Guérin," 223n; "Mycerinus," 190; "Obermann Once More," 198; *On Translating Homer,* 243–244; *The Popular Education of France,* 244–245; Preface (1853), 181–184, 221n, 222n; "Quiet Work," 186, 222n; "Resignation," 187–188; "Rugby Chapel," 198; *St. Paul and Protestantism,* 247–248, 282n; "Self-Dependence," 191–192; "Sohrab and

Rustum," 184, 222n; "Stanzas from the Grand Chartreuse," 198; "Stanzas in Memory of the Author of 'Obermann,'" 194–195; *The Strayed Reveller,* 185, 222n; "The Strayed Reveller," 188–190; "A Summer Night," 192–193; "Thyrsis," 198; "Tristram and Iseult," 195; "Written in Butler's Sermons," 186
Arnold, Thomas, 161, 162, 172, 176
Arnold, Thomas (MA's brother), 157n
Auden, W. H., 320
Augustine, *see* St. Augustine
Austen, Jane, 36, 87

Bagehot, Walter, 161
Bailey, Philip James, 176
Baker, Carlos, 100n
Baker, Ernest A., 39n, 41n, 45n, 102n
Baker, Richard M., 285n
Balzac, Honoré de, 37, 338n
Barnard, Robert, 284
Barrie, James Matthew, 329
Bartlett, Phyllis, 337n
Bate, Walter Jackson, xixn, 101n
Baudelaire, Charles, 37, 175
Baum, Lyman Frank, 336n
Beardsley, Aubrey Vincent, 321
Beckford, William, 9, 13–23, 30, 37, 39n, 41n, 44–45n, 86, 101n, 310; *Episodes of Vathek,* 14, 19, 20, 21, 41n; "Long Story," 16–18; *Vathek,* 13–23, 31, 39n, 41n
Beerbohm, Max, 330, 339n